Jim Craig made 234 appearances for Celtic Football Club between 1965 and 1972, earning winners' medals for seven league championships, four Scottish Cup finals, three League Cup finals and the 1967 European Cup final. This is his third book following his autobiography, *A Lion Looks Back*, and *Scotland's Sporting Curiosities*.

Pat Woods was born in Bangor, North Wales, and is the author/co-author of nine other Celtic books. He has watched Celtic at home and abroad over a period of half a century.

D1639035

WITHDRAWN FROM DÚN LAOGHAIRE RATHDOWN
COUNTY LIBRARY STOCK

BAINTE DEN STOC

CELTIC
PRIDE AND PASSION

JIM CRAIG *and* PAT WOODS

MAINSTREAM
PUBLISHING

EDINBURGH AND LONDON

Copyright © Pat Woods and Jim Craig, 2013

All rights reserved

The moral rights of the authors have been asserted

First published in Great Britain in 2013 by

Mainstream Publishing

Transworld Publishers

61–63 Uxbridge Road

London W5 5SA

A Penguin Random House company

Mainstream updated paperback edition published 2014

ISBN 9781780576817

Copyright permissions cleared by the authors. The authors have tried to trace all
copyright details but where this has not been possible the publisher will be pleased to
make the necessary arrangements at the earliest opportunity.

No part of this book may be reproduced or transmitted in any form or by any other
means without permission in writing from the publisher, except by a reviewer who wishes
to quote brief passages in connection with a review written for insertion in a magazine,
newspaper or broadcast

A catalogue record for this book is available
from the British Library

**Printed in Great Britain by
Clays Ltd, St Ives plc**

1 3 5 7 9 10 8 6 4 2

To my wife Elisabeth, my five children, my seven grandchildren and my teammates in the 1967 European Cup-winning side. We might not have been the best team the world has ever seen, but no group of players has ever had a better relationship with their supporters.

Jim Craig

To Lisbon Lions CSC and to my late parents, members of a generation who made great sacrifices to ensure their children had a better life than was possible for them.

Pat Woods

Both authors would like to place on record their appreciation of the excellent, dedicated work being done by the Celtic Graves Society in respect of the history of the club. The authors also wish to thank Jamie Fox, Jack Murray and the staffs of the Mitchell Library, the National Library of Scotland and the Bibliothèque Nationale de France (Paris) for their help and advice with particular aspects of the book. Thanks also to all at Mainstream involved in the commissioning and preparation of this book, particularly Bill Campbell, Graeme Blaikie, Ailsa Bathgate and Mary Tobin.

Contents

Introduction

Celtic, someone once said, seem fated ('like the race that bore them') to have moments of great joy – and of great sorrow. 'Weird and wonderfully Celtic' was how John Rafferty, a noted sportswriter for *The Scotsman*, described the atmosphere surrounding their greatest triumph, as both writers (one of them a Lisbon Lion) would also attest to with regard to that *annus mirabilis* of 1967. Heartbreaking was the sorrow that surrounded the untimely death of the 22-year-old goalkeeper John Thomson, the victim of an accidental collision while in action at Ibrox in September 1931. All part of the rich fabric of a story that has a fascination, we would assert, without parallel in the world of football. No club ever rocketed to fame as quickly as Celtic, whose reputation soon earned them invitations to undertake tours of the Continent, where their spirit of adventure and a desire to entertain made them many friends. Willie Maley, the club's manager for an incredible four decades, commented cryptically in the summer of 1922 on 'the trouble we have made in the minds and hearts of many ultra patriots here by our visit to Germany', a country that Celtic were the first British team to visit after the Great War, a gesture that earned them the title of 'the first doves of peace' from a newspaper in that Central European nation where the physical and mental scars were still as raw as back home. This at a time when he was all too aware of the incalculable depths of grief still being felt by his brother Tom, himself a dashing forward in the early days of the club, who had lost his son Joseph in the battle of Festubert in northern France in May 1915, but Willie's perception that such a barrier-breaking tour was essential 'if the world is to be rehabilitated' was typical of that tradition of broad-minded generosity for which Celtic have been noted down the years. Such is the pride in the club generated by the outlook of the 'Celtic family' that it should come as no surprise that some seven decades later the famous, socially conscious jazz musician, the late Gil Scott-Heron (the Scott came from his mother's maiden name), the son of a Jamaican forward – Gil Heron – who had left behind an indelible memory after playing for the club in the early 1950s, should find his concerts around the world populated by proud fans of the club waving scarves and chanting the name of himself and his father. The vast majority of them were too young to have seen the father play, but the memory had been passed down through the generations, an indication of the potency of Celtic folklore.

The authors have set out to distil the essence of the club through a determination to shed fresh light on various periods and aspects of its remarkable history, perspectives brought into focus, for example, by unearthing coverage of Celtic in the foreign press, much of the research on the 1967 European Cup final having been undertaken in Paris's Bibliothèque Nationale, whose incomparable newspaper resources span the Continent.

Jim Craig and Pat Woods

ABBREVIATIONS

QF — Quarter-final
SF — Semi-final
F — Final
FTQ — Failed to qualify

CHAPTER 1

Just Another Ne'erday . . .

In the latter decades of the nineteenth century, alcohol played an important role in Scotland's New Year celebrations, so there were probably quite a number of people with hangovers on the morning of Friday, 1 January 1892. One of these, though, had a most unusual background. Charging Thunder was a 24-year-old 'Lakota Sioux Indian' attached to 'Buffalo Bill's Wild West Show', at that time touring Scotland. To make matters worse, he awoke in a prison cell and, a few hours later, made an appearance in Glasgow's Eastern Police Court, Tobago Street, to answer to a charge of assault allegedly perpetrated the previous afternoon. The case was continued until the following Monday, when it was decided that Charging Thunder should remain in custody and the proceedings were referred to the Sheriff Court.

SEASON 1891–92

The first half of this season had gone well for Celtic Football Club. Admittedly, they had lost the first league match to Hearts at Tynecastle by three goals to one, but the team had then gone on to win the next nine, with both a healthy goals-for tally and an equally miserly goals-against figure.

PL	W	D	L	F	A	Pts
10	9	0	1	34	11	18

NB Two points were awarded for a victory in those days.

Celtic had also won the Glasgow Cup in fine style, the performance in the final at Cathkin Park a particularly impressive one, the players making light of the heavy rain, sleet and snow falling throughout the 90 minutes to pick up the trophy for the second successive year.

Celtic in the 1891 Glasgow Cup

Kelvinside Athletic (H) 11–1

Partick Thistle (A) 3–1

Northern (H) 6–0

Northern lodged a protest about the foggy conditions.

This was upheld and a replay ordered.

Northern (H) 3–2

SF: Linthouse (H) 9–2

F: Clyde (Cathkin Park) 7–1 Att. 6,000 (12 December)

The team had also played two matches in the Scottish Cup, with fairly comfortable victories over St Mirren and Kilmarnock Athletic, the lowly status of the Ayrshire side being reflected in the sparse attendance at Celtic Park on the day, for which conflicting figures were given in the reports of the match. The crowd was certainly well under 1,000.

Celtic in the 1891–92 Scottish Cup

28/11/1891 St Mirren (A) 4–2, Att: 4,000

19/12/1891 Kilmarnock Athletic (H) 3–0

The final league match before the end of 1891 had been on 26 December, when Celtic defeated St Mirren 2–1 at the first Celtic Park. That was followed by a hiatus in competition for the major trophies of the time, as the next match was not due until 16 January 1892, a home Scottish Cup quarter-final tie against Cowlairs (in the event, this tie had to be postponed due to frost and was played a week later). It was a good break for the players but it also meant the prospect of no income coming into the club for nearly a month and the committee was not happy about that. Ostensibly, all players in Scotland at this period were amateur, although not every club followed this dictate to the letter. The Scottish Football Association was supposedly monitoring the situation and, keen to protect its image, set up a sub-committee in season 1890–91 to check the books of the various clubs. Eventually, the committee reported that professionalism did not exist in Scotland, a finding that one cynic, writing under the pseudonym of 'Free Critic' in *Scottish Sport* in May 1891, obviously did not agree with:

> What a tribute to the skill and shrewdness of the various treasurers and secretaries! What sapient wisdom on the part of the Scottish Football Association! The club books proved that professionalism did not exist! Did the Scottish Association think for one moment that the managers of such clubs as the Rangers, the Celtic and the Third Lanark would allow their books to prove anything to the contrary?

Football clubs had various outgoings to pay for, and so, at holiday periods like this, their officials organised lucrative 'friendlies' against other Scottish clubs or English visitors to bring in extra money. Celtic, in particular, needed the income, as the committee in charge had decided to build a new ground from scratch, quite confident that 'the largest following of any team in Scotland' would continue to give the club its support.

The first Celtic Park was compact, with one stand on the east side and rough earthen mounds serving as viewing areas round the other three. Many fans would climb up the eastern boundary wall of Janefield Cemetery to get a better view of proceedings. The ground may have been basic but it suited Celtic's early needs. Unfortunately, in 1891, the landlord asked for a massive eight-fold increase in rent, a rise the committee regarded as totally unjustified, hence the decision to build a new ground. By the beginning of January 1892, work was already under way, on a site just across the street from the first stadium. A large piece of waste ground, a brickfield in fact, which had a huge 40-ft crater in the middle that was filled with water, was being transformed into a top-class stadium with a playing pitch of 'bowling-green' quality.

This was the reason that income levels needed to be kept up, and so as the New Year period of 1892 approached the committee went to work to arrange matches against suitable opposition, teams that would tempt the supporters out of their homes. On the first day of 1892, the Celtic committee would no doubt have been delighted to see their choice of opponent vindicated by a 15,000 turnout, a huge attendance in those days. The 'Sons of the Rock' – Dumbarton FC – were one of the top sides of the era, joint winners of the first-ever League Championship the previous season and close behind Celtic in the title race of 1891–92. It was a prestigious encounter and the match was fully advertised in the sporting press of the era:

The Occasion
From the pages of *Scottish Sport*, a well-regarded publication of the era:

GRAND FOOTBALL MATCH.
Today Friday 1st January
CELTIC v. DUMBARTON
Celtic Park, Dalmarnock Street, Parkhead.
Kick-off 2 p.m.
Admission sixpence. Ladies free.
Grand stands sixpence extra per person

What made it a Memorable Match?
First, the teams involved were the two best sides in Scotland at that time. Second, it was the first time that goal nets had ever been used in a match at Celtic Park. Third, the kick-off was performed by Major John M. Burke, the manager of 'Buffalo Bill's Wild West Show'. And, finally, there was the little problem of . . .

. . . *The Final Result*
When the final whistle blew, the scoreline was Celtic 0 Dumbarton 8. Actually, the Celtic keeper had to pick the ball out of the net eleven times but three goals were disallowed. Even so, it was a bit of a thrashing. The *North British Daily Mail* report described this as

an 'ordinary' (i.e. friendly) match in which the 'strangers' (i.e. visitors) were 'in splendid fettle' from the outset and, with the wind in their favour, were five [NB – a correction] up at the interval. In the second half, 'the Celtic were again driven up on their goal' and conceded another three [NB – a correction] goals. The Dumbarton-based *Lennox Herald*, revelling in its 6 January 1892 edition in what its reporter clearly regarded as a highly prestigious, 'crushing' triumph for a local team, noted that, in comparison to the efforts of the Celtic forwards, who were 'remarkably weak and not in consonance with their usual smart work', their opponents 'swarmed like bees around Duff' in front of 'an immense gathering of spectators'. Such was the mastery that their first-half display had brought them, said that same match report, that 'Dumbarton's sons jauntily trooped from the pavilion' after the interval and the 'nimble, fleet-footed' visitors – 'eager to make the defeat an overwhelming one' – continued to force the pace as they completed an 8–0 rout during which the inside-right, Taylor, scored a hat-trick.

Initial Reaction from the Supporters

Quite naturally, the fans were not happy at seeing their team on the receiving end of such a heavy defeat, Celtic's biggest since a 2–5 loss to Renton in the Charity Cup in 1889.

The Celtic team on this shocking Ne'erday – laid out in the 2-3-5 formation of the time – was:

Duff

Reynolds   Doyle

W. Maley   Cherrie   Dowds

McCallum   Brady   Madden   McMahon   Campbell

Much of the blame for the defeat was heaped on two players, John Cherrie, the Clyde centre-half and captain, who was able to play for Celtic – in the absence of the injured James Kelly – because he was technically an amateur who could play for any club, and goalkeeper Tom Duff.

Further Reaction from the Supporters
Within the following 24 hours, however, the atmosphere among the support turned more sulphurous. Rumours swept the East End of the city that the Celtic players had been out drinking on the eve of the game and that more than a few were feeling the effects during the match. One individual came in for particular criticism for his performance on the day.

Reaction in the Press
In its own rather subtle fashion, the periodical *Scottish Sport* made it clear that something odd had been afoot among the Celtic players. 'Footballers – no more than ordinary mortals – cannot serve two masters,' it thundered, 'the members of the Celtic team, or at least a sufficient number of them – and we say it more in sorrow than in anger – made the attempt and failed.' The reason for this allusion becomes clear in the response to the question as to why Celtic had suffered such a heavy defeat: 'Because they eight [ate] nothing! – which, we have reason to believe, is a falsehood – at all events, it is not to be denied that, at least, some of them drank.' The publication was, however, particularly harsh in its condemnation of the performance of the home side's goalkeeper: 'Duff for the day spelt his name D-U-F-F-E-R. It will take a lot of his best saving to recover the reputation lost.' Given the savage – and damning – nature of this verdict, it is no surprise that this would turn out to be Tom Duff's last match for Celtic. It does, however, say a lot for the character of the Celtic players as a whole that they should go on to redeem themselves by turning it into an unprecedented 'Season of the Three Cups' by adding the Scottish Cup (beating Queen's Park 5–1 in the final) and the Charity Cup (2–0 victory over Rangers in the final) to the Glasgow Cup triumph. Their hopes of a clean sweep of the honours by annexing the League Championship were thwarted by an eventual two-point margin in favour of . . . Dumbarton!

Why Did the Team Play So Badly?

Several mitigating factors must be taken into account. First, it was a friendly and the committee in charge of team selection took the opportunity to field John Cherrie at centre-half. In the 2-3-5 formation of the period, the centre-half was more of a playmaker than a 'stopper' and a crucial member of any team. A new boy coming in surely disrupted in some measure the balance of the side. Second, there can be little doubt that goalkeeper Tom Duff had a nightmare and, when that happens, the goals-against tally soon mounts up. However, there is some evidence that Duff may not have been fully fit. Early in the Celtic v. Dumbarton league match at Celtic Park on 26 September 1891, torrential rain had forced the referee to call a temporary halt to the proceedings and the players to seek shelter. As a result of his soaking, Duff experienced a bout of rheumatics, which meant that he only played in three of Celtic's matches in the following three months, with Charlie Kelly and Mick Dolan deputising in goal. Certainly, Willie Maley was quite sympathetic to his former teammate in his memoirs in the *Weekly Mail and Record* of 11 September 1915: 'Until he fell a victim to rheumatics that season, Duff was unbeatable at times.' However, other papers were less charitable in their judgement. The *Glasgow Observer* of 27 April 1895, in a profile of the current incumbent in Celtic's goalkeeping jersey, Dan McArthur, was particularly forthright: 'Everyone remembers the fatal New Year's Day when, in the presence of some 20,000 people, the Celts had to submit to the ignominy of a 8–0 defeat, owing to the extraordinary and erratic behaviour of Duff in goal.' Whatever, the experience was a personal tragedy for Tom Duff, who was highly regarded by 'Bedouin', the pen name of the much-respected football writer Robert M. Connell, whose knowledge of the early days of organised football in Glasgow was encyclopaedic and who referred to the keeper as 'The Cowlairs Orangeman' in the *Scottish Weekly Record* of 18 July 1908. Duff had played for Cowlairs from the north-eastern area of the city for over three years before joining Celtic. A third mitigating factor might have been the staging of the match on New Year's Day, only a few hours after the biggest celebration of the year for everyone living in Scotland, when an over-indulgence in alcohol was a national sport. But there can be no justification for the obvious fact that the Celtic players just did not seem up for the match on the day.

Were the Rumours of Drinking True?

Almost certainly. At that time, the festival of Christmas was not celebrated to any great extent, with shops always open and many people working on the day. By contrast, the New Year was a real holiday, the drinking bouts beginning during the afternoon of Hogmanay and continuing through the night and into the next day – or even two! The Celtic players would have found it difficult to avoid the company of drinkers during the 24 hours prior to the game and probably, in the knowledge that the match against Dumbarton was a friendly, a few might have succumbed to the occasional glass, with the inevitable consequences. As to why the Dumbarton players were not similarly affected, one can only assume that, during that particular New Year festival, to use a Glasgow colloquialism, there were more 'bevvy-merchants' among the Celtic side!

* * *

When Charging Thunder's case was eventually heard, on 12 January 1892, he pled guilty through an interpreter hired by his boss William F. Cody, better known as 'Buffalo Bill', although in mitigation the defendant claimed that the 'lemonade' he was drinking had been 'spiked with whisky'! Unfortunately, the sheriff was unimpressed by his explanation, particularly his inability to identify the pub in which he had been drinking, and sentenced Charging Thunder to 30 days in Barlinnie Prison!

* * *

What a spectacle it must have been for the citizens of Glasgow! During the late autumn and winter of 1891–92, 'Buffalo Bill's Wild West Show' enthralled the crowds that flocked to the 7,000-capacity East End Exhibition Building off Duke Street in Dennistoun. 'Buffalo Bill, with his picturesque following of cowboys, Mexicans and American Indians, and horses, mules and buffaloes, arrived in the city a fortnight ago,' reported the *Glasgow Herald* of 6 November 1891, the writer adding that 'nearly 300 people and 175 head of stock' would take part in 'entertainments', which included, rather gruesomely, 'the destruction of an emigrant train'. The covered wagons needed for the latter segment of the show had been unloaded along with another 'prop', namely the famous Deadwood Stage – found abandoned and neglected on the plains by Buffalo Bill himself, who secured its ownership – and the livestock at the still extant Bellgrove Station (15 minutes or so from Celtic Park) when the company, which featured the renowned sharpshooter Annie Oakley, arrived by train from London. The buffaloes in particular must have been an awesome sight as they were herded through the narrow East End streets to their stables, far from the prairies in which they once roamed in their multitudes before coming close to extinction, not least as a result of the marksmanship of the show's celebrated impresario.

CHAPTER 2

Hot Off the Press

The Celts on their arrival from Edinburgh had a great reception at the Central Station. Crowds followed the members of the team, cheering lustily as they left the station. A flute band was waiting outside, and their strains were added to the general rejoicing.

Scottish Referee, 25 November 1895, on Celtic's return to
Glasgow after their 4–1 victory over Heart of Midlothian
at Tynecastle Park had brought them neck-and-neck
with Rangers at the top of the league table.

'PHENOMENAL DISPLAY OF THE CELTIC AGAINST DUNDEE. RECORD LEAGUE SCORE.' This was the banner headline in the sports pages of the first-ever edition of the *Daily Record*, above a match report with the byline of 'Bedouin' (Robert M. Connell), who had been poached from the newspaper *Scottish Sport*. In that first edition of the daily, dated 28 October 1895, the editor of the new broadsheet complained about 'a most unjust effort' having been made by an unnamed rival journal to induce local newsagents to refuse to sell the newspaper (circulation wars are nothing new!), before outlining what he believed was the ethos of the newcomer: 'a constant striving to make our pages readable and attractive . . . not to furnish forth a mere dull chronicle of events from day to day, but to give a picture, vivid, accurate and varied, of the web of human life as it is.' It was, therefore, clearly going out of its way to avoid the pomposity of other newspapers of the day, particularly in its coverage of football at a time when its place of publication, Glasgow (with premises in Renfield Lane), was developing a good conceit of itself as the hub of the football universe, soon coming take for granted the record crowds flocking to the three biggest temples of the sport in Britain (Celtic Park, Ibrox Park and Hampden Park) prior to the onset of the First World War in 1914. The popularity of the *Daily Record*, a daily that reflected football's broader appeal as the transition from an amateur to professional sport took hold, can be judged by the fact that its easier-to-read, less cluttered layout (not to mention quicker results and match reports) soon rendered obsolete the specialist newspapers that had earlier reigned supreme in their coverage of the native game, namely the twice-weekly *Scottish Sport* and *Scottish Referee*, whose densely packed pages were absolute treasure troves of information and comment but whose style and presentation became increasingly outmoded.

And 'Bedouin', surely, could not have believed his luck that his debut report in his new paper could be mined from such sensational material, namely the unparalleled 'extraordinary events which transpired at Celtic Park in the return fixture between Celtic and Dundee' two days earlier. With many years of experience in writing about football behind him, he confidently backed his assertion that 'nothing approaching it' had ever taken place in connection with the game in Scotland:

> We have had occasional crushing defeats inflicted in League competitions, but never did a disaster of such magnitude befall a club whose preceding form showed such merit and evidence of power and skill as that which, unfortunately, is associated with the latest appearance of the Dundee club. Fresh from triumphs over such redoubtable opponents as Heart of Midlothian and Rangers, the visitors were expected to emerge from this contest with some degree of merit, but, strange to say, they tumbled completely to pieces, and 'went down at the ropes' [presumably a boxing analogy].

He, like the rest of a population that had looked forward eagerly to a clash between title contenders, felt confident in the capability of the men from the east to administer a jolt to the ambition of 'The Irishmen', as the press had been wont to call Celtic from their inception, albeit the latter had been getting their league challenge back on track after two potentially morale-shattering defeats in mid-September 1895, when they had lost 0–5 at home to Heart of Midlothian and 0–3 at Logie Green, Edinburgh, to St Bernard's. As a result, they had been relegated to fourth place, behind the three clubs from the capital – Hibernian, St Bernard's and Heart of Midlothian – but, significantly, they had made an immediate recovery, netting twenty-four goals in their five intervening competitive matches before facing Dundee on 26 October:

21 September 1895: Linthouse 1 Celtic 7 (Glasgow Cup tie at Govandale Park, Govan Cross).

28 September 1895: Dumbarton 2 Celtic 3 (league match at Boghead Park, Dumbarton).

5 October 1895: Celtic 3 Hibernian 1 (league match at Celtic Park).

12 October 1895: Clyde 1 Celtic 5 (league match at Barrowfield Park, French Street, off Main Street, Bridgeton, Glasgow).

19 October 1895: Celtic 6 Cambuslang 1 (Glasgow Cup tie at Celtic Park).

Dundee were seeking their first league victory over Celtic since the Jute City club's formation in June 1893 as the result of a merger between the Old Boys and East End clubs, though they had inflicted a shock Scottish Cup defeat on their famous Glasgow visitors at their dockside Carolina Port ground in January 1895. Celtic had won four of their five league meetings, including a 2–1 away victory on the opening day of season 1895–96. After a sticky start to the season and, particularly, on the strength of an impressive 5–0 demolition of Heart of Midlothian, Dundee were being touted as potential champions, a status underlined by a glance at the top of the league on the morning of that fateful 26 October:

Hibernian: Played 10, Points 15 (2 points for a victory).
Heart of Midlothian: Played 10, Points 14.
Celtic: Played 10, Points 14.
Dundee: Played 10, Points 12.
Rangers: Played 7, Points 10.

The teams lined up as follows on a Celtic Park surface that was somewhat tricky as a result of the sun melting the snow that had fallen overnight, though the weather was sufficiently congenial to attract the largest crowd to that date to watch Dundee in Glasgow, a large attendance for its day of 11,000:

Celtic: McArthur; Meechan and Doyle; W. Maley, Kelly and Battles; Madden, Blessington, Martin, McMahon and W. Ferguson.

Dundee: Barrett; Darroch and Burgess; Dundas, Longair and F. Ferrier; Thomson, Sawyers, Vail, McDonald and Keillor.

There was a rather bizarre prelude to the kick-off, as 'Bedouin''s report noted: 'The Celts, after emerging from the pavilion to commence the fray, had to return again, in order to change their colours, owing to the similarity of Dundee's stripes.' The latter normally played in blue and white striped jerseys, while Celtic normally played in green-and-white stripes, and thus the cause for concern. (There is no description in the newspapers checked of Celtic's substitute strip.) This minor hiccup had no effect on the early proceedings, with Dundee seeming to shrug off the absence of the injured Bill Hendry, their left-half and captain, by making a brisk start and forcing Celtic goalkeeper Dan McArthur to display his renowned 'cat-like agility' to deal with a fierce Keillor shot in the very first minute. One account stated that 'For a time the play was pretty even, and held out the promise of a close game', but, gradually, Celtic assumed control of the match, passing up a couple of scoring opportunities before, suddenly, on the quarter-hour mark, cutting loose in devastating fashion. A much-anticipated battle suddenly turned into a procession for the home side. Unbelievable as it would seem to us today, though the lack of numbers on the strips was a factor in the confusion (see Postscript to this chapter), there was no unanimity in match reports as regards the identities of the players who hammered 11 nails into the Dundee coffin. Guesswork based on piecing together several accounts has produced the following (likely?) list, together with a description of the goals where available:

1: 15th minute – 'from a smart run and good passing by the front division, Blessington had the leather passed to him in the right place and he sent it spinning into the net'.

2 and 3: Scored, apparently, within the next ten minutes, first 'from the foot of Ferguson' followed by a goal 'scored out of a scrimmage, Ferguson and Blessington being last on the leather'. (Blessington appears the more likely scorer.)

4: On the half-hour mark, apparently by McMahon, who was 'in irresistible form'.

5 and 6: Scored in the final stages of the first half, with Madden, described in *Scottish Referee* as a player who 'time and again brought the ball within shooting range of Barrett', being apparently the scorer of the fifth, and Willie Maley appears to have scored the sixth from a free kick ('dropped one in'). Curiously, Maley does not credit himself with the goal in his 1939 *The Story of the Celtic*, perhaps out of modesty. He contented himself, after attributing the fourth goal to McMahon, with the statement that 'by the interval Celts had six goals to their credit'.

[Dundee emerged after the interval with only nine men, the result of injuries to centre-half Longair and left-half Ferrier, Hendry's deputy.]

7 and 8: Martin, it seems, scored twice in the opening minutes of

the second half, first by 'sending in a high shot, which took effect' and then 'three or four minutes later, that same forward put in another'.

9 and 10: Maley's account of a 'farcical' second half states that Martin 'scored twice in the first few minutes [i.e. numbers 7 and 8], adding other two shortly after [i.e. numbers 9 and 10]'. Certainly, the newspapers checked agree in crediting Martin with the ninth.

11: The result, apparently, of a free-kick ploy – the second of two goals 'scored off a foul', as one newspaper put it – which was rounded off by Battles, 'to whom Doyle just tipped the ball', to make the final score 11–0 over 'a dispirited and crushed' Dundee side.

What was the cause of Dundee's downfall? While admitting that the 'element of luck was not entirely absent' (a reference to the loss of Longair and Ferrier for the second half), 'Bedouin' homed in on the crucial factor, namely the impact of Celtic's 'earnestness and brilliance, which was astonishingly effective', with the forward line being singled out for particular attention: 'From first to last Madden, Blessington, Martin, McMahon, and Ferguson exhibited a perfection in combination which was altogether phenomenal, and against which Dundee were of no use. Individuality was discarded for the attainment of combination, and this was achieved by one of the finest displays of accurate football ever seen from a Celtic team.' It is worthwhile pausing here to reflect on the individual qualities of the demolition crew that had inflicted such humiliation:

Johnny Madden – 'Genial Johnny', so called because of his popularity both at Celtic Park and at his other place of employment, in Glasgow's Whiteinch, where in 1895 he worked as a shipyard riveter, was a pacy forward noted both for his long-distance shooting and for several tricks that were peculiarly his own. One favourite move described by the *Glasgow Observer* was 'the feint of pretending to stop the ball and then letting it roll to the right man'. An all-round sportsman of sorts who dabbled also in 'championship-class' speed cycling and cricket, he was also 'a tenor singer whose sweet voice and varied repertoire are in great demand at club socials'.

Jimmy Blessington – 'Blessy' to his teammates and the fans, a whole-hearted forward whose 'manly, robust, conscientious style fairly fetches the Parkhead habitués, who simply idolise the fair-haired laddie', according to the same newspaper, whose profile of the player added that Blessington was 'not one of your madcap, rushing, bull-in-a-china-shop, bully wee Michael sort of player' but one who allied 'cultured, reposeful' method to 'masterly manoeuvres and cool, crafty cuteness'.

Allan Martin – recently signed from Hibernian, he became a prolific centre-forward (the proverbial 'goal a game' striker) in his only season with Celtic before returning to Hibs. His short stay at Parkhead was marked by an extraordinary experience that underlines the fact that the game in Scotland was not a full-time calling for all: 'Allan Martin fainted clean away after the cup tie on Saturday. The popular Celtic centre is an ironworker, and prior to playing he had been employed continuously for 24 hours at the furnaces. It was enough to have paralysed the average mortal' (snippet in *Scottish Sport* of 24 September 1895, after Celtic's 7–1 away Glasgow Cup tie victory over Linthouse). He had worked a double shift in order to get time off to play the match.

Sandy McMahon – 'The Duke', so called after either the Duke of Wellington, to whom he bore a physical resemblance, or Duc Patrice de Mac-Mahon, the late President of France (take your pick), could be regarded as the first Celtic 'superstar'. He was considered a genius of a player by the *Glasgow Observer*, which once profiled him as a player with outstanding heading ability – 'endowed with extraordinary cervical elasticity' – and one who 'danced dances with the sphere at his toe, and generally indulged in such mazy gyrations that the opposing half-back was often prepared to swear that "McMahon was in three places at once"'.

Willie Ferguson – 'The Bag o' Tricks', probably the least celebrated of this front five, an outside-left who formed a deadly partnership with McMahon in this match and who had come to the attention of the press on the same day that Allan Martin fainted after the Linthouse cup tie. Playing for a Celtic eleven in a friendly away to Preston North End, his unorthodox style caught the eye of an English critic as he 'paddled down the wing like an athletic over-grown duck [yet] showed that, despite his ludicrous appearance and gait, he could play "fuitba" [sic]'.

Praise for Celtic's feat elsewhere was rather grudging. *Scottish Referee* damned it with faint praise, complimenting the victors on 'a performance which speaks for itself' while lambasting Dundee for playing into the hands of their opponents by 'close passing and dallying on the ball', which suited Celtic's 'smart tacklers'. Only right-back Darroch could be absolved from blame, 'playing throughout a plucky, manful game, but what was he amongst so many dolts and against such masters?' In similar vein, the rival *Scottish Sport* stated that 'Dundee's defence was no match for the Celtic sharp-shooters, who outmanoeuvred them almost every time . . . but the merit of the record performance is discounted by the fact that they were scored against a reduced and disorganised team.' The 'Dundee View' in this newspaper was allocated to 'A Dundee Traveller', who saw the match and rejected claims from the east that 'the game was rough and our men were abused' by stating that 'we certainly were not beaten by roughness, and I freely attribute the accidents [i.e. injuries] from which our men suffered to sheer ill-luck, combined with a little too much eagerness at the start of the game . . . never in the wildest dreams of either opponents or supporters was such a terrible beating looked for'. Predictably, it was left to the *Glasgow Observer*, admittedly the *Celtic View* of the time, to redress the balance in its assessment of a match whose outcome was received with incredulity and consternation throughout Scotland. While not neglecting to mention that Celtic had actually 'notched thirteen, and one of the brace disallowed was the prettiest and fairest goal of the match', it exulted in its favourites' goalfest: 'It would seem that our forwards have shaken off the tig-toying mania with which of old they were cursed, and set themselves seriously to the task of goal-scoring . . . grand, sustained and effective combination was there, with just enough dazzling individualism to emphasise the brilliancy of Celtic's play.' There are shades of 'Custer's Last Stand' about the writer's comment that 'so thoroughly did the Celts' rear rank o'ermaster the aggressive Dundonians that, towards the close, they were all playing forward', and he dismissed the excuses of the losing side, stating that Longair 'retired with injury – or pique' and that Burgess was 'never too disheartened as to take flying kicks at Johnny Madden'. Nevertheless, he was not so bowled over by Celtic's display as to forsake the opportunity to administer a rebuke for a perceived degree of carelessness with an assertion that implied that, had Celtic applied themselves fully, they would have approached (or even surpassed) the British record margin (36–0) by which Arbroath had overwhelmed the hapless Aberdeen Bon Accord in their September 1885 Scottish Cup tie: 'I do not exaggerate when I say that for every goal scored against Dundee, two certain chances were thrown away.' Some people are never happy . . .

* * *

POSTSCRIPT

a.) Celtic's victory remains a record for the top Scottish division. According to *Scottish Sport* of 29 October 1895, it broke the record set by Leith Athletic in their 10–0 rout of Vale of Leven on 19 September 1891. Incidentally, Willie Maley seems to suggest, while not endorsing the censure, that the observation of the *Glasgow Observer* writer regarding Celtic passing up goal-scoring chances in the annihilation of Dundee was not an exaggeration: 'To their credit be it said, Celtic teams throughout the years were never guilty of "rubbing it in", and even on this occasion there were times when they actually refused to score' (*The Story of the Celtic*, 1939).

b.) The lack of unanimity as regards the Celtic goal-scorers can be seen in the undernoted alternatives (no. 9 excepted) culled from a perusal of six sources. In the early days of football reporting, it was not unknown for the term 'the ball was sent through [the posts]' to be used when the goal-scorer could not be identified:

1. McMahon/Blessington
2. Madden/Ferguson
3. Blessington/Ferguson
4. Madden/McMahon
5. Madden/McMahon
6. Maley/Kelly
7. McMahon/Martin
8. Madden/Martin
9. Martin
10. Battles/Martin
11. Battles/Martin

Intriguingly, in a profile of Johnny Madden in *Der Kicker* (Stuttgart), 7 June 1922, it was stated that he had scored seven goals in the match. Given that the profile was part of the sports newspaper's extensive coverage of Celtic's tour of Central Europe (featuring matches in Prague, Berlin and Cologne), it is reasonable to assume that Johnny – by then Slavia Prague's coach (nicknamed 'the iron grandfather' for his emphasis on discipline) – had made this claim in an interview. Amusingly, the writer ('Beda') described the match as a 'Celtic–Dandy [sic]' one!!

The confusion certainly owes a lot to the absence of numbers on strips, a situation that was only rectified in British football some four decades later with the application of numbers on the backs of shirts. Celtic shunned this development out of a sense of righteousness, with mutterings about the 'defilement' of a sacred jersey, their initial concession to progress coming as late as 1960 with the introduction of numbers on the shorts.

c.) Celtic's record victory laid down a marker in the title race, acting like a booster rocket to propel the club to a championship that they eventually won by a four-point margin over Rangers, thus bringing the league flag to Parkhead for the third time in the first six years of the competition. In winning their remaining seven matches in a ten-club league, they scored twenty-seven goals.

CHAPTER 3

Game for Another*

'The people here take sport too seriously, and, first of all, took little notice. One man, who had fallen fifty feet, even got up and watched the match through to the end. But this man, although he picked himself up straight away, seemed afterwards to be very ill. This is the last time I will go to a football match.'

An extract from a postcard sent by a Herr Dieckmann, a German studying in Glasgow, to his mother in Altona, near Hamburg, on 7 April 1902, two days after witnessing the Ibrox Disaster.

Since the second-last decade of the nineteenth century, the city of Glasgow has hosted six International Exhibitions – in 1888, 1901, 1911, 1938, 1951 and 1988. They all proved very popular, with the first two, in particular, catching the attention of the public. In those far-off days, Glasgow was the second city of the Empire and the (self-styled) 'workshop of the world'.

---

* The chapter title is taken from a statement attributed to the organising committee after the success of Glasgow's 1888 Exhibition. That aspiration came to pass in 1901, and of course Celtic and Rangers were 'game', given the circumstances, for another match to decide ownership of the trophy first put up for competition at the 1901 Exhibition.

CELTIC: PRIDE AND PASSION

Glasgow's Exhibitions

	1888	1901
Opened	8 May	2 May
Closed	10 November	9 November
Opened by	Prince and Princess of Wales	Duke and Duchess of Fife
Attendance	5,748,379	11,497,220
Admission	One shilling for adults, sixpence for children	One shilling for adults, sixpence for children
Profit	£41,700	£39,000

Both these events were held in Kelvingrove Park and both featured a football tournament. In fact, Celtic's opening tie in the 1888 competition was the club's first official match in their inaugural season of 1888–89.

1 August 1888: Celtic v. Abercorn, 1–1.

Unfortunately, there is no mention in the newspapers of the period of any replay, although it is noticeable that 20 days would elapse before Celtic's next tie. Perhaps a replay did take place during this time or it could be that Abercorn – a side from Paisley – just scratched from the tourney.

21 August 1888: Celtic v. Dumbarton Athletic, 3–1.
29 August 1888: Celtic v. Partick Thistle, 1–0.
6 September 1888: Celtic v. Cowlairs (final), 0–2.

The result against Cowlairs might have disappointed some fans but the team from the north of the city was a strong force at the time and, two years later, alongside Celtic, became one of the founder clubs of the new Scottish Football League.

By the time of the 1901 tournament, with the invited clubs competing for a 'magnificent silver trophy', the growing Celtic support was full of expectation but again their hopes were dashed. The top eight sides in Scotland had been invited to take part and

GAME FOR ANOTHER

Celtic reached the final of the Exhibition Trophy/Cup by disposing of the two major Edinburgh teams:

21 August 1901: Hibs, 1–0
5 September 1901: Hearts, 2–1

That put Celtic through to the final of the tournament, against Rangers on 9 September 1901. In his report in the *Glasgow Observer*, 'Man in the Know' regarded it as – in modern parlance – a match too far for a squad that was playing its sixth match in the space of ten days, as follows:

Saturday, 31 August 1901: league match v. Third Lanark (H).
Monday, 2 September 1901: challenge match v. Aston Villa in Birmingham.
Wednesday, 4 September 1901: benefit match for ex-Hibs forward Pat Murray at Easter Road.
Thursday, 5 September 1901: Exhibition Trophy semi-final v. Hearts, mentioned above.
Saturday, 7 September 1901: league match v. St Mirren at Paisley.
Monday, 9 September 1901: Exhibition Trophy final v. Rangers.

All the ties in the Glasgow Exhibition tournament (as in 1888) were played at Glasgow University's Recreation Ground at Gilmorehill and it was on that pitch that Celtic ran out to face Rangers. Celtic opened the scoring through outside-left Johnny Campbell in 15 minutes; Rangers equalised a few minutes later. Unfortunately, the play then became tousy and bad-tempered, which did not improve the atmosphere among the watching crowd. The Light Blues seemed to cope better with the prevailing ambience, in contrast to the two young stars making up Celtic's left wing. Inside-left Jimmy Drummond (20) and outside-left Jimmy Quinn (23) were well held by their immediate opponents, giving a lop-sided look to Celtic's attacking opportunities.

By contrast, Rangers appeared very comfortable, showed a lot of confidence and scored two further goals in the second half to give them a 3–1 win plus a very handsome trophy to take back to Ibrox. The Rangers directors were so pleased with their acquisition that they insured it for £100, a large sum of money for that period.

'Man in the Know' acknowledged the quality of the Rangers forwards. However, the admittedly partisan columnist's verdict was: 'is it any wonder the cup was won after half an hour's play? . . . The Celts were never a match for the fresher opponents; they never looked like winners even when leading, and it was only by the most marvellous good luck that McFarlane [Celtic's goalkeeper] was not beaten at least half-a-dozen times.'

A letter written in the same edition was sympathetic to this viewpoint and, for good measure, also complained about the state of the pitch and the prevalent atmosphere: 'The soft, crumbling ground, the early darkness, and the shamefully hostile crowd also told against the Celtic, and especially against the youngsters [a reference to the likes of Quinn and Drummond] . . . the Rangers triumph at Gilmorehill on Monday will vastly please the section of the public which dearly loves to witness a Celtic humiliation.'

In the very early days, relationships between the Celtic and Rangers officials were very cordial. Indeed, the future Celtic chairman J.H. McLaughlin, a keen organist, accompanied the Rangers Glee Club for several years! By the beginning of the twentieth century, though, that relationship had cooled somewhat as the rivalry between the clubs deepened. There is little doubt that Celtic's experience at Gilmorehill reinforced a growing suspicion that had already been highlighted in a reference in the *Glasgow Observer* of 16 March 1901 to a 'pro-Rangers and anti-Celtic feeling existing among legislators as among all other sections of the football community'.

This sentiment was only aggravated by two fractious episodes in the autumn and winter of season 1901–02. First, there was some controversy over a decision to hold the replayed final of the Glasgow Cup at Ibrox. Rangers' ground had been awarded – by ballot – the final, when a crowd of 30,000 watched the Old Firm draw 2–2. Celtic's contention that the replay should be at Celtic Park was over-ruled by the Glasgow Association, so they scratched from the competition in protest. It has to be said, though, that Rangers did offer to play the replayed match on neutral territory.

The Ne'erday league encounter of 1902, watched by a 40,000 crowd, also caused controversy. At that time, the First Division sides played an 18-match league and, as the teams ran out at Parkhead, the table situation read:

	Played	Points
Celtic	17	26
Rangers	14	20

Victory in their final league match of the season would have given Celtic an unassailable lead (at that time, two points were awarded for a win) but they lost 2–4 in highly controversial circumstances. The Celtic players, apparently with some justification, hotly disputed three of the Rangers goals and were handicapped by the loss of their talisman after Rangers' second, when, in the midst of the home side's protests about the award of the goal, the referee – Mr Nisbet of Cowdenbeath – sent off the gifted and prolific forward Sandy McMahon in the belief that the latter had deliberately tripped him! Rangers went on to take the title by winning their three remaining league matches. Willie Maley, in his secretary-manager's report in the following edition of the *Celtic Football Guide* asserted that 'Celtic would have been champions but for the vile treatment we received at the hands of the referee on New Year's Day, when the Rangers were practically given the match.'

On 5 April 1902, a large crowd (at least 75,000) packed into Ibrox Park for the annual Scotland–England encounter, in that era the most important fixture on the international calendar. At what is now called the Broomloan Road (west) end of the ground was a renovated stand, not for people to sit in but for 'standing', the structure made of wood with a staircase leading up to it. During the first half of a match that finished 1–1, the flooring of the stand gave way without any warning, and hundreds of spectators plummeted through the resultant (estimated) 70 foot by 10 foot gap onto the concrete below, many either falling to their death or being crushed in the resulting panic. Almost unbelievably, after a 20-minute delay, the play was allowed to continue, the authorities assuming that an abandonment of the match would lead to more panic and further problems. Equally surprisingly, upon resumption of the contest, there were still people standing on the terracing surrounding the area of the accident. The casualty figures were later put at 25 dead and 517 injured (categorised as '24 dangerously injured', '168 seriously injured', '153 injured' and '172 slightly injured'). One English observer, a Mr Radford, recorded a poignant scene: 'A wee Scotch laddie, his face like wax, lying upon the floor with his leg crushed. He was crying and a young companion, also terribly injured, was heard to say, "Don't take on [i.e. grieve], Jamie. Cheer up, our team is winning."'

The Corporation of Glasgow immediately inaugurated a relief fund to which the SFA subscribed all their available assets. Over £30,000 was raised and all claims settled without recourse to law. The fund also benefited early on (within three weeks of the disaster) from the donation of the stand takings at the Celtic v. Hibernian Scottish Cup final played at Celtic's ground.

The disaster shook Glasgow very badly. All those connected with Rangers FC were devastated, particularly as the name of Ibrox Stadium came to be mentioned throughout Britain for all the wrong reasons. Since there had been some bitterness among the Celtic camp over losing the ballot for – and thus the income from – this international fixture, it is perhaps not surprising that one or two injudicious comments were made publicly . . . and just as quickly regretted. The atmosphere was soured even further when the *Glasgow Observer* columnist, unashamedly pro-Celtic, pointed out that Celtic's 'splendidly equipped ground, which had stood the test of previous record grounds . . . would have safely accommodated Saturday's mammoth muster'.

To their eternal credit, Rangers took full responsibility for the tragedy that had befallen so many people and attempted to raise money for compensation purposes. They decided to put up for competition the Glasgow Exhibition Trophy they had won the year before. It was renamed the 'British League Cup' and the Ibrox club invited Celtic plus two English clubs, Sunderland and Everton – first and second in the English First Division of the 1901–02 season – to take part. The semi-final draw paired Celtic with Sunderland and Rangers faced Everton.

On 30 April 1902, with 4,000 in the ground, Celtic defeated the English Champions, Sunderland, 5–1 at Celtic Park in the first of the ties. One day later, Rangers drew 1–1 with Everton at Goodison Park, in front of a crowd of 8,000, then won the replay at Celtic Park on 3 May 3–2, when 12,000 were watching. So, the scene was set for another epic contest between the perennial rivals and this went ahead at Cathkin Park on 17 June 1902.

In an early form of football sponsorship, it was reported that, in order to defray expenses for the final, the Bovril Limited Company would pay the advertising costs and also supply 'splendid gold medals' for the winners. A crowd of 7,000 turned up for what the papers were calling the 'British Championship Final Tie'. The Rangers side ran out in their normal light blue, while Celtic were in the green-and-white striped shirt. The teams were:

Celtic: McPherson/McFarlane, Watson/Davidson, Battles, Loney, Marshall, Orr, Crawford, Campbell, Quinn, McDermott, Hamilton.

[Alternative names of both goalkeeper and right-back, due to conflicting newspaper line-ups. McFarlane and Watson were the probable occupants of their respective berths]

Rangers; Dickie, A. Smith, Crawford, Gibson, Stark, Robertson, Lennie, Walker, Hamilton, Speedie, N. Smith.

Referee: J. Hay (Greenock).

It is difficult to imagine that Celtic did not approach this particular match with a sense of grievance as a result of their recent dealings with the Ibrox club. In addition, the players must have been keen to atone for what Willie Maley described later as 'the worst season, from a playing point of view, that it has ever been the lot of this club to report'. Rangers started the tie as the favourites but it quickly turned into a typical 'Old Firm' clash, where grit and determination were as important as ability. Willie Maley surprised many by playing Jimmy Quinn at centre-forward instead of his customary position – at that period – of left wing. And how Quinn relished the change!

He was immense, a real thorn in the flesh of the Rangers defence, to whom he gave no quarter. After 90 minutes, the score was level at 2–2, Jimmy Quinn having got both of Celtic's goals, one from 'a diagonal shot', the other a 'close-in finish after Campbell's shot re-bounded from the crossbar'.

Anyone reading the following morning's *Glasgow Herald* report would have been left in the dark as to what happened next, a newspaper deadline being the probable cause of the lack of clarity: 'At Cathkin Park last night, what should have been the final match of the British Championship was played but the game resulted in a draw.' In fact, as the *Evening Citizen* reported, there had been a 'consultation' in the pavilion, which resulted in a decision to play extra time. It took the report of the *Herald*'s sister paper, the *Evening Times*, to clear up the matter: 'Twenty minutes of extra time were played. Close on time, Lonie [*sic*] initiated a grand effort and a corner resulted, from which Quinn scored the winning goal.' According to the recollections of a Celtic supporter some two decades later, Quinn notched the winner by putting his hands on the shoulders of his teammate Tommy McDermott to gain extra height before powering home a last-minute header for his hat-trick.

The Celtic fans in the crowd were ecstatic, delighted that such a prestigious trophy was going to Celtic Park. The match report in the *Glasgow Observer* of 21 June 1902 revelled in the achievement of the men in green-and-white stripes: 'The play of the Celtic was worthy of the best traditions of the club; despite the very forcible play of their opponents they held the whip hand throughout.' Unfortunately, that was not the end of the matter.

Rangers appeared to think that the Cup would be returned to them the following season and made this request not once but several times. They even suggested that Celtic put the trophy up for competition again but Celtic dug their heels in. The source of this dispute may have been an observation in the 'Realms of Sport' column in the *Evening Times* on the day after the final: 'Having won it in the hardest of fights, it would be a graceful act on their part [Celtic's] to hand it back to the Rangers, the object of the competition having been realised in a most satisfactory way.'

Celtic's continuing refusal to hand the trophy back was a source of friction between the clubs for many years. When a *Football Weekly* writer visited Celtic Park in 1936, he was struck by the extraordinary care the club took to safeguard the trophy. Intrigued to learn that it was kept in a huge safe, he soon discovered how touchy Willie Maley was on the subject of the trophy and the notion of its being the object of another competition: 'No, no! The cup is ours. We won it outright. We regard it as a treasured possession and, unless some very special occasion arises, we do not intend to risk losing it.'

* * *

POSTSCRIPT

In the 'Milestones' chapter of his book *The Story of the Celtic*, published in 1939, Willie Maley states erroneously that the match on 17 June 1902 finished level at 2–2, resulting in a replay two nights later. According to the former Celtic manager, 'this game was simply a repetition of the first' (2–2) and then extra time was played, during which Celtic scored the winner. To add to the confusion, Maley also mentions another match between the clubs two months later for the same purpose, although he does not specify the date. This was not a final, as his reference to the outcome being 'to secure the medals' would imply, but was in fact a first-round encounter in the 'Rangers Benefit Tournament', also known as 'The Ibrox Disaster Fund Benefit Tournament'. Celtic beat Rangers 7–2 at Hampden Park on 20 August 1902 (Quinn notched another hat-trick), then edged out Partick Thistle by two goals and six corners to two goals and two corners a week later at the latter's ground, Meadowside, located in what was then the burgh of Partick. In the final, held at Ibrox Park on 24 September 1902, two-goal Willie Loney (a standout as an attacking centre-half), Tommy McDermott and Davie

Hamilton netted for Celtic, who came from behind to run out 4–2 victors over Morton. Three days later, the *Glasgow Observer* report commented wryly, and somewhat censoriously, that 'The Parkhead forwards contented themselves with a brilliant exhibition of midfield trickery, and their chiefest anxiety was to avoid goal-scoring.' Gold watches were the prizes for the winning side.

CHAPTER 4

'A Condition of Seething Excitement'*

Football has become the natural game of the kingdom and I am thankful that it has done so, because there is an outcry for recreation. To me there is no more delightful sight than to see an exhibition of manly skill, strength and endurance.'

A section of the speech made by Sir John Ure Primrose, Bart., Lord Provost of Glasgow, when he officially opened the new (present) Hampden Park in October 1903 prior to the Queen's Park v. Celtic match that followed the ceremony. Commenting on the event, the sports newspaper Scottish Referee took great satisfaction in reporting that 'The joy of the Queen's Park players, officials and everyone connected with the club was the common joy of the people.'

After Saturday's riot I would suggest the withdrawal of all policemen from football matches and substitute a regiment of soldiers with fixed bayonets.

From a letter to Glasgow's Evening Times

A disgraceful exhibition . . . the most fiendish outburst of inflamed passion ever seen in a civilised country . . . no matter under what circumstances the affair occurred, public opinion would very soon demand the cessation of a pastime capable of converting a crowd of human beings into an army of savages.

From a Daily Record and Mail *editorial*

---

* The chapter title is taken from the description in *The Scotsman*, 19 April 1909, of scenes inside the stadium during the 'Hampden Riot' and in the district afterwards.

CELTIC: PRIDE AND PASSION

Two quotes published in the wake of the 'Hampden Riot' Scottish Cup final, April 1909.

Why did Scottish football, which had been basking in popular acclaim in the first decade of the twentieth century (notwithstanding the 1902 'Ibrox Disaster'), suddenly become the target of such opprobrium? Why had its followers suddenly become, in the words of various newspapers, 'hooligans', 'ruffians', 'downright malevolent, cowardly and brutal' individuals, as well as being 'criminals and thieves', the latter stemming from reports that cited the use of coshes and pokers – in addition to corner flags, bricks, bottles and stones – as weapons by the estimated 5,000 to 6,000 rioters? Why, to judge from the aforementioned editorial, was the future of the game as a spectacle fit for public consumption suddenly under threat? And, finally, what did this all say about a city whose character was eviscerated by the London-based *Daily Telegraph*, which prefaced its account of what took place at Hampden as follows: 'Glasgow, which holds the record for football disasters, was on Saturday afternoon and evening the scene of a riot which will take rank as one of the most disgraceful blots disfiguring the game.' Even 60 years later, writing in the annual *Charles Buchan's Soccer Gift Book*, the English journalist Basil Easterbrook inserted into his account of the match this observation: 'The great city, sprawling on both banks of the Clyde, has however a reputation for being more prone to accident, disaster and civil disorder than any other community in Britain.'

Certainly, this particular Scottish Cup final, the first match of which was played on 10 April 1909 at a windy Hampden Park in front of a 70,000 crowd, had the added edge of being an 'Old Firm' meeting, representing for the aforesaid Easterbrook 'something apart from all other demonstrations of partisanship in sport' and described by him as 'an unhealthy emanation of religious bigotry, intolerance and slum mentality', but it was played with both a verve and a sporting spirit that also characterised the replay a week later. The prolific Jimmy Quinn opened the scoring on the half-hour mark by getting his head on the end of an Alec McNair 'long punt' or 'high lob', but, just when Celtic seemed set fair to win the trophy for the third successive year, they were shocked by a quick Rangers double in the shape of Gilchrist equalising in the seventy-second minute and ex-Celt Alec Bennett ending a fine solo run by putting the Ibrox men in front three minutes later. There was a touch of desperation about Celtic's equaliser when, ten minutes from time, their right-winger Dan Munro fired what appears to have been a cross-cum-shot towards the Rangers goal that Harry Rennie decided not to palm out of harm's way (a technique he described as 'panic and crude goalkeeping, unworthy of the standard of play usually associated with the Glasgow Rangers Football Club') but instead to stretch up his arms to grasp it, in the process of which his attempt to evade the attentions of the inrushing Jimmy Quinn meant that he appeared to step backwards over the line with the ball. The referee awarded a goal, much to the indignation of Rennie, who maintained afterwards – somewhat bizarrely – that it was not only 'a high-class and effective bit of goalkeeping' but also 'one of the most artful and artistic saves in my merry football career'. Nevertheless, many would soon be given reason to wonder how things might have turned out but for his theorising and perfectionism. The match ended 2–2.

Celtic: Adams; McNair, Weir; Young, Dodds, Hay; Munro, McMenemy, Quinn, Somers and Hamilton.

Rangers: Rennie; Law, Craig; May, Stark, Galt; Bennett, Gilchrist, Campbell, McPherson and Smith.

Referee: J.B. Stark (Airdrie).

A couple of days after this first match, the Celtic secretary-manager Willie Maley, during a casual conversation with a Rangers director in the city centre's The Bank restaurant, of which Maley later became the proprietor, seems to have raised the question of the replay being played to the finish (i.e. the use of extra time, if necessary), with a view to the matter being discussed by the Ibrox board of directors. Thereafter, Maley, perhaps encouraged by what he heard during the conversation, had a meeting with his own board at a function held in the Grosvenor Restaurant to celebrate director Tom White gaining his B.L. degree from Glasgow University, the outcome of their deliberations being the following snippet in the *Daily Record and Mail* of Wednesday, 14 April 1909, three days before the replay:

> An important decision was arrived at by the directors of the Celtic Football Club last night when it was agreed to approach the Scottish Football Association and the Rangers club with a view to having the match played to a finish on Saturday. With a heavy league programme still to be faced, the desire of the Parkhead management to arrive at a definite conclusion in the final can be easily understood. According to the rules of the Association, in the event of a draw the match [i.e. the second replay] would require to be played in the following mid-week, but should such an arrangement be made as that emanating from the Celtic Football Club be come to there is every possibility of another game being obviated.

Celtic's motive was understandable, since – due to their involvement in several Glasgow Cup and Scottish Cup replays – after the Scottish Cup final replay (and not allowing for a third match) they faced a schedule of eight league matches in the space of twelve days as they strove for a record fifth successive title. At the time of the directors' meeting, the position at the top was as follows (two points for a victory):

	Played	Points
Dundee	33	48
Rangers	30	43
Celtic	26	39

Glasgow's *Evening Citizen* endorsed the suggestion as being a popular one, stating that there should be little objection to the proposal, even though the Scottish Football Association rules stipulated that a third game take place, and asserting that if all parties concerned were agreeable 'the rule is one that may be broken with impunity'. However, that newspaper was not to know that on that very Wednesday afternoon Willie Maley had met Rangers director A.B. Mackenzie in the 'Association Rooms', where he learned that the matter had not been discussed by the Ibrox board. Indeed, it seems that there was no question of that happening, according to John Allan in his *The Story of the Rangers* (1923): 'The question of extra time had never been discussed by the directors for the simple reason that the SFA rules stipulated for extra time only when a third game became necessary.' There seems to have been no official approach to the Association in time for a change to the rule before the replay, since on the eve of the match the *Daily Record and Mail* reported that 'Nothing fresh has transpired with regard to the Scottish Cup final.' John Allan, commenting in his book, issued an implicit rebuke to Willie Maley for what Allan regarded as an irresponsible role in implanting a notion in the public domain: 'It is quite likely, therefore, that many of those who attended the second game were under the belief that, in the event of another draw, extra time would be played. The presumption amounts almost to a certainty.' Fatal error number one.

Celtic made only one change for the replay on Saturday, 17 April in front of a 60,000 gathering, fielding Willie Kivlichan in place of Munro, while Gordon replaced May for Rangers, who also made two changes in the forward line: McDonald for Gilchrist and Reid (signed two days before the match from Portsmouth) for Campbell. One of those changes brought an early reward when Gordon gave Rangers the lead with 'a powerful slanting shot' on twenty minutes, but Jimmy Quinn's famed persistence drew Celtic level some twenty minutes after the interval with a headed goal from a Jimmy Hay corner. Thereafter, the fear of losing was predominant, with the teams behaving like boxers too wary of their opponents' craft to land a knockout punch, and the match ended 1–1. In his report to the SFA, the referee, again Mr J.B. Stark, gave his version of what happened after he blew the whistle for time-up. He said that he found himself having to cross the whole breadth of the pitch to reach the pavilion. When he neared the pavilion, he was approached 'to know if extra time was to be played' by someone who was not identified and his reply was that he had no official instruction in regard to that. Noticing players still standing on the pitch, he 'signalled for them to retire'. One policeman present, an Inspector McKay, told the *Daily Record and Mail* that, after the final whistle, 'The Celtic team remained on the field as if with the intention of playing an extra half-hour, the Rangers players leaving the field. The Celtic team shortly afterwards followed. The spectators, being under the belief that an extra half-hour would be played, remained in their position.' In fact, a newspaper showed that eight Celtic and two Rangers players had remained on the pitch. This hesitancy was undoubtedly a crucial factor in what happened next, attributed by the watching Sir John Ure Primrose to the 'very great mistake that there was no definite announcement before the match commenced as to whether there would be an extra half-hour'. A verdict endorsed by Jimmy Quinn in his recollection of the episode in the *Scottish Weekly Record* in July 1914:

> When the second game finished as a draw the public were of the opinion that the game would be played to a finish. This, of course, was not thought of, but the public ought to have been told the exact position. This was not done, however, and gave a chance to the hooligans, who are always ready to embrace an opportunity to ply their vile trade.

Fatal error number two.

According to one account, the expectancy of a crowd shouting 'Play on' and 'Extra time' was soon dashed by the sight of an official emerging from the pavilion to begin removing the corner flags, but the signal for spectators to take matters into their own hands was apparently the sight of a policeman dealing roughly with one of the crowd who ran towards the pavilion to demand the match be played to a finish. There were around a hundred policemen on duty at the replay, but the officer-in-charge deployed them to protect the stand, a seated area patronised by the wealthier members of society, with the result that, initially, there were no policemen on hand to attempt to hold back the angry multitude pouring out of the terracings, largely from the section opposite it appears. Fatal mistake number three. This act of deference reinforces the impression that the post-match newspaper coverage, particularly the tone and language in which it was couched, was a manifestation of the syndrome known as 'moral panic', defined as an intensity of feeling (most notably expressed in terms of alarm, indignation and loathing) expressed by the more privileged section of the population about an issue or event that appears to threaten the social order. It is difficult to avoid the impression, however one deplores the events that day at Hampden Park, that this was class warfare of a sort, a form of revenge on the part of the proletariat, for want of a better word, on the broadly middle-class ethos that controlled (and to a lesser extent still controls) the sport, with administrators and club directors treating the working man as mere turnstile fodder. When combined with the prevalent suspicion about the number of drawn cup ties between the two clubs, instanced by the previous season's three Glasgow Cup final matches averaging crowds of 63,000 and drawing enormous receipts for the day, this resentment was a heady brew. Simply put, the police soon found themselves overwhelmed as they struggled to contain what one newspaper described as 'mob rule', even with the aid of the reinforcements who were quickly summoned. Baton charges were repelled in hand-to-hand combat and by 'a fusillade of stones, bottles, brickbats and every conceivable missile of which the roughs could become possessed'. Mounted police brought in to contain the situation met a similar reaction. The rioters also cut the hoses of fire brigades attempting to put out pay-box fires and, in another demonstration of an improvised scorched earth policy, dragged a 'road roller' onto the pitch, a piece of machinery that they rolled up and down the playing area, turning it into 'a ploughed field'. Meanwhile, Willie Maley watched the events unfolding, his recollections of which he detailed in *Thomson's Weekly News* in July 1936. He prefaced his account by neglecting to mention his role in fostering the 'erroneous impression [that] got around that an extra half hour would be played in case of a draw', but went on to say:

I watched the progress of the rioters, and I watched how certain officials tried to handle them. I think now, and I thought then, that if more judgment and a lot more tact had been employed when the trouble first broke out, all the destruction and damage would have been avoided. Had the two competing clubs been consulted right away, I am certain the combined efforts of manager Wilton, of Rangers, and myself would have soothed the savage breasts of the multitude. But we were treated as negligible quantities. The riot was now on, and the rioters getting into their stride.

Indeed they were, and it took nearly three hours to bring matters fully under control and enable the referee to emerge from the safety of his dressing-room, but not before, in the words of *The Scotsman*, the culprits departed the stadium in triumph, carrying souvenirs such as the crossbar of one of the goalposts, leaving behind among the debris littering the ground a number of policemen's helmets that 'had been lost in the day's struggle' but many of which had been cut up into strips and also carried away as mementos. According to another report, this scene of exultation caused alarm in the surrounding suburban streets where residents cowered at the sight of the rioters 'brandishing their improvised weapons [goalposts, pieces of wood, etc.], smashing windows behind which householders huddled in terror, and breaking every street lamp they saw'.

In the aftermath, the host club, Queen's Park, took immediate steps to secure the ground and allay the anxieties of the still-nervous local inhabitants by arranging for 30 policemen to patrol the stadium and its surrounds on the Saturday evening and on the following day, when they were also needed to deter sightseers who turned up at Mount Florida to view the destruction that had taken place. An army of joiners were brought in on the Sunday morning to make temporary repairs to the stadium. An eyewitness described the scene that greeted them: 'All the woodwork at the Somerville Drive entrances had been burned away or charred and what was left was a mass of torn, twisted or bent galvanised iron. The enclosure was a litter of stones and broken bottles and scarred patches where the fire had been at work.' The total damage was assessed at £1,000, of which the SFA paid half and the other £500 was 'evenly divided among the finalists and the ground club', an arrangement that has to be set against the fact that the two matches of the final had taken in a total of around £4,000 at the gate. The SFA met two days after the fiasco and, after learning that both clubs had already met to make a pact ('within their right, according to rule', said their spokesman, Celtic director Tom White) not to participate in a third match, the upshot was that the following motion proposed by the SFA president, John Liddell, was carried by the rather narrow margin of 15 votes to 11: 'That to mark the Association's disapproval of the riotous conduct of a section of the spectators at Hampden Park, and to avoid a repetition, the Cup competition for this season be finished and the cup and medals withheld.' However, provision was made in time for the 1910 final (and subsequent ones) for extra time to be played at the end of a replay if needed to decide the destination of the trophy. Indeed, it was used in the replay of that year's final before Dundee prevailed over Clyde in a third match.

Celtic now turned their attention to the arduous matter of retaining their title, winning five matches, drawing two and losing one in the aforesaid twelve-day period to pip Dundee by one point. Celtic in those days relied on a small, compact squad marked by an 'all-round versatility' yet also stamped with top-class, match-winning performers such as the infinitely subtle but unselfish 'brains' of the side, Jimmy McMenemy, described by *Scottish Referee* in April 1909 as 'the master-key of Celtic's clock-work passing play'. McMenemy would turn goal-scorer to clinch that title at Hamilton at the end of the month, netting the winner in a 2–1 victory with an adroit manoeuvre to gain himself space before 'placing the ball inside the post' from some 12 yards out. Allied to a demanding captain in Jimmy Hay, whose stentorian voice, it was said, could be heard during matches in the lofty press box perched atop the 'Grant Stand' at Celtic Park as he drove his men to pull out that little extra which wins championships, it all added up to making the Parkhead side a formidable outfit, probably the best in Britain. No wonder that the veteran reporter writing under the pen name of 'Bauldie' was moved to reflect in *Scottish Referee* of 29 April 1910 – after Celtic had created a new Scottish record of six titles in a row – on the reasons for this remarkable consistency and set it down to three factors: 'First, good management; second, good players; third, harmony.' It all sounds so simple . . .

CHAPTER 5

The March of Time

Goalkeeper: 'Safety first' should be the motto of every goalkeeper; for this reason he should use his hands whenever possible.
Inside-Forward: When they performed at inside-forward 30 years ago, they always played a little behind the centre-forward, and had to do a good deal of 'fetching and carrying'.

'Individual Positions', Association Football, *F.N.S. Creek, 1937*

The position of goalkeeper has always been an important one in any football team with aspirations of success. To be regarded highly in the role, many qualities are required. Some are obvious, like athleticism, a keen eye for the ball and good judgement. Others, such as anticipation or a dominating personality, are less so. But in the late nineteenth and early twentieth centuries, bravery was another essential requirement, as assaults on the last line of defence were a regular feature of the game.

In the first 20 years or so of Celtic's existence, over a dozen keepers played a part in the history of the club.

Mick Dolan, the first man between the sticks, was at the time with Drumpellier but, as an amateur able to play for whomsoever he wished, turned out for the new club when the invitational select ran out to face Rangers Swifts in Celtic's first-ever match on 28 May 1888. He signed shortly afterwards and played seven matches for the club, three in the Scottish League, one in the Scottish Cup and three in the Glasgow Cup. The Scottish Cup tie was against

St Mirren at Westmarch, Paisley, on 28 November 1891 in front of a crowd of 4,800. The *Scottish Referee* match report of 30 November 1891 stated that the referee, Mr Hay of Dumfries, 'clad in a Harris [Tweed] suit, ornamented with a heilan' cape, a brass whistle and a summer smile, set the tie going prompt to time, 2.30'.

Willie Dunning was brought in from Johnstone Juniors just in time to make his first-team debut against Shettleston in Celtic's first-ever Scottish Cup tie on 1 September 1888. Willie played in six Scottish Cup ties that season of 1888–89, although he was also in goal for three Glasgow Cup ties, two matches in the Glasgow International Exhibition Tournament at Gilmorehill plus a tie in the North Eastern Cup (a competition for clubs in that area of Glasgow).

Willie Dunning eventually ended up at Aston Villa with whom he won a League Championship medal in 1894 but retired the following year through ill health. Shortly afterwards, pulmonary tuberculosis was diagnosed and he died from the disease in 1902, shortly after his 37th birthday.

John Kelly was next in, making his debut in a friendly against Mitchell St George's in December 1888. He made four competitive appearances (two Scottish Cup, one Charity Cup, one North Eastern Cup) and was the first keeper to represent Celtic in a Scottish Cup final (February 1889). His career with the club was effectively ended by an indifferent performance in the Charity Cup defeat (2–5) by Renton three months later.

James McLaughlin made his first-team debut as a full-back against Albion Rovers in a Scottish Cup tie on 13 October 1888 and his goalkeeping debut when Celtic won the North Eastern Cup at Barrowfield Park by beating Cowlairs 6–1 on 11 May 1889. James also played – as a goalkeeper – in three Glasgow Cup, one Charity Cup and another five North Eastern Cup matches.

James Bell was Celtic's first regular league goalkeeper. Unfortunately, he joined Celtic in rather rushed circumstances. In those days, players had to be two weeks clear of any attachment to their former club – in Bell's case, Dumbarton – and Celtic were found guilty of infringing this rule when he made his debut against

Hearts in Edinburgh on 23 August 1890, and were deducted four points for this transgression.

James Bell kept his place during the first league season of 1890–91, playing fifteen matches, as well as making seven Scottish Cup, three Charity Cup and five Glasgow Cup appearances, one of the latter being when Celtic beat Third Lanark 4–0 at Hampden in the 1891 final.

For some reason, Jim McLaren, usually a wing-half, was chosen as keeper for the club's first league match against Renton on 16 August 1890. Celtic lost 1–4 but the result was later expunged from the record books as a result of Renton dabbling with professionalism and the management brought in James Bell for the game against Hearts the following week.

Tom Duff joined Celtic from Cowlairs in the summer of 1891 and took over from James Bell for Celtic's league campaign at the start of the 1891–92 season. However, in his sixth outing, against Dumbarton at Celtic Park on 26 September 1891, he received such a soaking when torrential rain hit the ground that rheumatics set into his hands, a condition that did not help his performances. This poor form reached its nadir in the friendly against Dumbarton at Parkhead on New Year's Day 1892, when Celtic were beaten 0–8 and Tom Duff never played for Celtic again (see Chapter 1). His overall record was eight Scottish League, one Scottish Cup and two Glasgow Cup appearances.

Another Kelly, this time **Charles Kelly**, replaced Duff during his period of illness, making two Scottish League and one Glasgow Cup appearances in October 1891 before moving on to Busby Cartvale. Charles died of dropsy (oedema) in 1898 at the age of 31.

Joe Cullen, Celtic's first long-serving goalkeeper, signed from Benburb in 1892 and became the first Celtic keeper to win a Scottish Cup medal (v. Queen's Park, 9 April 1892) and also the first to play at the new Celtic Park (v. Renton, 20 August 1892). Joe played ninety-six times in total for the club (fifty-eight Scottish League, five Glasgow League, fifteen Scottish Cup, thirteen Glasgow Cup and five Charity Cup) before he moved to Tottenham Hotspur in 1897.

Dan McArthur was the next incumbent and a real star in a tough age. Dan made 123 appearances in League and Scottish Cup between 1894 and 1901 – with 42 shut-outs, a 34.1 per cent success rate – and also played 20 Glasgow League, 11 Inter City League, 21 Glasgow Cup and 13 Charity Cup matches. Dan was between the posts for the league victories of 1895–96 and 1897–98, the Scottish Cup wins of 1899 and 1900 plus several Charity and Glasgow Cup successes.

The Inter City was an expansion of the Glasgow League to incorporate Edinburgh and Dundee clubs. The Glasgow/Inter City League only lasted a decade (seasons 1895–96 to 1905–06).

In between the regulars were the keepers who got occasional chances when the stars were injured. These included:

John Docherty, originally signed from Dumbarton on a loan deal when Dan McArthur was injured in February 1896. He signed full forms for Celtic in 1887 and played nineteen times in total (eleven Scottish League, three Glasgow League, one Inter City League, two Glasgow Cup, two Charity Cup).

Willie Donnelly made six appearances (three Scottish League, two Scottish Cup, one Charity Cup) in place of Dan McArthur in season 1900–01 before returning to Northern Ireland and Belfast Celtic.

Robert McFarlane replaced Willie Donnelly in that season of 1901–02 and made twenty-three appearances with four shut-outs (17 per cent) in League and Scottish Cup (plus six Inter City, two Glasgow Cup and three Glasgow Exhibition Cup outings) before moving on to Aberdeen and Motherwell. Robert later emigrated to Australia.

Andy McPherson was another to be given a run, making forty-four appearances between 1902 and 1904 (twenty-seven Scottish League, five Inter City League, five Glasgow Cup, six Charity Cup and possibly one British League Cup/British Championship). Andy may have been in goal when Celtic beat Rangers in the final of the latter in June 1902, but newspaper accounts differ as to whether he or McFarlane was the occupant. He was definitely the first Celtic custodian to wear the Hoops instead of the Stripes (goalkeepers wore the same jersey as the rest of the team in those days, their only identification coming in the form of wearing a cap) when Celtic beat Patrick Thistle at Parkhead on 15 August 1903.

There were also three other keepers with a handful of appearances between them during this period. Both **Willie Howden** (1 app) and a keeper called **Forbes**, whose first name is not known (2 apps), got their chances in the 1897–98 Glasgow League; while **Hugh Edmonds** played his only match for the club in the 5–1 British League Cup/British Championship victory over Sunderland in April 1902.

While all of these players deserve credit for having sufficient talent for the club to sign them in the first place, it would also be true to say that they were not always to the liking of even partisans of the club. In the *Glasgow Observer* of April 1895, for example, in a profile of Dan McArthur, widely regarded as the first really good or outstanding Celtic keeper, the writer was fairly uncomplimentary about some of the early custodians: 'For some seasons, the Celtic club was indifferently served in the matter of goalkeepers. Dunning, McLaughlin, Bell and Duff were very fair in their way, but, as the saying is, "nothing patent".' A few weeks later, in a profile of Joe Cullen, the newspaper was even more frank, describing Willie Dunning as 'very second-rate' and James McLaughlin as 'mediocre', while reserving its particular scorn for Duff: 'Duff went up like a rocket, and, after a brief period of fitful brilliance, came down like the proverbial stick.'

The one aspect that every club likes in its goalkeeper is consistency and, with 18 keepers in nearly the same number of years, that was obviously not the rule at Celtic Park. Then **Davie Adams** arrived and brought a well-needed security to the position.

Davie made his debut in an Inter City League match against Hibernian in April 1903 and, after initially deputising for McPherson, soon became the man behind one of the best defences in Celtic's history. During the next eight years, the club picked up Scottish Cups in 1904, 1907, 1908 and 1911; six consecutive league titles between 1905 and 1910; plus five Glasgow Cups and two Charity Cups. Overall, Davie Adams made 337 competitive appearances

(248 Scottish League, 43 Scottish Cup, 5 Inter City League, 27 Glasgow Cup and 14 Charity Cup). In fact, during the years 1903 to 1911, only a touch of rheumatics and the occasional bout of pneumonia kept him out of the side. It was a remarkable level of consistency. Davie was also the last Celtic keeper to wear the Hoops and thus the first to don a distinctive (yellow) jersey in season 1910–11, after the wearing of a cap to identify a goalkeeper was abolished.

In one of Davie Adams' more serious spells out with injury, in season 1906–07, when he was injured during a testimonial match for Rangers player Finlay Speedie, Celtic accepted an offer from Rangers and took their reserve-team keeper **Tom Sinclair** on loan. Sinclair made nine appearances in total (six Scottish League, three Glasgow Cup), picking up a Glasgow Cup winners' medal in the 3–2 victory in the final against Third Lanark, his only competitive match for Celtic in which he did not keep a clean sheet.

Unfortunately, as season 1911–12 got under way, there were rumours coming from within the club that Davie Adams was having some problems with his eyesight. And, while nothing official was said at that point, there was some evidence that he definitely did have a problem.

At Motherwell, on 25 November 1911, two of the goals he conceded were attributed in the *Daily Record and Mail* match report (27 November) to errors on his part. McStay, the Motherwell right-half, opened the scoring with a 40-yarder: 'the wonder of many (in the 10,000 crowd) was that a man of Adams' undoubted ability could have allowed such a long-range shot to take effect'. Of Motherwell's third goal, in the 55th minute, the *Daily Record and Mail* report said, 'Lindley's long drive from an acute angle passed Adams.'

The existence of a problem was further suggested by a comment from 'Man in the Know' in the *Glasgow Observer* of 2 December 1911: 'Adams was again unfortunate but if my readers knew how handicapped he has been for the past few months, sympathy and not resentment would be shown this old and tried servant.'

However, in time-honoured fashion, a new hero was about to

emerge to ease the fans' concerns about Celtic's indifferent form. Of the first eighteen matches of that season of 1911–12, Celtic won ten, drew three and lost five. The usual back three of Adams, McNair and Dodds was in place but, in the forward line, there had been much chopping and changing of position, with players like Willie Nichol (16 apps in total for the club), Paddy Travers (22), John Black (4) and Andy Donaldson (17) all given chances alongside old warhorses such as McMenemy, Quinn and Hamilton. Another was now about to appear in the frame for possible selection up front.

In the early days of organised football, the systems used by football teams were evolving slowly, the number of defenders increasing at the expense of the forwards. Thus, the cavalry charge of the initial years in the 1-1-8 formation soon changed to a more guarded 2-2-6 layout and this eventually developed into a 2-3-5 system that lasted right up to the change of the Offside Law in 1925. The playmakers in this formation were initially the centre-halfs but, as time progressed, the inside-forwards became the main providers and every club was desperate to find players of quality who were comfortable in those positions. They were few and far between, but, just occasionally, a club was fortunate enough to spot one in the most unusual of circumstances.

In the spring of 1910, a 19-year-old youth called Patsy Gallacher from juvenile side Renfrew St James was selected to play for Renfrew Juveniles against their Paisley counterparts at Love Street, the home of St Mirren. He obviously did well, as he was then chosen for the Rest of Scotland side to face Lanarkshire at Fir Park in May 1910.

Any match like that attracts scouts from all the major – and minor – clubs and they would have all been impressed that night by Gallacher's enthusiasm, stamina, ball control and dribbling skills, although there would have also been some serious reservations about whether his puny frame, 5 ft 7 in. and under 10 st., could cope with senior football. Clydebank Juniors was one club willing to give the laddie a try and Patsy played for them during the 1910–11 season.

Over at Celtic Park, secretary-manager Willie Maley was feeling a trifle depressed. After six consecutive seasons of league title success, his side had disappointed in the most recent campaign, finishing fifth in the table, a distant eleven points behind champions Rangers. Certainly, Celtic did win the Scottish Cup, beating Hamilton 2–0 in the 1911 final replay, after a 0–0 draw in the first match. And the Bhoys had reached the final of both the Charity and Glasgow Cups, though had lost to Rangers on each occasion. However, Maley still felt that an injection of fresh talent was essential and his extensive network of scouts was on the lookout throughout the country.

The name of Patsy Gallacher was one put forward and the Celtic manager decided to try him out in a friendly against a Dumfries Select on a local holiday called Rood Fair Day in October 1911. Celtic won 6–1, with Patsy scoring twice and obviously impressing those watching. On the train home, he received another invitation to play for the club, this time against an Army XI. Celtic won again, this time by 5–0, with Patsy getting a hat-trick. Any reservations the Celtic management and board of directors might have had were swept aside by these performances, and Patsy was asked to sign for the club on part-time terms, an offer he gratefully accepted.

He arrived at a time when the team was not playing particularly well. In September, Celtic had lost to Partick Thistle in the first round of the Glasgow Cup; of nine league matches during October and November, Celtic had won four, drawn two and lost three; and, just to make matters worse, Jimmy Quinn had been out injured, playing only a couple of games since the start of the season, and Jimmy McMenemy had missed six consecutive matches. By late November, Celtic were in second place in the table, having 21 points from 17 games (2 points for a win then). Second place might not have seemed a bad position to be in, but Willie Maley was a realist; on top were Rangers, with 27 points from only 14 matches. If Celtic wanted another league title, immediate improvements were required. Might this new boy Gallacher be just what the side needed? Should he give him an early chance?

The next league match was against St Mirren at Parkhead and after much thought Maley decided to give Patsy Gallacher a run-out. 'Man in the Know' of the *Glasgow Observer* was obviously given the nod in advance from the manager, as he enthused about the young man: 'He had the crowd in raptures over his play' was his description of Patsy's display at Dumfries; while he 'had quite a good time against the "sojers"' was his verdict on the youngster's performance on the day Celtic had beaten the Army XI.

A crowd of 12,000 made its way to Celtic Park on Saturday, 2 December 1911 for the contest, an attendance boosted by the knowledge that Jimmy Quinn would be returning after injury. The full team was:

Adams, McNair, Dodds, Young, Loney, Johnstone, McAtee, Gallacher, Quinn, Donaldson, Brown.

Celtic won 3–1, a victory made all the more sweet by the information that Rangers had suffered their first league defeat of the season against Morton. However, for two of the Celtic players who took to the field that day in all-green jerseys and socks, with white shorts, there were conflicting emotions. Unfortunately, when St Mirren opened the scoring, the evidence seems to suggest that Davie Adams may have been at fault – again. Certainly, that was the impression given by the *Daily Record and Mail* match report, which stated, 'probably nobody was more surprised than Callaghan (St Mirren's right-winger) himself when he saw the ball which he had evidently intended as a centre curl past Adams'.

For Patsy Gallacher, however, the emotions would have been entirely different, as the press went into raptures over his performance.

Daily Record and Mail, 4 December 1911: 'With as many tricks in his box as would almost make Cinquevalli [Paul Cinquevalli – a famous juggler, acrobat and trapeze artist of the time] green with envy, Paddy Gallacher established himself as a favourite in his first match at Celtic Park.'

Glasgow Observer, 9 December 1911: 'Gallacher, while playing well, merely gave a hint of the football that is in him . . . I can promise some hot work on the right wing once he gets to know what Quinn and McAtee want . . . young Gallacher has no superior as an accurate passer and when it comes to shooting, well, one wonders where he gets the strength.'

Scottish Weekly Record, 9 December 1911. Jimmy Quinn was not a man to go overboard in his judgement of players. In his regular column for the newspaper, he said this of Patsy's debut: 'little Gallacher put in a power of work and, once he steadies down to the regular game, I consider he will take a lot of beating. He is clever with the ball, very plucky, and exceedingly quick to take an opening, but he is too keen on work, and is thereby apt to roam too much for the benefit of the forward division, where it behoves us all to keep our places . . . I believe he is a real asset to our club and I look forward to his taking his honoured place among the clever players the Celts have reared.'

So, it was a poignant occasion that afternoon of 2 December 1911, with one great Celtic career coming to an end as another was set to bloom. Patsy Gallacher went on to score 196 goals in his 464 matches in the major, national competitions for his beloved Hoops, won 6 League Championships and 4 Scottish Cup honours plus 12 caps for Ireland. Davie Adams never played for Celtic again and was forced to give up the game altogether in March 1912. Ring out the old, ring in the new . . .

* * *

The particulars of Patsy Gallacher's career are well documented and he is rightly remembered as one of the finest players ever to wear the green-and-white strip. The name of Davie Adams, on the other hand, is not recalled quite so effusively, so how good a goalkeeper was he? Well, he did make 291 appearances for Celtic in the major competitions, the custodian in one of the most successful sides in Celtic's history, so he certainly had a pedigree that should never be forgotten.

This might come as a surprise to many fans but, in the 125 years since Celtic played their first official competitive game against Abercorn in the Glasgow International Exhibition Cup in 1888, only 20 goalkeepers have played more than 100 matches for the club in the major competitions – the Scottish League, the Scottish Cup, the Scottish League Cup and European competitions. When the playing records of these stars are listed, it is customary to state the number of appearances along with the number of clean sheets, i.e. the matches during which that particular goalkeeper prevented the opposition from scoring. Listed below, up to the end of season 2013–14, are the relevant records for those 20 Celtic goalkeepers; the names are in chronological order:

	Period	Appearances	Clean Sheets	% Success
Dan McArthur	1892–1903	123	42	34.1
Davie Adams	1903–12	291	126	43.3
Charlie Shaw	1913–25	444	236	53.2
Peter Shevlin	1924–27	105	36	34.3
John Thomson	1926–31	188	66	35.1
Joe Kennaway	1931–39	290	81	27.9
Willie Miller	1946–50	123	29	23.6
John Bonnar	1946–58	178	51	28.7
Dick Beattie	1955–59	155	42	27.1
Frank Haffey	1958–64	200	61	30.5
John Fallon	1958–72	185	61	33.0
Ronnie Simpson	1964–70	188	91	48.4
Evan Williams	1969–74	148	59	39.9
Peter Latchford	1975–87	272	82	30.1
Pat Bonner	1978–95	641	253	39.5
Gordon Marshall	1992–98	136	63	46.3
Jonathon Gould	1997–2003	158	69	43.7
Robert Douglas	2000–05	162	86	53.1
Artur Boruc	2005–10	221	85	38.5
Fraser Forster	2010–	193	100	51.8

Based on information –since updated – in *Charlie Shaw* brochure, Celtic Graves Society, 2013.

CHAPTER 6

Two in One

Mr Maley has no equal in getting the best from his players. I think that will go uncontradicted.

'John O' Groat' in the Scottish Weekly Record
of 14 October 1916

No greater honour could be paid the Celtic than the desire of other clubs to beat them. The sensation of beating the Celtic is a sensation unequalled by victory over any other club and thus it is that the Parkhead team find greater effort put forward against them by opposing clubs than is generated at any other time . . . They go out to win all the time, and no club does more to keep alive the interest in our national sport. They would be foolish, however, to think that they can never be beaten, and I don't believe they regret an occasional reverse after the first pang is over. Monopoly in football, or anything else, is not for the general good.

'John O' Groat' in the Weekly Mail and Record, *30 March 1918, after
Celtic's 1–3 home defeat at the hands of Third Lanark severely dented their
hopes of making it five successive titles. Rangers thwarted that ambition,
edging out Celtic by one point.*

The 'war to end all wars' was dragging on in its already weary way that spring of 1916, with no end in sight to a conflict already seemingly embedded in stalemate on a Western Front where the losses were so heavy that conscription had been introduced in Britain earlier that year, and now its effects were being felt on the very doorstep of Celtic Park. With the military gearing up for the looming offensive on the Somme, Clydeside – and particularly the city of Glasgow – was crucial to the war effort. The gigantic Beardmore's steelworks (popularly known as Parkhead Forge, and where Celtic defender Joe Dodds worked in the shell factory as a condition of carrying on as a professional footballer in wartime) was deemed so indispensable to the production of armaments that an alarmed government took severe and decisive action when a three-week strike there resulting from rumbling discontent about restrictions on trade union activity and the issue of dilution, namely the bringing in of women and unskilled men to do the work of time-served engineers, spread to munitions works in the rest of the city. Such was the determination to limit the role of trade unions at such a critical juncture of the war by exiling its leaders from their sphere of influence that in the early hours of the morning of Saturday, 25 March the chairman of the shop stewards at Parkhead Forge, Davie Kirkwood (the locally born son of a labourer), became one of six members of the Clyde Workers' Committee who were arrested at their homes, imprisoned (one of them was then released) and 'deported' to Edinburgh by armed police. The police were acting on military instructions authorised under the terms of the 1914 Defence of the Realm Act, which gave legal sanction to extensive control of areas of life in wartime Britain; one of its provisions included the banning of bonfires lest they alert Zeppelins. Although the men were released in June 1917, the Glasgow-based left-wing newspaper *Forward* articulated its outrage at this perceived infringement of civil liberties in its 1 April 1916 edition: 'No charge! No bail! No trial! Men whose families have lived four generations in one district, men whose personal character is unblemished, men who have the respect, the esteem and the confidence of their fellows, simply whipped off – as if we did not live in a free country.'

In its report of the deportation, the newspaper noted that 'a Siberian touch' had been added to the proceedings by the weather being 'bitterly cold and snow was falling fast', a development that led to a fruitless journey by the players and directors of Celtic FC that very same day. Scheduled to play a league match at Motherwell that afternoon, the Celtic party had already set out for the steel town despite having received a message to the effect that the match had been cancelled due to the weather. They could not afford to treat such a communication from an unofficial source (not identified in the press) as official. It was only when they arrived at Fir Park that they learned for certain that the pitch was 'unplayable' due to a snowstorm. This postponement meant that Celtic were now faced with the problem of completing their league programme by 30 April, as was the rule then, and matches could only be played on Saturdays and 'recognised public holidays' in order not to interfere with the demands of war-related industries. However, thanks to some shrewd negotiation on the part of Celtic secretary-manager Willie Maley, an arrangement was made for both Celtic and Motherwell to play two matches on the same day, Saturday, 15 April 1916. He circumvented Ayr United's reluctance to play Motherwell at Fir Park that afternoon by offering them a financial 'sweetener' to allay their concern about the potential impact on the 'gate' of two matches at the same venue within the space of some six hours, with Motherwell hosting Celtic in the evening.

And so it was that, two days after the legendary Glasgow revolutionary socialist John Maclean had been sentenced to three years' penal servitude (reduced by nearly a half after various forms of protest) for anti-war speeches and writing against what he regarded as 'a capitalists' war', Celtic and Raith Rovers lined up at Celtic Park at 3.15 p.m. on 15 April. Celtic had two objectives in mind that day. First, there was the prospect of clinching the league title for the third year in succession should they win their two matches and Rangers falter that afternoon and, second, there was the opportunity to create a new Scottish League goal-scoring record by eclipsing Falkirk's 1907–08 feat (103 in a 34-match First Division, albeit as runners-up to Celtic). Celtic's match against Raith Rovers that afternoon would be their 34th in a 38-match programme. In their previous 33 league matches that season, Celtic had notched 98 goals and were well set to overhaul Falkirk's tally, for they were cloaked in an aura of free-scoring invincibility. Although at that stage they were not yet halfway through their record-setting run of 66 matches undefeated spanning the period November 1915 to April 1917 (62 League, 2 Glasgow Cup, 2 Charity Cup – the Scottish Cup competition was suspended during wartime), Celtic were so dominant that, according to 'Man in the Know' of the *Glasgow Observer* of 25 March 1916, some bookmakers were leaving them out of their coupons while others were treating them as the home team at places like Paisley, Falkirk and Motherwell.

Celtic: Shaw; McNair and McGregor; Young, Dodds and McMaster; McAtee, Gallacher, O'Kane, McMenemy and Browning.

Raith Rovers: Brown; Inglis and Robson; Hutchison, McKerley and Foster; Archibald, Abbott, Newbigging, Turner and Gibson.

Referee: J. Binnie – also listed as Bennie – (Falkirk).

In his regular column a week later in the *Weekly Mail and Record*, Jimmy McMenemy stated that before the match Willie Maley had given the Celtic players a little homily: 'It was the one about the dog with two bones, and they were advised not to lose sight of the first match, because of the second [v. Motherwell in the evening]. "You can get the necessary number of goals if you go the right way about it" were the words he used.' The players soon demonstrated that they had no need of such pleading. Despite a promising opening by a visiting side that was languishing at the foot of the table but which was seemingly intent on countering the prevailing impression in football circles that Celtic's opponents were beaten before they took the field – their defence keeping the Celtic forwards at bay by their early brisk tackling and forwards 'who beat up well against the wind' showing a determination to make their mark against the champions – the homesters were not to be denied, as detailed in these descriptions pieced together from various newspapers whose accounts of the goals give varying degrees of satisfaction:

15 mins: shortly after missing a 'sitter' by lofting the ball over the

bar from close in, Joe O'Kane (deputising for the injured, prolific centre-forward Jimmy McColl) opened the scoring, sweeping a low McAtee cross past the keeper.

25 mins: the alert O'Kane took advantage of a defensive misjudgement following a throw-in to net his own second goal (and Celtic's 100th that league season): 'The visiting backs, evidently under the impression that Brown would run out to clear, made no effort to intercept the centre as he ran in to tip the leather between the goalkeeper's legs.'

Untimed: Patsy Gallacher's 'clinching [of] a nice cross from Browning' made it 3–0 for Celtic before the interval. Mention of Gallacher having 'bobbed on' Browning's cross might suggest a headed goal.

Despite playing against the wind in the second half, Celtic swarmed all over a Raith Rovers side that, apart from the odd breakaway, simply wasn't in it, having to rely on the goalkeeping heroics of Brown to keep the score down.

Untimed: shortly after retiring to the touchline for attention by the trainer, Patsy Gallacher (who had felt unwell before the match) 'put the finishing touch to a hot Celtic attack' to make it 4–0. One account says he 'netted from a free kick', though whether he took it or got a touch to it is unclear.

Untimed: with the bombardment of the visitors' goal reaching a crescendo, Patsy Gallacher (five minutes after his second goal) brought Celtic level with Falkirk's 103-goal record in appropriate and characteristic fashion, scoring a brilliant solo goal for his hat-trick: 'Getting the ball on the Rovers side of midfield, he wormed his way through the entire defence' and, although fouled twice, referee Binnie's use of his discretionary powers (the 'advantage rule') allowed Patsy to 'go on and drive the ball past Brown'.

83rd minute: with the atmosphere in the ground bordering on hysteria, shortly after Gallacher had a headed goal disallowed for an infringement and both O'Kane and Browning had contrived to miss 'an open goal' from a perfectly judged McAtee cross, centre-half Joe Dodds brought relief to the 10,000 crowd [the wartime exigencies had affected attendances] when he jumped with glee as his 40-yarder 'sailed under the bar' and created a new record. 'Man in the Know', on a page in the *Glasgow Observer* headed 'Greatest day in Celtic history', was almost lost for words in depicting the finale to a 6–0 victory: 'It is beyond me to describe the scene when Joe got the ball home. The crowd simply went mad and, but for the iron railing, I fear the players would have had trouble getting off the field and into their clothes for the joy ride to Motherwell.' According to the *Glasgow Herald*, the sixth goal was also the signal for 'several hundreds' to 'take train for Motherwell' in expectation of seeing Celtic win the match postponed from 25 March, and annex the championship for the third year in succession.

In fact, Celtic's trouncing of Raith Rovers while Rangers were succumbing to a heavy (2–5) defeat at the hands of Partick Thistle at Firhill had already stripped that evening match at Motherwell of tension and drama. Those results meant that Rangers were now ten points behind Celtic, with only five matches remaining for the Ibrox men. The best that Rangers could hope for was that they won all those matches (two points for a victory in those days) and pray that Celtic lost their four remaining ones, thus forcing a title play-off, the system used up to the early 1920s to decide the destination of the championship in the event of teams finishing level on points. A remote prospect, indeed, especially given the mood that this Celtic side was in. 'A dizzy motor run' and Celtic reached their industrial Lanarkshire destination shortly after 6 p.m. for a match against opponents whose current plight had been outlined in the *Motherwell Standard* two days earlier: 'Motherwell have fallen on evil days. Not since 22 January, when they defeated Clyde, have they won a match, and even that victory was an isolated one in a preceding series of defeats. As a matter of fact they have only won two out of their last seventeen games, and bagged eight points and lost 26.' It was a daunting prospect for them to face a side whose third league defeat that season, on 13 November 1915, would be their last in a season in which they dropped only nine points. The writer's underlying suggestion that the match would be akin to a walkover for the reigning champions seems to have been shared by those in charge of Celtic, since the decision to play the on-leave 'Trooper' Joe Cassidy in place of O'Kane (the only change from the afternoon match) was made, according to 'Man in the Know', because he was so anxious to play that 'the directors decided to let him have something to talk about when he rejoins his regiment'. The home side had no such scope for whimsy, their injury problems being such as to lead to three enforced changes from the afternoon defeat by Ayr United, with one of the replacements, according to the *Motherwell Standard*, seeming to have been the product of an emergency measure: 'They had to hunt for a centre forward and found one in Johnnie Robertson, who at one time played for Motherwell.' Perhaps he was a spectator plucked from the crowd, one of the soldiers or sailors on leave who had been admitted to the terracing area of Fir Park at half-price (3d). The teams lined up at 6.30 p.m. in front of a crowd estimated at 8,000 or 9,000, a healthy attendance in view of the *Standard*'s reference to there 'being gold if not goals in it for Motherwell':

Motherwell: Rundell; Penman and McSkimming; McStay, Finlayson and Archibald; F. Kelly, Waugh, Robertson, Gray and R. McNeil.

Celtic: Shaw; McNair and McGregor; Young, Dodds and McMaster; McAtee, Gallacher, Cassidy, McMenemy and Browning.

Referee: G.H. McKenzie (Glasgow).

The match commenced 'amid the slanting rays of the setting sun and concluded under the pale moonlight' in an era when artificial lighting was not in operation at football matches in Britain due to technical doubts and, in any case, its use would have been banned under the wartime regulations. Despite their previous exertions that day, both sides put on a much livelier display than had been anticipated. As the *Daily Record and Mail* reporter noted, instead of a dreaded flat and lifeless encounter 'the magnetic presence of the Celtic seemed to put life and metal in the heels of the Motherwell men', an observation with which his *Motherwell Standard* counterpart concurred: 'From what cause I know not, but the very presence of Celtic seems to electrify the Motherwell men.' The latter appears to have been a trifle understated for, quite apart from Motherwell striving to avoid the embarrassment of an unwelcome entry in the record books as a side that lost two matches on its own ground on the one day, Celtic had not won a league match at Fir Park since December 1909 (losing three and drawing two) and there was the additional 'hostility factor'. Celtic fans had had experience of not feeling entirely welcome in the town. Before and after the Scottish Cup tie there in March 1914, they had been the target of verbal abuse and physical assault (including stone-throwing) at a place called 'County Corner', where Orange flags were displayed from many windows. Regardless of this background, Celtic were set on ending the hoodoo as quickly as possible and the Motherwell goal had two narrow escapes inside the opening five minutes, with full-back Penman just managing to clear a goal-bound effort off the line and Celtic's Andy McAtee shooting past 'with an empty goal in front of him'. Despite the home side's spirited resistance, there was a certain inevitability about 'the initial rush which wild horses could not have held back' producing the early goal that duly arrived on the quarter-of-an-hour mark when McMenemy headed in a well-placed corner kick. McMenemy and Gallacher (still trying to shake off his queasiness) were delighting the crowd with some sublime touches, but their artistry was lost on a Motherwell defence battling to contain a rampant Celtic who made it 2–0 before the interval after, according to the *Motherwell Times* report, 'Cassidy got well away on his own, but was unfairly brought down inside the penalty area', leaving Joe Dodds to convert the award.

Because of concerns about the fading daylight, 'the teams about-turned without leaving the field', according to one report, which gave no indication as to whether the teams enjoyed any period of rest, however brief. The second half started as the first had ended, with the 'sweet-moving' Celtic in total command, forcing the 'magnificent' Rundell, who had made his senior debut only that afternoon in the 0–3 loss to Ayr United, to keep the score down with some marvellous saves. The *Motherwell Standard* reporter ('Orpheus') waxed lyrical about the visitors: 'One could not fail to observe the thorough understanding that exists between the Celtic players.' The valiant home side threatened the Celtic goal only occasionally, but at least the Motherwell fans could take comfort in the display of Frank Kelly, a pacy right-winger who was showing himself capable of crossing a highly accurate ball. Given the proximity of Fir Park to the family home in Blantyre, it would be a surprise if his performance was not watched by a proud father in the shape of the legendary James (Celtic's very first captain and now a director of the club) and by an equally proud younger brother, the teenage Bob, a future chairman of Celtic who would become Sir Robert Kelly in 1969. Frank played briefly for Celtic on a loan basis later in the war years, but his football career was cruelly cut short when he lost his life (aged 26) in May 1919 as the result of a train accident while serving with the Army in post-war France. But sentimentality on the football field was lost on this Celtic side, which demonstrated its ruthlessness when Joe Cassidy and Johnny Browning combined to seal the two points after the latter was enabled to beat the brave Rundell for the third goal. Although the pace had visibly decreased, the thrills did not end with that third counter, for in the last five minutes, with the match now being played in 'semi-darkness', Cassidy passed up a great chance to make it 4–0, but with only Rundell left to beat he shot for goal at point blank range, only to see the keeper bring off an unlikely save at the expense of a corner. Robertson, the Motherwell centre-forward, missed an equally good opportunity before making amends by rounding off some fine approach play by the left-wing pair of Gray and McNeil to put a more respectable gloss on the (3–1) scoreline.

'Man in the Know' was exultant in the *Glasgow Observer* as he put forward his theory for the club's phenomenal success:

Thirteen times league champions; as many flags at Parkhead as are held by all the other Scottish clubs put together; that is where the Celts stand today. How marvellously consistent they have been since they first electrified the football world by their glorious football in the late 'eighties'! It is given to few teams to be both brilliant and consistent, yet one has only to glance over the long list of Scottish, Glasgow and Charity Cup victories to realise that our players would rise to the occasion and pull off a cup final with real Irish enthusiasm, or go through a long series of 38 league matches and hang on with Scottish dourness until they reached the topmost rung of the ladder.

He commended Alec McNair, the 'cool and crafty' full-back, and Joe Dodds, 'our very best all-round player, at home in any position, shooting goals when he is not saving them', but reserved particular praise for the captain, an individual with a justifiable claim to top any poll as the greatest-ever Celt, namely the inimitable 'Sunny Jim' Young, who had been a standout in both matches:

He was as full of enthusiasm and energy as to make one wonder where he gets his running from. Had it been possible to fix up a moonlight match about ten o'clock at Lanark or Biggar, Young would have been the first man out of the pavilion for the third game [of the day], the last to leave the field, and then be found muttering to himself what a pity it was that Scots sabbatarianism prevented another game next day . . . The club has had many faithful players, but never a more loyal than Capt. James Young, who with McNair and McMenemy can claim to have helped to win 9 league championships and cups galore.

After the Motherwell match, the Celtic party headed for 'a snack and a chat' at The Bank restaurant in Glasgow's Queen Street, described by Jimmy McMenemy as 'our town headquarters' and an establishment in which Willie Maley (later its proprietor) may already have had a stake – no pun intended! In keeping with the times, there was no raucous celebration, just a quiet satisfaction in a job well done. This was not a group of men whose heads would be swollen by the words of the captain of arch rivals Rangers, Jimmy Gordon, which appeared the following weekend in a newspaper:

> The Celts appear to have the magic power of obtaining new players, some of them nothing special at the time, but in a few short months they become infected by the Celtic atmosphere and thus form part of a very smoothly running football machine, and proceed to do their best in the way of creating more and greater club records.

In any case, there was still some work to do, for, apart from completing the league programme (116 goals notched and only 23 conceded in their 38 matches), there was the small matter of a Charity Cup to be won in order to complete a clean sweep of the honours available to them that season. This they accomplished in some style with victories over Rangers and Partick Thistle. Twelve days after the final, military duty called for the popular and highly versatile Peter Johnstone, who had been 'doing his bit' for the war effort in the mines while still donning the Celtic jersey before he enlisted on 25 May 1916 in the Argyll and Sutherland Highlanders, transferring later to the Seaforth Highlanders. While on leave, he managed to play four games for Celtic (including helping the club to retain the Glasgow Cup). The shocking news reached Glasgow in May 1917 that he was 'missing in action', it later being confirmed that he had been killed in the Battle of Arras, an offensive designed to 'end the war in forty-eight hours' but whose six-week duration failed to achieve the major breakthrough needed to break the deadlock on the Western Front. He left behind a wife and two young children. The all-conquering Parkhead outfit had been touched by tragedy, a stark reminder that success and fame could be fleeting. It was as if, for them, it was a period that could be described in the words of a Charles Dickens novel: 'it was the best of times, it was the worst of times'.

CHAPTER 7

The Rift in the Lute

In recent years the rivalry between Parkhead and Ibrox has extended from football to athletics, and the result has been the same in both forms of sport – Celtic have taken a long lead; Rangers, bar an exceptional season, have had to be content with second place. Just as Parkhead led the way in assembling an all-conquering eleven, so has Mr Maley out-distanced all rivals in bringing from both sides of the border and each side of the Atlantic the foremost sprinters and distance men, the fleetest cyclists, and all that is worth having in the way of cross-country and hurdle experts.

Glasgow Observer, *12 August 1916. The Celtic Sports meeting that day attracted twice the attendance of the Rangers one the previous Saturday.*

'Man in the Know' found it 'painful at times to listen to the conversation of those who think and talk of nothing but Celtic and Rangers, of the thousands who cannot give a thought to what has happened and is about to happen in France and Flanders'.

A comment in the Glasgow Observer *of 19 January 1918 on what many believed to be an unhealthy obsession with the fortunes of the 'Old Firm' at a time of war.*

'In 1912 the rift in the lute appeared,' said Willie Maley rather dramatically, in his *The Story of the Celtic*, of the origins of the bitter edge to the 'Old Firm' rivalry. Before that, he claimed, the fans of both clubs were the best of friends, their brake clubs wending home together from 'Old Firm' contests in a spirit of harmony, whatever the result. Perhaps he felt the need for circumspection at the time in expanding on the nature of the rift, given that the book came out in 1939, a year that began with an IRA bombing campaign in mainland Britain, focusing initially on London, Manchester and Birmingham. However, in the 'Willie Maley story' that appeared in Glasgow's *Evening News* during January and February 1955 (the third such serialisation, in different newspapers, of his life and times with Celtic), he felt sufficiently relaxed, as someone no longer connected with the game, to respond to his ghostwriter, Jack House, when challenged on the topic:

> There's no use beating about the bush, Jack. The reason for the trouble between Celtic and Rangers starting in 1912 was that a new shipbuilding yard was opened on the Clyde, and the owners brought over a big number of workers from Belfast. These workers had what they regarded as religious ideas for opposing a team they thought of as entirely Roman Catholic, although even then we were fielding many Protestant players.

Significantly, Harland and Wolff opened their yard in Glasgow at a time when Protestant feeling against the looming prospect of Home Rule for Ireland was reaching fever pitch back in the company's home town of Belfast, so much so that its chairman Lord Pirrie (ironically, a Liberal backer of the proposed constitutional change) was at one stage pelted with rotten eggs and he was regularly derided as a 'traitor and a turncoat'. In September 1912, close on half a million Unionists in Ulster – and a large number of sympathisers in other parts of the United Kingdom, mainly exiles from Ulster working and living in cities such as Glasgow – signed a covenant in which they pledged to defend 'civil and religious freedom' by all means necessary (including their own lives, was the perceived subtext). Home Rule, a form of devolution akin to that which now exists in the Scottish parliament, was, they asserted, really 'Rome Rule'. The Protestant population of Ulster also feared what they firmly believed was the inevitable eventual outcome: an

Ireland that was both independent and predominantly Catholic, with a government in Dublin that discriminated against the northern, largely Protestant and industrial part of the island (including the shipbuilding city of Belfast) in favour of the rural economy of the south. Plans drawn up for a 'Provisional Ulster Government', enrolment for an 'Ulster Volunteer Force', and gunrunning from continental Europe brought the near certainty of civil war, before the intervention of the First World War defused (but, in fact, merely postponed) the crisis. It is most unlikely, however, that Maley was aware of a crucial aspect of these developments, one revealed by Robert McElroy in 1998 in his *The Spirit of Ibrox* and which can now be perceived as clearly a major factor in boosting the fortunes of a club that had been trailing in Celtic's slipstream:

> Rangers were the natural home for the many [Ulster shipyard workers] attracted to football – the club represented the indigenous Protestant population of Scotland, a country which in the eighteenth century had embraced the protestant Reformation more thoroughly than any other in Europe. The owners of Harland and Wolff [Lord Pirrie apart, it seems] were undoubtedly themselves as one with their shipyard workers, and it was therefore a sound business deal to advance to Rangers – a club still struggling financially from the aftermath of the 1902 Disaster – a loan of £90,000 [the equivalent of nearly £4 million in today's money, and a fortune then], the terms of which included a clause which stated that the agreement was 'subject to those private agreements made between the parties but not subject herein'. The demarcation lines had been clearly laid out between the two Glasgow giants – for more than half a century each would have a clearly defined community from which to draw their support.

However obliquely framed, was this transaction (undated in the book) the source of the long-standing signing policy associated with the Ibrox club for many years? Certainly, before that shipbuilding company arrived on the scene, several Catholics (most notably Willie Kivlichan) had played for Rangers, a club that had turned out for

Catholic charities, one example being their match against Hibernian at Easter Road in May 1903 for the benefit of the Leith Catholic School Building Fund. What is not in doubt is the hardening of attitudes that developed in the West of Scotland during the First World War. This was highlighted in the differences in treatment accorded at Ibrox Park within the space of a year to two personalities connected with Celtic. On 27 September 1915, Willie Angus, who had been on Celtic's books and was one of the five Catholic First World War holders of the Victoria Cross from 'the Glasgow area' listed in the *Glasgow Observer* in January 1919 (he was actually a Carluke man), was still feeling the effects of his rescue of a wounded officer, which earned him his award, when, two days after receiving a hero's welcome from the crowd when making a personal appearance at Celtic Park, he was given a rousing cheer as he hobbled onto the Ibrox turf to 'kick off' the Rangers v. Glasgow Highlanders match for the benefit of the regimental fund and the Red Cross. But, in August 1916, the Celtic star Patsy Gallacher was outraged by the 'biased reception' that awaited him and other members of the Celtic five-a-side team at the annual Rangers Sports meeting, with particular reference to their defeat in the final by Morton. He made his feelings known to a reporter from the *Weekly Mail and Record*. Below the article's heading – 'Would crowd cheer the Huns [i.e. the Germans]? I think they would if up against Celtic' – Gallacher condemned the barracking they had endured from the patrons of the stand 'from the moment they went on the field till they left it'. He seemed genuinely hurt and bemused by it all:

I am quite aware of the antagonism between Celtic and Rangers, and know that 'opposition being the life of trade' the club finances gain by it, but on Saturday when we turned out in full strength to honour the Rangers' meeting we had hoped and were entitled to expect a welcome as generous as that given to other contestants. I cannot help expressing my opinion of their lack of fair play and firmly believe that, if a team of Huns [derogatory term for the Germans] opposed Celtic at Ibrox Park, the crowd that 'goosed us' on Saturday would cheer our deadly enemies.

Perhaps the Donegal-born Gallacher was an early victim of the backlash set in train four months earlier by the Easter Rising in Dublin, which had fostered considerable antipathy to the Irish in Scotland, despite an editorial denouncing the 'unpatriotic' and 'stupid' insurrection as the 'madly criminal action of pro-German plotters' that appeared in a Catholic newspaper, the *Glasgow Observer*. However, Arthur Murphy, chairman of the Home Government branch of the United Irish League in Glasgow, may have been a more accurate barometer of the opinion of the local Irish Catholic population, particularly after the execution of 15 of the rebels by firing squad, when he asserted that 'the Sinn Fein rising' was the inevitable outcome of 'the seditious speeches of Carson and his followers'. Certainly, the chief constable of Paisley would have been reflecting a change of outlook caused by the British government's failure to introduce Home Rule, and their subsequent attempts to thwart Irish independence, when he wrote to the Secretary of State for Scotland in July 1922: 'At the outbreak of war, the young men of the Catholic religion in Paisley enlisted in greater proportion than the rest of Paisley's inhabitants; they were apparently loyal but their attitude has changed since the Dublin rebellion.' The *Observer*'s regular and proud wartime recording of the ultimate sacrifice paid by, and the valiant deeds of, 'Our Catholic soldiers' came to naught in the face of sentiments such as those expressed in a contemporary novel, John Buchan's *Mr Standfast*, where one character says, 'Glasgow's stinkin' nowadays with two things, money and Irish . . . I'm not speakin' about Ulster which is a dour, ill-natured den but our folk all the same.' Patsy Gallacher was in no doubt about the motives behind the punishment meted out to him a few months after his Ibrox outburst when, on top of a fine imposed on him by a munitions tribunal for 'bad timekeeping and attendance' at the Dalmuir factory where he was employed during the week, he was suspended for nearly six weeks by the Scottish Football League (and Celtic fined for continuing to field him once they became aware of the offence). Gallacher regarded both verdicts as vindictive, pointing out that he was taking his punishment 'openly', unlike certain players who 'left their work and played under assumed names'. The clear inference was that this was a case of victimisation of a Celtic player of Irish Catholic stock. The implication that this was not a breed to be trusted was underlined in the eyes of many of his 'compatriots' the following autumn by the anxiety of the British monarchy to play the patriotic card in its attempts to distance itself from its Germanic family associations by renaming itself 'The House of Windsor' and striving to cope with the more democratic (and potentially threatening and radical) forces emerging during the war by remodelling the honours system. Ironically, the Celtic secretary-manager Willie Maley was as ardent a Royalist as they come, but the nearest a reigning monarch (or spouse) had come to Celtic Park was in July 1914, when King George V and Queen Mary had alighted at Parkhead Railway Station (later re-named Parkhead Stadium Station, being only some 200 yards from the ground) for their visit to Beardmore's Forge, adjacent to Parkhead Cross, where a 'Royal Arch' with the words 'Parkhead workers welcome you' had been specially erected. However, the royal couple returned to Glasgow in mid-September 1917 for the first ceremony of its kind in Scotland, when Ibrox Park was accorded the honour of housing a public investiture, the awarding of decorations and medals to war heroes and (in the case of the fallen) their next-of-kin being combined with a ceremony to honour the recipients of the Order of the British Empire, newly created with outstanding contributions to the war effort in mind, particularly production work in the munitions industries. Thus it was that a crowd estimated between 70,000 and 80,000 people packed Ibrox Park 'like herring in a barrel' on 18 September 1917, when one of the loudest cheers went up for Lizzie Robinson, a 'munitions lassie' dressed in her uniform of khaki tunic and trousers as she went forward to receive her medal 'for devotion to duty in a national projectile factory'.

As he departed, the King, accompanied by the Lord Provost of Glasgow (Sir Thomas Dunlop, Bart.), thanked the Rangers manager William Wilton and the club chairman, Sir John Ure Primrose, for the 'perfection' of the arrangements. It has long been contended that Rangers FC is the 'establishment' club of Scotland and this event may well have represented its baptism in that role (by royal appointment, as it were), as a piqued *Glasgow Observer* was quick to sense:

> In Glasgow apparently no Catholic citizen was presented to the King
> – that is to say from the municipal list. But His Majesty encountered
> a few notwithstanding. Among the recipients at Ibrox Park (why not
> Celtic?) on Tuesday were W. Maloney, Royal Scots . . . and Sergeant
> McCafferty, Argyll and Southern Highlanders, to take only a few
> names from the official list as showing (incidentally) how the bearers
> of such typical Irish names have by their bravery brought distinction
> to the Scottish regiments to which they have been posted.

The sense of exclusion from the mainstream of Scottish life is palpable, and it was reinforced by the comments of 'John O' Groat' in that same day's *Weekly Mail and Record* (22 September 1917):

> I have heard people of narrow outlook occasionally express surprise
> that so much notice should be taken of the Celts in connection with
> our national game. They might as well ask why so much attention
> should have been paid to the King whilst being among us. Men and
> organisations at the top must always be noticed, and so it is with
> the Celts in football . . . Don't you think they deserve credit?
> Whenever a team comes along to equal or surpass their achievements
> due praise awaits them under my nom-de-plume.

Rangers were now shaping up to be that team, and served due notice of their credentials that very day at Celtic Park when they won the Glasgow Cup semi-final 3–0. 'Man in the Know' of the *Glasgow Observer*, who was wont to observe that 'to build up is the Parkhead motto, to buy up is the Ibrox way', poured scorn on this 'victory for Rangers' variety troupe' (or the 'All-Scotland Eleven' as he also called it), but it was a triumph for a recruitment drive that illustrated the Light Blues' determination to eclipse Celtic. After their resolution took them all the way to the title in April 1918 (pipping Celtic by one point), Patsy Gallacher criticised Rangers for their 'working' of the Scottish League's wartime temporary loan system 'not being in keeping with the spirit of the rule as introduced by the League', but Willie Maley was even more scathing, sniping at the 'piebald champions'. The heavyweight contest for post-war supremacy was well and truly under way, but even though Celtic regained the championship in season 1918–19 (by one point from Rangers), their fans could not rid themselves of a nagging feeling that the status Rangers enjoyed as 'Scotia's darlings' would bring them unfair dividends, and nothing would convince them otherwise after the events surrounding the 1919–20 battle for the title. Celtic's bid to retain the title got off to a flyer as they reeled off nine successive victories, averaging three goals a game, but Rangers punctured that self-belief with a 3–0 victory at Ibrox in mid-October. Knocked off their stride somewhat, Celtic drew seven of their next fifteen matches before losing at Clydebank and Dundee in late January 1920. Eight successive wins then put Celtic right back into contention, but they blew an opportunity to come within two points of Rangers (with both having four matches to play) when they drew (2–2) their game in hand against St Mirren, defensive frailties (of the 'wait-and-see, leave-it-to-the-other-fellow' variety) allowing the visitors to snatch a late equaliser at Parkhead on 22 April. A body blow, no doubt about it, but the fans clung to the hope that Dundee, one of the sides near the top of the table, would put a spanner in the Ibrox works two days later. Celtic did their bit on 24 April to keep their title ambitions alive, beating Ayr United 4–0, but then news came through that all but snuffed out any remaining flickers of optimism. Rangers had beaten Dundee 6–1 at Ibrox Park. Reports of Dundee's collapse only darkened the mood of Celtic fans. They were not mollified by comments about the Dens Parkers having had 'an off-day' and their goalkeeper Vallis having been the proverbial bag of nerves in the 'troublesome wind', or claims that the visitors had simply been outclassed and overwhelmed by 'a nippier, faster and more forceful' 11. Instead they latched on to the Glasgow *Evening Times* reference to Dundee, generally considered the biggest remaining obstacle to Rangers' championship prospects, putting up 'such a poor show' at Ibrox ('contrary to expectations') and the comments of a writer in the *Dundee Advertiser* about expecting 'a desperate battle for the points' but finding 'nothing of a heroic character in the play at all', plus reports of 'weak defending' such as that which had enabled Bowie to head a goal 'with the visiting defenders as spectators', making 'no great effort to prevent this score'. Suspicions of collusion between the clubs were dismissed by Dundee wing-half Bert McIntosh as 'utter rot', but there was no mistaking the anger, mixed with sullen resignation, in the air as McIntosh and company turned up at Celtic Park on Monday, 26 April 1920, two days after the Ibrox debacle.

Celtic: Shaw; McNair and Livingstone; Gilchrist, Cringan and W. McStay; McMaster, McKay, Craig, Cassidy and McLean.

Dundee: Watson; Raitt and Thomson; McIntosh, Nicol and Jackson; Rawlings, Downie, Bell, Slade and Troup.

Referee: T. McMillan (Hamilton).

Dundee took the field to a typical Glasgow 'sherracking', but shrugged off the antipathy, and early injuries to Jackson and Bell that required lengthy off-field treatment, to come strongly into the game against a more methodical Celtic side that was nevertheless handicapped by a lack of pace on the right wing. The deployment there of Johnny McMaster was a source of angst to 'Man in the Know', for whom the whole-hearted player was 'a daisy of a half-back, but as a wing forward – !' The visitors took advantage of the unsettled look about recent Celtic performances to edge in front six minutes before half-time through Slade after 'a cleverly concerted move' with Rawlings, but the home side hit back immediately when Willie McStay converted a penalty awarded for a handling offence. Dundee continued to hold their own thereafter, surviving scares such as Nicol almost putting through his own goal (the ball struck the crossbar) and Cassidy having a goal struck off for offside, and came very close to restoring their lead when a Rawlings shot crashed against the crossbar 'with Shaw nowhere'. After Craig missed a golden opportunity to net the winner for Celtic but instead 'headed past' with only Watson to beat, Dundee looked certain to leave Parkhead with a draw as a reward for their stubborn resistance when, in the words of the *Dundee Advertiser*, the following occurred around five minutes from the final whistle:

> McLean [Celtic] was careering along the left wing when he was cleverly dispossessed of the ball by McIntosh. The Celtic outside left brought McIntosh down, and ere one could realise what had happened a crowd of ruffians invaded the field. McIntosh was the target and he came in for some rough usage. McLean endeavoured to pacify the crowd, but his endeavours were of no avail. The referee was also made at, but luckily for him he was safely escorted to the pavilion. The game was then declared off, with the score standing at one goal each.

The *Daily Record and Mail* reported that the incursion came from almost every part of the ground and that 'severe blows and kicks' were aimed at the referee and the Dundee players, with – according to various reports – the referee sustaining a facial cut 'from which blood flowed', Raitt being 'in a prostrate condition' once he reached the pavilion, and McIntosh receiving 'a severe bruising'. Celtic players and officials, prominent among them Alec McNair, who grabbed and threw aside a 'mad man striking the referee', and chairman Tom White (the victim of 'rough handling' for his pains), exerted 'every protective effort' possible to prevent the situation attaining more serious dimensions.

In the aftermath, at least one newspaper acknowledged that Celtic had been 'at a disadvantage on and off the field' recently because of illness on the part of Willie Maley, but 'Craigpark' of the *Daily Record and Mail* pinpointed failings on the part of the host club, noting that 'not one policeman was present' and suggesting that 'the incident would not have happened had the iron railing which surrounded the field a couple of months ago still been in existence'. The latter aspect of the fiasco was taken up by 'Man in the Know' in his 1 May post-mortem in the *Glasgow Observer*:

Since the iron railing disappeared, the small fry has become unpleasantly conspicuous at Parkhead. Not content with free admission – they burrow under the turnstiles – this vast army of tiny ragamuffins has made a practice of dashing across the field and capturing the enclosure terracing in front of the Grant Stand. It is from that coign [sic] of vantage that they launched their attack on Monday night.

Clearly anxious to play down the implications of the 'wild disorder' for the club, he stated that 'a few adults of the hooligan class' joined in a 'sudden' invasion for which he could detect no cause, although judging from the frenzied nature of the incident it is inconceivable that anything other than a welling up of frustration on the part of those Celtic fans involved (most notably the adults) led to their venting their anger on Dundee players whom they suspected of lying down to Rangers. Bizarrely, the *Dundee Advertiser* postulated an unlikely theory for the break-in a few days later, citing 'an authoritative source' that claimed it was an affair organised by a large gang of pickpockets, and not by Celtic supporters: 'The idea was to get the crowd on the field and pick their pockets. In this they were successful, and it is estimated that over £56 was stolen from several members of the crowd.' On the day following the abandoned match, Tuesday, 27 April (a day when the Celtic chairman Tom White described the pitch 'disturbance' as 'a disgrace and a scandal'), baton charges by police dispersed a Sinn Fein demonstration held in Glasgow's George Square to protest against the treatment of hunger-strikers in London's Wormwood Scrubs prison, an indication of the recent intensification of 'The Troubles' in Ireland. Later that day, Rangers disposed of Third Lanark 2–0 at a packed Cathkin Park, leaving them four points ahead of Celtic with both contenders having only two games left. The best Celtic could now hope for was a total Rangers collapse and for them to acquire all four available points to force a title play-off. Celtic beat Airdrieonians 1–0 at home on the Wednesday (28th), taking no risks in the process by having the ground 'guarded like a stronghold by a strong force of policemen'. All to no avail, for Rangers acquired the solitary point needed for the title with a 0–0 draw at Dumbarton in their penultimate league match of the season. The upshot was that, as a result of Rangers finishing three points clear of Celtic (two points being awarded for a victory then), the score at the time of the abandoned match against Dundee (1–1) was allowed to stand and the SFA meeting held on 5 May also decided that Celtic Park be closed to eleven-a-side football until the end of August. It certainly helped that Tom White was also the SFA chairman, for it was widely construed as a light sentence, given that the season was virtually over (Celtic had been drawn away in the upcoming Charity Cup semi-final, and the final was at Hampden Park) and the ban did not cover the five-a-side tournament at the annual pre-season Celtic Sports. As it transpired, the fixture list was rejigged in order that Celtic played their first three league matches of season 1920–21 at Hamilton, Coatbridge (Albion Rovers) and Aberdeen.

During the close season, the *Glasgow Observer* reported that Celtic's profits for the season just past amounted to a healthy £8,275. 'Celtic's prosperity is still at floodtide,' the writer proclaimed, but it was to be threatened, undermined in fact for over three decades, by a man who was to cement Rangers' new-found status as what one writer would describe in 1968 as 'the chosen representatives of Protestantism' in the eyes of the mass of their supporters, their notions of supremacy attained under his regime having been reinforced by the club styling itself in official publications as 'The Rangers Football Club', whose home matches took place at 'The Stadium'. Bill Struth, the successor to William Wilton, who was killed in a boating accident only a few days after that championship was clinched at Dumbarton, was a man for whom the term 'second best' was anathema. He was into ascendancy.

CHAPTER 8

'Aye . . . But You Should Have Seen Patsy!'*

Because the First Division was essentially non-competitive, Rangers had quite often won the championship by late January with severely adverse effects on attendances, including their own. Gates of only 12,000 for run-of-the-mill matches at Ibrox and Parkhead were by no means uncommon. Great crowds would come out to watch cup-ties but by their very nature they provided an uncertain form of income and Rangers were going through a spell when a quarter of a century would separate their Scottish Cup win of 1903 from that of 1928. Even the most prestigious clubs therefore had to watch the income flow and it should occasion no surprise that Celtic were censured in October 1925 for admitting the unemployed through the boys' gate. In his defence Willie Maley claimed that the practice was common among all Glasgow clubs. Common or not, Celtic were peremptorily invited to discontinue it.

Extract from The Scottish Football League: The First 100 Years
by Bob Crampsey, 1990 (comment on the inter-war years)

In terms of trophies won, there can be little doubt that Celtic held the upper hand in the first two decades of the twentieth century, the figures below taking into account the suspension of the Scottish

---

* The chapter title is taken from a common reaction by 'old-time' Celtic fans in the pre-Stein era when pressed about the merits of various great players who had donned the green and white.

Cup competition during the First World War.

	League	Scottish Cup	Glasgow Cup	Charity Cup
Celtic	11	6	8	11
Rangers	7	1	8	6

The respective managers – Willie Maley for Celtic and William Wilton of Rangers – were friends as well as rivals but even those who supported the Light Blues recognised the extra ingredient that Celtic seemed able to conjure up on the special occasions. A criticism often applied to Rangers teams of that era was 'unreliable' although others, slightly harsher or perhaps more perceptive, suggested that they 'choked' at vital moments.

Then, in May 1920, on the first day of his summer holiday, William Wilton was drowned in a boating accident off Gourock. It was a tragic and unexpected occurrence, which caused considerable grief at the football club. Wilton was popular with both his players and those who worked at Ibrox and his passing was much mourned. A replacement was quickly needed, though, and, within a few days, Bill Struth, the trainer at that time, was appointed. Struth had never played football but, having been an athlete in his youth, he recognised the value of certain qualities. He immediately adopted a strict regimen in which discipline, hardness and fitness were all-important. The new manager also insisted that the players, management and directors travel in style, first-class preferably, and made the players dress accordingly. The impact was immediate.

After four seasons of the 1920s, a comparison of the Old Firm's relevant records shows a tilt in the balance towards Rangers.

	League	Scottish Cup	Glasgow Cup	Charity Cup
1920–21	Rangers	———	Celtic	Celtic
1921–22	Celtic	———	Rangers	Rangers
1922–23	Rangers	Celtic	Rangers	Rangers

'AYE . . . BUT YOU SHOULD HAVE SEEN PATSY!'

1923–24   Rangers   ————————   Rangers   Celtic

Just when Rangers were in the ascendant, the Celtic board of directors made a monumental decision. Apparently on the grounds of cost, they decided in 1922 to withdraw the reserve team from the 2nd XI league. The predictable outcome was the drying-up of an assembly line of young talent and a reliance on players already within the club.

A closer look at the league tables for 1922–23 and 1923–24 gives more credence than ever to the theory that, while Celtic had some fine players, they lacked the solidity of Rangers, particularly in defence.

1922–23

	P	W	D	L	F	A	Pts
(1) Rangers	38	23	9	6	67	29	55
(3) Celtic	38	19	8	11	52	39	46

1923–24

	P	W	D	L	F	A	Pts
(1) Rangers	38	25	9	4	72	22	59
(3) Celtic	38	17	12	9	56	33	46

The goal-scoring rate was low at this period because defenders were exploiting the offside law to great effect. The main problem for Celtic, however, is quite apparent from the figures. In these seasons, they simply were not scoring as many goals as their main rivals and conceding far more; hence, they were losing more matches.

In addition to the parsimony displayed by the withdrawal of the reserve team, other problems concerning money continued through the early 1920s. The harsh economic climate was having an effect on attendances. There were fewer jobs available and a fairly rampant sectarianism prevailed. Celtic fans, given the background of the huge majority of them, suffered more than most and eventually a

'Buroo' gate for those not working was instituted at Celtic Park.

Behind the scenes, there seemed to be dissension between players and officials. The vast majority of footballers have always been gregarious characters, very willing to meet socially with players from other clubs, and no doubt the subjects of wages and bonuses would have received an airing. Possibly, Celtic's players might have found out that they were not as well paid as those in other clubs and wished to challenge the existing financial structure. Certainly, in the early part of season 1923–24, the dressing-room was an angry place. The captain, Willie Cringan, was asked by his teammates to approach the chairman, Tom White, and put some proposals to him. The players wanted a bonus of £1 per point in league matches, a not unreasonable request in their eyes. The board refused. A very unhappy team lost the next home match to Partick Thistle on 1 September and, on 5 October, after a Celtic career of 214 appearances in the major competitions, Cringan was transferred to Third Lanark.

In season 1924–25, the dominance of Rangers continued, as they picked up the Glasgow Cup, the Charity Cup and the League Championship (for the League Championship, see table below: two points for win):

	P	W	D	L	F	A	Pts
(1) Rangers	38	25	10	3	76	26	60
(4) Celtic	38	18	8	12	77	44	44

Only one goal difference in respect of total of goals scored for both but just look at the difference in goals against and matches lost!

Rangers' Achilles heel at that period was the Scottish Cup, which they had not won since 1903. Even more surprisingly, they had suffered some surprise defeats in the final at the hands of lesser-regarded sides, like Partick Thistle in 1921 and Morton in 1922.

In that season 1924–25, both sides had moved through to the semi-finals stage of the Scottish Cup, Celtic finding St Mirren stubborn opponents in the quarter-finals:

Celtic

24/1/25 Third Lanark (A) 5–1, Att. 42,000

7/2/25 Alloa Athletic (H) 2–1, Att. 12,000

21/2/25 Solway Star (H) 2–0, Att. 7,000

7/3/25 QF, St Mirren (A) 0–0, Att. 47,428

10/3/25 Replay, St Mirren (H) 1–1, Att. 36,000

16/3/25 Replay, St Mirren (Ibrox) 1–0, Att. 47,492

Rangers

24/1/25 East Fife (A) 3–1, Att. 10,000

7/2/25 Montrose (A) 2–0, Att. 4,000

21/2/25 Arbroath (H) 5–3, Att. 15,000

7/3/25 QF, Kilmarnock (A) 2–1, Att. 30,500

Dundee and Hamilton were the other two semi-finalists but, when the draw was made, it paired Celtic against Rangers at Hampden, with Easter Road the venue of choice for the Dundee/Hamilton clash.

On the days leading up to the Celtic v. Rangers encounter, the papers were full of comments and assessments of the game. There was little doubt that Rangers were the form side but would that much-publicised Cup hoodoo prevent them from fully showing their best form? Celtic, on the other hand, were noted for their Scottish Cup record (having a tally of ten at that point to Rangers' four), although the team was inconsistent, with several youngsters in the side. On the whole, press opinion seemed to favour the Light Blues.

The teams that ran out that afternoon of 21 March 1925 in front of 101,714 were:

Celtic: Shevlin, W. McStay, Hilley, Wilson, J. McStay, McFarlane, Connolly, Gallacher, McGrory, A. Thomson, McLean.

Rangers: Robb, Manderson, McCandless, Meiklejohn, Dixon, Craig, Archibald, Cunningham, Henderson, Cairns, Morton.

Like most British managers of that era, Willie Maley was not one for detailed tactical discussions before a match. It was more or less assumed that the players knew what to do, whom they would be marking, etc. On that particular Saturday, he would have made his usual declarations about the need to do one's best, to rise to the challenge and to maintain at all times the good name of Celtic. He would then have left the dressing-room and, being a man 'wi' a guid conceit o' himsel', most probably headed for the boardroom.

Back in the dressing-room, though, Patsy Gallacher was keen to give the players a little pep-talk of his own. Apparently, he checked that Willie Maley was well out the road, then laid out his ideas. Now, after all these years, we do not know the precise wording of his message but players there that day recalled that his theme was a two-fold one. First, they would play on the Rangers players' fears, talking to them about their record in the competition, of jinxes and hoodoos. In other words, unsettle them. And second, for the first part of the match, they would sit back a bit and try to absorb Rangers' attacks.

From the kick-off, on a bright but slightly windy day, that is exactly what happened. Celtic left Jimmy McGrory upfield almost on his own and pulled back Alec Thomson, Patsy Gallacher, Paddy Connolly and Adam McLean into the Celtic half. Rangers swept into the attack, attempting to utilise their wings, Sandy Archibald and Andy Cunningham on the right, Tommy Cairns and Alan Morton on the left. However, because of the sheer number of Celts packing what we now call the midfield, they found it difficult to settle and could not find their rhythm.

As Rangers became frustrated, Celtic became more confident and slowly began to push more players forward. Against the run of play, they got their reward in the 30th minute. Right-half Peter Wilson robbed Alan Morton of the ball and passed it down the wing to Paddy Connolly. The Celtic winger merely pushed it past his immediate opponent – Irishman Billy McCandless – and used his pace to get to the byeline, from where he crossed for Jimmy McGrory to score.

To say the goal came against the run of play would be no understatement but it gave Celtic a crucial lead, which they held to half-time. At the interval, Willie Maley seems to have been astute enough to keep his comments brief, recognising that Patsy Gallacher had the ear of the players that day. Patsy appears to have again stressed to his teammates that they could give Rangers a real thrashing if they again went about matters in the right way. It was a tribute to the regard in which his colleagues held Patsy that such a statement was not immediately laughed out of court. He believed they could do it and his sheer force of personality made them believers too.

Naturally, Rangers started the second half by throwing everybody forward to draw level. Initially, though, Celtic returned to their defensive formation and held them. The turning point of the match may have come early in the second half, when a fierce shot by Davie Meiklejohn hit the post and rebounded to the head of Tommy Cairns, normally deadly in such situations. Perhaps Cairns had too much time to ponder his next move, though, as eventually he sent a weak header right into the grateful hands of Peter Shevlin and Rangers' best chance had gone.

Relieved by that let-off, Celtic stepped up a gear and went into attacking mode, Patsy Gallacher in particular, who was here, there and everywhere, urging his men on. Just before the hour mark, with three men marking Jimmy McGrory at a corner, Paddy Connolly sent his kick right onto the head of Adam McLean. 2–0. Number three came in the sixty-fifth minute; Gallacher to McGrory, the ball quickly out to Connolly, who again beat McCandless before whipping the ball across for McGrory to score his second. 3–0.

And the final two in the 5–0 rout were the fault of goalkeeper Willie Robb. First, he failed to hold a high ball and Alec Thomson was quick to knock it home; then, as he struggled to pick up a back-pass from Bert Manderson, Adam McLean pounced for his own second.

By this time, one half of the stadium was nearly empty and the other was in raptures, singing the praises of their side. It had been a superb afternoon for Patsy Gallacher, who had demonstrated a whole range of skills both on and off the pitch. He had worked out a plan to cope with the best team in the country; cajoled – and sometimes berated – his teammates into, first, believing in the idea and, second, putting it into operation; and finally, during the play, he was an omnipresent, there to help, advise and also play a crucial role.

The 5–0 victory put Celtic into the final, where their opponents would be Dundee, victors over Hamilton in the other semi-final at Easter Road. Patsy Gallacher would play a major role in that game too . . . but that's another story!

The magnificent performance against Rangers in the semi-final of the Scottish Cup in 1925 is recalled to this day. It became a very special moment in the club's history, though, for another reason. In the years that followed, a song about the match was made up, with the tune unashamedly pinched from the Ibrox repertoire. The more vulgar version of the words I (Jim Craig) can well remember from my own teenage years. The original was:

Hello! Hello! We are the Timalloys!
Hello! Hello! You'll know us by the noise!
We stuffed the Rangers in the Cup,
'Twas great to be alive,
Not one, not two, not three, not four but five!

James Sanderson, in his *Scottish Daily Express* (24 August 1960) profile of 'Peerless Patsy', admitted that he nearly ran out of superlatives to describe the player he regarded as the greatest forward Scottish football had ever seen, but the following effusions indicate that he did not fail to convey the extent of his admiration for the Celt:

His unorthodox style, his elusiveness, his wriggles, slips, swerves and hops, were wonderful to watch and baffling to play against . . . Gallacher's small, fragile form looked out of place in First Division football, only his supreme cleverness saved him from serious injury . . . If Jimmy Wilde, the tiny fly-weight boxing champion of the world, who weighed a mere seven stones, was called the 'Ghost with a hammer in his hand' as a tribute to his frailness and power, then surely Gallacher was 'THE GHOST WITH THE MAGIC FEET'.

CHAPTER 9

A New World

The Colours

A rainbow arched across the sky,
With many a colour bright,
Imparts to the artistic eye
A thrill of pure delight.

The gifted artist with his brush
Can make his picture speak,
Depicting rosy tints that flush
On some fair sitter's cheek.

Italian skies, oft we are told,
Can boast a vivid blue;

A sunset in a blaze of gold
Has its admirers, too.

Rich colours that Dame Nature blends
Give pleasures that won't cloy.
The plumage of our feathered friends
Can bring an inward joy.

But to my partial Celtic eyes
There's no more lovely sight
A sunny day on the 'Paradise',
Ten jerseys Green and White.

Poem by 'J.C.' published in the Glasgow Observer, *6 June 1931. Since it
was published while Celtic were on tour in America, it would have struck a
chord with exiled fans there.*

The 'Celtic brand' is much to the fore these days, when merchandising revenue is so crucial to football clubs' finances, but you could be forgiven for believing that it was already in vogue way back in 1931. A New York magazine, *Soccer Star*, dedicated its 21 May edition – printed throughout in green and white – to a 'Special Glasgow Celtic number' whose content could have come straight out of Madison Avenue:

The world renowned Glasgow Celtic FC . . . The accomplishments and the record of the Glasgow Celtic are international bywords . . . Perhaps no other soccer team in the world can boast of being better known than the Glasgow Celtic . . . It is unquestionably true that no club of such youthful origin has achieved the world-wide fame of this great Irish club . . . The famous Glasgow Celtic soccer team is with us at last, the greatest team in the world, bar none.

The North American continent had beckoned Celtic for the first 30 years of the twentieth century. In January 1910, secretary-manager Willie Maley and director Tom Colgan had travelled to New York on the Anchor Line's SS *California* to make arrangements for a summer tour, but discovered that association football was not a potentially viable spectator sport there at the time, particularly when pitted against the burgeoning popularity of baseball. However, two decades later such a venture seemed a better prospect, given the influx of immigrants from the British Isles (Scotland being notably high in proportional terms) as a result of the pre-First World War recession, the aftershocks of the war itself and of 'The Troubles' in Ireland. And so it was that, on the evening of 13 May 1931, a twenty-three-man Celtic party consisting of seventeen players, four directors, secretary-manager Willie Maley and trainer Will Quinn set off from Glasgow's Yorkhill Quay on the SS *Caledonia*, which was bound for New York. Several thousand supporters turned up to wave them off, giving a rendition of 'all the old Celtic songs' as they waited for the off and whooping with delight as captain Jimmy McStay displayed the recently won Scottish Cup from on board the ship. His teammate Jimmy McGrory, in an opening entry for his private diary of the tour, noted wryly that the trophy 'received an ovation all to itself', but it was to be as nothing to the level of (often tearful) veneration it became for the exiles who followed Celtic on the tour. The sense of adventure for the Celtic party was reinforced by a telegram of 'good wishes and safe return' from Rangers FC, the strains of 'Will Ye No' Come Back Again?' as the liner weighed anchor and set course for the Atlantic and, in the words of the *Glasgow Observer*, 'the crowds occupying every point of vantage from

Yorkhill to Greenock to cheer their heroes on their journey to the Far West'. As the liner moved downriver, its passengers were given a stark reminder that they were leaving behind a country beset by economic crisis, indeed 'sailing through some industrial graveyard', as the city's *Evening News* described the state of shipbuilding on the upper reaches of the Clyde in its 13 June edition: 'Seven shipbuilding berths occupied out of a total of 75; five shipyards out of a dozen with no ships in the stocks at all; and two famous shipyards closed for ever.'

A frenzied reception awaited them when the liner, its arrival delayed by bad transatlantic weather, docked nine days later in New York, where the Statue of Liberty was shrouded in mist but also where, as Jimmy McGrory noted in his diary, the green-and-white dockside banners 'made us feel as if we were back home amongst umpteen brake clubs'. That indefatigable promoter of all things Celtic, 'Man in the Know' of the *Glasgow Observer*, may have been a tad guilty of exaggeration when he said of this welcome that 'Then and since, New York has been green-and-white mad', but there is no doubting the giddy feeling of being treated like VIPs that is conveyed by the Celtic chairman Tom White in an early dispatch for the *Daily Record and Mail* (as its 'special correspondent') where he commented on the events that surrounded the first match of the tour, in Philadelphia on the day after they had set foot in the USA: 'What a country! Never, surely, have a soccer touring party been given such a reception. Since we landed we have been feted and feasted, feasted and feted; it has been one continual round of joy-making . . . so much junketting are we having that the boys are afraid of attaining aldermanic proportions before the time comes for the homeward sail.' At this early stage, however, Celtic were able to shake off the effects of all this, and of the nautical equivalent of jet lag, to overwhelm the Pennsylvania All Stars by a 6–1 margin. Tom White went into raptures about the performance: 'A grand exhibition of true Celtic football . . . [the 15,000 crowd] was seeing football they had enjoyed before they left home, Scots football they have been telling the Americans all about since coming over here.' The *Glasgow Observer* of 1 August

1931 gives us an insight, based on a letter from America, into that diaspora on which Celtic would have drawn during the tour with its profile of the Rochester Celtic team that played in upper New York State and whose players, officials and 'many followers' motored to Toronto to see 'the dear old Glasgow Celtic' play Ulster United in a later stage of the tour:

> Peter Carlin of Arbroath and T. Tomany of Kilmarnock last saw the Celtic twenty years ago . . . we have Frank Toner at centre and, as you know, Frank is from Tollcross [Glasgow] and played for King's Park. Dan, his brother, is at left half, and Jim Murray, also from Tollcross, is at left back. Paddy Cairney, at inside-right, is from Parkhead [Glasgow], and Bobbie Stewart from Coatbridge. Jimmy Northcote from Stevenston is at inside-left, and Johnny McMillan from Shettleston [Glasgow] at outside-left. Danny Spencer at centre-half is from St. Francis, Glasgow. The president of the club is Mike Hanley from dear old Ireland, treasurer Pat Meechan from Maryhill [Glasgow], and secretary-manager Jim Campbell of St. Francis and St. Paul's, Shettleston.

These were people who had come to the land of opportunity, but the Celtic tourists were arriving in the New World at a testing time for the American dream, as the Great Depression was tightening its grip. Tom White was a witness to great suffering, but was sufficiently perceptive as to detect an underlying optimism in this melting pot of a country:

> Many men are selling apples; others have nothing to sell; here a man falls exhausted on the kerb by sheer want. There a poor devil is sat on a chair on the pavement, where crowds gather round to gaze on his pinched and haggard face. Everywhere, in this great city of millions, are unemployed – and this is no city in which to live with little or no money. But all of New York's citizens are not unemployed. Irish, Jews, Italians, Poles, Slavs and even Scotsmen are tunnelling for subways, erecting bridges and viaducts, hewing the solid rock of Manhattan for the foundations of still more

'skyscrapers'. All are preparing for the day of the glorious revival, of the great 'come back'.

The sheer size and scale of the continent and of the places they visited (albeit confined to the eastern seaboard and midwest), not to mention the near-overpowering sense of energy and bustle therein, fairly took the visitors' breath away, coming as they did from the tight little island of Britain. The 21-year-old full-back John Morrison, from the mining area of Kilsyth, confessed to being 'absolutely astounded' by his first sight of New York. Tom White could not disguise his awe and envy when he viewed its Grand Central Station, 'a small city in itself' with its huge marble entrance hall of chocolate and gold, its luxurious waiting rooms, its many and varied shops and restaurants, all in 'glorious illumination'. There was a clear note of nostalgia (anger, even, in at least one respect) for the colonial past in his thoughts after the Pullman train taking Celtic to a match in Montreal touched the shores of Lake Champlain: 'Stations en route are Fort George, Fort Ticonderoga, Montcalm Landing, Roger's Rock and many others known in the history of nations. What a change in the world's history there surely would have been had this great country been retained by the old land. Yet I don't remember reading that anyone was shot or hanged for losing it . . . ' In less philosophical vein, the likes of Celtic winger Bertie Thomson, a man who aspired to living life to the full, waxed lyrical on his return home about a 'great and fascinating experience', one that had 'almost made him a Yankee', even eliciting from him a hint that he would like to make New York his home: 'Simply marvellous. Broadway? – something to dream about. Niagara Falls? – nothing more wonderful.' Only Willie Maley, it seems, failed to extract the maximum satisfaction and enjoyment from the trip, despite the protestations to the contrary in his 1939 history of the club. He appears to have been a bit of a party-pooper aboard the SS *Caledonia*, pleading seasickness for the most part to account for a failure to enter into the spirit of things while others enjoyed the round of deck games, concerts, etc. designed to while away the boredom. His curmudgeonly disposition did not endear him to the club directors, the more so when his 'plight' enabled him to badger them into extending an invitation to his brother Tom to come over and join him on the tour. It was an episode that would not be forgotten (or forgiven) during the rest of the decade, and it was a contributory factor in the removal of this most stubborn of men from his post in January 1940, thus robbing him, in his own words, 'of the very tang of life'. In any case, he gave the game away in respect of his true feelings about the tour in one of his articles in Glasgow's *Evening Times*, for whom he was covering Celtic's sojourn in North America: 'The rush of things here is not to my liking, and I would not give a day on the Braemar road via the Devil's Elbow for a week in any place I have seen here yet' (11 June 1931). His humour would not have been enhanced by a chance meeting, a few days earlier, at a place called Lynn near Boston, with a character who brought back unhappy memories of the blackest day in Celtic's history to that date, namely a Mr McVicar, the referee of the embarrassing Scottish Cup defeat by Arthurlie in January 1897. Shades of the Humphrey Bogart character in the movie *Casablanca* – 'Of all the gin joints in all the towns', etc.!

This note of tension in his relationship with the directors would not have been eased by the implicit criticism of his handling of the tour – for which he had ultimate responsibility – by chairman Tom White in the *Evening Times* on the return to Glasgow. The chairman was pleased that Celtic had come out of it well financially, but added:

> I thought the arrangements made for us might have been much better. The fixtures that had been made necessitated long train journeys, and sometimes the players had to take the field without having had adequate rest. This affected the form of some of the boys; but it was no wonder. Sometimes they had to play in a temperature of 94 in the shade.

In that same day's *Daily Record and Mail*, he said that, due to the travelling and excessive heat, all of the players had lost weight, 'and it might have been a serious matter if the tour had been prolonged'.

As it was winding down, Maley himself confessed that it had been 'five weeks of strenuous travelling and playing'. The logistics of the tour on the American side were entrusted to one T.J. 'Terry' McKenna, described by Maley as an irrepressible 'Garscube Road product' from Glasgow's Maryhill district who had emigrated to New York, and his 'henchman' Joe Jones, an 'American-Welshman' who 'at times got a little bit mixed with Eastern Standard Time, Central Standard Time, and Summer Time'. Certainly, there was more than a hint of muddle when one considers that the term 'fixtures' when applied to this tour seems to have been inappropriate (or, at the very least, flexible); there is a touch of exasperation in Tom White's statement in mid-June that 'Celtic's card has again been reshuffled'. In its 23 May edition, the *Glasgow Observer* printed a match schedule that projected two matches in St Louis in mid-June that never took place, as was the case with a match in either Cleveland or Pittsburgh on 20 June that was mooted in another newspaper. It appears that it was only shortly after the tour itself was under way that arrangements were fixed to play in Canada (Montreal and Toronto). Furthermore, it was originally scheduled for Celtic to play three matches against the New York Yankees – first in Boston, second in Brooklyn or Philadelphia, and the final one in New York the following day. As it happened, only two took place, in Boston and New York. Finally, and most bizarrely of all, the tour was originally scheduled to end with that New York meeting with the Yankees, but consideration was given to a (floodlight) return match with Hakoah All Stars on 30 June as a sort of healing process after their tousy 14 June encounter, though that was rejected in favour of a match that took place in Baltimore on the same day, on the eve of Celtic's sailing for home. And what is one to make of the 'phantom' match that came to light recently with the surfacing on the Internet of a match ticket for a contest scheduled for 29 June: 'Glasgow Celtics [*sic*] v. Newark Americans' in an 'International flood light soccer game' at Bears' Stadium, the home of a baseball team in the New Jersey town? Confusing? You betcha. In fact, the US Football Association refused to sanction the match, perhaps because it was proposed at short notice, thus raising the question of the wisdom (and expense) of printing the tickets. And, for all Mr McKenna's claims that on the long railroad journeys the players were 'like a lot of boys, chock-full of good nature and fun', the twenty-four-hour one from New York on 'The Rattler' (his description) to play Bricklayers FC in Chicago was hardly the height of comfort. Jimmy McGrory records in his diary that the heat and dust was such that it necessitated the changing of shirts two or three times before the train arrived at its destination, where the populace was coming to terms with the beginning of the end for Al Capone's blood-stained fiefdom in the midwest city. 'Scarface' had pleaded guilty to charges of income taxation evasion and of violations of the Volstead Act, which prohibited the transport, production and sale of liquor; it was a ploy designed to bring him a light sentence but one that backfired spectacularly, ultimately leading to a long stretch in federal prison.

Incidentally, Maley did not mention that McKenna (who appears to have been some sort of football agent some six or seven decades before the term became common, judging by an apparent involvement with fellow Glaswegian Jack Coll, a trainer/coach in both Scotland and the USA, in the transfer of Celtic goalkeeper Charlie Shaw to New Bedford Whalers in the USA in 1925) and Jones had, in partnership with Sam Mark (a Massachusetts-born promoter of basketball, baseball and soccer), underwritten the Celtic tour, during which McKenna and Jones acted in an 'advisory capacity'. Unfortunately for them, although Celtic were paid in full, the enterprise came at a time when soccer's efforts to gain a foothold in America as a spectator sport were torpedoed by a debilitating combination of rival leagues, power struggles surrounding the US Football Association and, above all, the Great Depression. The partnership was dissolved amid much recrimination and messy litigation, with McKenna and Jones, dismayed by the level of their share of the profits, alleging 'fictitious expenditures and receipts' in their lawsuit against Mark.

It says much for the players that in such circumstances they should perform creditably, with the exception of a few matches, on the hard-baked pitches that were the norm throughout. Jimmy

McGrory was the cynosure of attention in the early encounters. Tom White displayed a quick grasp of the native lingo when he referred to our 'little centre-forward' being 'full of pep', adding that 'he was almost unholdable at the moment'. However, White was no match for the reporters from the New York newspapers who watched Celtic snatch a last-minute victory over the New York Giants on 24 May at the Polo Grounds, where the 40,000 present contained thousands of spectators who 'sported favours in green and white, the Scottish club colours'. McGrory led the line superbly, inspiring a rousing comeback from a 1–2 deficit at the interval, a performance that led to him, in the words of the *Evening Post*, being 'lifted on the shoulders of hero-worshippers, who all but smothered the great centre-forward with embraces'. McGrory himself recalled of the Celtic players' struggle to reach the dressing-room that 'everybody seemed to want souvenirs, because I was left with only half my football shirt'. The enthusiasm was pardonable, given the sheer drama as the game entered the final minutes, with the score tied at 2–2, and then this happened, as described in the *Daily News* account of the 3–2 victory by 'Scotland's fighting Irish': 'Jock Brown [the Giants keeper] fumbled a roller that passed the marker for a corner flag-kick [*sic*]. This started the trouble. R. Thomson sent the flag-kick across. Bart McGhee miskicked, the Celtic captain [Jimmy McStay] tapped to the speedy McGrory, and before anyone could realise it the damage was done. An unsaveable shot: no goalkeeper could have saved it.' It was, said the *World Telegram* match report, 'just like a story-book fable, but this was true, and Jimmy McGrory was the booter who booted over the winning goal'. Incidentally, there would have been spectators in the crowd who would have been aware that the unfortunate McGhee, who had been a member of the USA side that reached the semi-finals of the first-ever World Cup, held in Uruguay the previous year, was the son of Jimmy McGhee, a member of the Hibs side that had hanselled the first Celtic Park in May 1888 (in a match against Cowlairs), a couple of years before he joined the Glasgow club.

Celtic had hoped to emulate Rangers' highly successful North American tour of the previous year, when their great rivals won all fourteen matches, but they quickly came to earth with a bump six days later at Fenway Park, Boston, the home of the Red Sox baseball team. The match against New York Yankees was played in a temperature of 92 degrees in the shade on the grass-covered outfield and Tom White was unhappy with the lightweight 'US ball', a familiar complaint during the progress of the tour. In separate articles for the *Evening Times*, Willie Maley observed that 'the terrible heat' left his players 'limp' at the outset, trailing by three goals after twenty minutes, 'but we got level with twenty to go, and looked like winning', then 'a breakaway and a simple shot that deceived Thomson lost the game, with no time to make up leeway again'. He admitted of their 4–3 victory that 'the Yanks played a good game', but castigated the referee for tolerating roughness on the part of several of their players. The outstanding player afield was a son of Portuguese immigrants, namely the 6 ft, 13 st. Yankees forward Adelino William ('Billy') Gonsalves, an adept dribbler and a clever exponent of long passing, which opened up the Celtic defence repeatedly. His goal-scoring menace was acknowledged afterwards by a young man only a few months away from an untimely death, namely Celtic goalkeeper John Thomson, who was beaten by two of his long-range shots yet whose brilliant save from a penalty kick prevented the hat-trick hero from notching four goals. Willie Maley would later describe Gonsalves as 'the finest forward I have seen in years', and it was reported in the American press that after this match Celtic had offered him a contract. Maley was not quite so generous in respect of the victors' other scorer, describing him as 'a fellow named Patenaude'. Bert Patenaude was the player credited recently by FIFA with scoring the first-ever hat-trick in the World Cup finals tournament, having recorded this feat in Uruguay the previous summer, where he played in the same forward line as Gonsalves and the aforementioned Bart McGhee. British football, it should be said, was pretty insular then, ignorant to the point of indifference about developments abroad, staying aloof from the World Cup, but its self-proclaimed status as the masters of football was already being undermined, with Scotland's prestige-shattering Continental tour in May 1931 being marked by defeats at the hands of Austria (a humiliating 0–5) and Italy. The following day proved to be no better for Celtic, with another loss coming against Fall River FC at Mark's Stadium, North Tiverton, Rhode Island. On a pitch bare of grass, Celtic pressed continuously throughout, but despite 'a harvest of corners' could not score and they were hit by a sucker punch three minutes from time-up after 'Peter' McGonagle conceded a free kick just outside the penalty area. For the second match in a row, John Thomson was shown to be fallible, misjudging the flight of Watson's lob from the corner of the penalty box, 'jumping just a second too soon' and succeeding only in tipping the ball onto the underside of the bar (and thence into the net) as he scrambled desperately to clear. Frank McGrath, reporting for the local *Herald News*, added to his description of that 'big surprise' for the 'highly touted Glasgow Celtics' with a colourful summary of the play after the interval: 'With the wind in favor of the Celtics in the second half, little hope of a Fall River victory was held out. The dope went wrong, however, for the locals tied up McGrory, the most dangerous forward, and the others were unable to break through, despite the wind advantage.' The only consolation that Celtic would take from this reverse came in Willie Maley's dispatch to the *Evening Times*: 'Our people at home fancy John Thomson, but they have his equal at Fall River, where their goalkeeper saved them time and time again by brilliant work.' Maley did not name him, but undoubtedly the seeds were planted there and then for Joe Kennaway to become John Thomson's successor within a matter of months, albeit in the most tragic of circumstances. Even at this early stage, Maley was hinting that something had gone awry with the tour arrangements, stating in the same article, 'We have had too much football all at once, and four hard games in eight days in climatic conditions like what we are having has taken the vim out of our fellows, but we will recover in time.' Jimmy McGrory said that the pitch was like concrete and that the whole Celtic team was now suffering from blisters on their feet, and so they were relieved that there was a six-day interval before the next match, but it turned out to be a brutal contest in what McGrory described as 'easily the worst place – and the worst crowd – we have seen yet'.

On their return visit to Rhode Island, this time to the Providence Cycledrome at Pawtucket on 6 June, Celtic lost 1–3. Tom White's *Daily Record and Mail* report summed up the match with this heading: 'Rough and tumble match in tropical heat on a pitch only two thirds regulation size – bad ball and worse refereeing – desperate opposition – last minute penalty'. Celtic may have had two goals disallowed for offside against Pawtucket Rangers, originally (before their renaming) the company team of the local factory of the Scottish multinational textile firm J. and P. Coats, but the match report by Dave Scott of the *Boston Post*, rather triumphalist in its tone, left its readers in no doubt as to the merit of the home side's victory over a 'disjointed and hesitant' visiting team: 'Skill, speed and experience were thought to be the assets of the Scottish Cup holders. But in today's game the boot was on the other foot, with the boys from "Little Rhody" easily outguessing the wearers of the famous green and white.' With Celtic striving to regain parity despite Charlie Napier, Peter Wilson and Alec Thomson struggling with injuries, McAuley closed out the game for his team with an 88th-minute penalty after McGonagle was adjudged to have handled the ball, though the Celtic players claimed that Sam Kennedy, an ex-Clyde forward, had fouled Willie Cook beforehand. This seems to have lit the touch-paper for the mayhem that ensued in the dying seconds, with an altercation involving Cook, McGonagle and Kennedy not only resulting in Cook's front teeth being loosened (for which he apparently extracted retribution on Kennedy), but also prompting spectators to invade the pitch. The police had to be called in to restore order and enable the players to reach their dressing-rooms safely.

Three successive defeats had jolted Celtic's confidence, but the players demonstrated their resilience – and a determination to recover wounded pride – the following day at Ebbets Field, the home of the Brooklyn Dodgers. Providentially, the weather was cooler for a change and Brooklyn Wanderers, their opponents (who included the diminutive ex-Celt Willie Crilly), proved to be the ideal opponents for frazzled nerves. The only downside to Celtic's 5–0 victory was the loss of McGrory after 70 minutes. He was prevented from attaining a hat-trick by a collision with the Wanderers goalkeeper that kept him out of the next three matches with a jaw injury, which in turn meant his missing out on a trip to Montreal (where Peter Scarff netted five goals against Carsteel in a 7–0 'exhibition stuff' win). But he considered himself fortunate to have to sit out on the next fixture, a fiery meeting at the Polo Grounds in New York the following day, Sunday, 14 June, after an overnight train journey from the Canadian city, with a team he considered as even rougher than Pawtucket Rangers, namely Hakoah All Stars. This was a team formed from a merger of two clubs that had been founded by former players of SC Hakoah Wien, a Jewish club in Vienna, following a 1926 US tour. A 30,000 crowd saw a 1–1 draw that was characterised by weak finishing on Celtic's part, despite what one writer described as their 'best and brightest display' on the North American continent. A degree of coarseness and niggly ill feeling crept into the contest early in the second half, leading to the match degenerating into a 'bloodthirsty melee', according to 'Man in the Know', who put the blame squarely on Celtic's opponents – 'Who put the hack into Hakoah?' Another writer attributed the trouble to the players' tempers being affected by the blazing heat, but the upshot was the dismissal of four players – Charlie Napier and Peter Scarff of Celtic, Rudolph Nickolsburger and Bela Guttmann of Hakoah. The latter, a midfielder/defender, was a fascinating character, a man who had lost virtually all of his savings in the 1929 Wall Street Crash but was sufficiently single-minded and resourceful to shape successful careers both as a player and a manager with many clubs, most notably as a coach at Benfica where the Portuguese club broke the Real Madrid hegemony in the European Cup with their twin triumphs in 1961 and 1962 and where he snatched the legendary Eusebio from under the noses of their great rivals Sporting Lisbon. An equally colourful character, the dapper Jimmy Walker (immortalised in the 1957 Bob Hope film *Beau James*), a songwriter turned mayor of New York and a man with an eye for the ethnic vote, had chosen the event as a vehicle for some pre-match politicking, taking part along with 'a body of Tammany bigwigs' (the Democratic Party machine) in a parade headed by the local police band before kicking off the game. Little good did it do him, for 15 months later he was forced out of office amid allegations of corruption and cronyism in his administration.

After all this excitement and razzamatazz, Celtic's progress was almost prosaic, uneventful even, before they headed for home. The aforementioned match against Bricklayers in Chicago ended with praise for Celtic's classy performance in a 6–3 victory and brickbats for the nervous home keeper from a local newspaper. This was followed four days later by the club's first-ever match under floodlighting (in the modern sense). Indeed, the visibility at the University of Detroit Stadium on 25 June during the visitors' 5–0 victory over Michigan All Stars was so good that the players told Tom Maley, accompanying his brother Willie on the tour, that 'once the game had started they knew no difference to playing in the ordinary daylight of a fine day'. However, later, Tom did draw attention to certain drawbacks to playing in North America when he penned an account of the tour for the October 1931 issue of *The Journal of the RMS Transylvania*, the ship on which he made both his outward and return journeys: 'The "diamond" in the field of play and the existence of confusing ground marks associated with baseball and kindred games made for confusion and handicap for our players and they suffered thereby. Very much lighter are the balls used in games. In the interpretation of many of the rules of the game there is a difference.' A few days later, following a visit to Toronto where Ulster United were defeated 3–1, there was the welcome opportunity for revenge over the New York Yankees, this time at Yankee Stadium (the ground of the famous baseball team of the same name), and Celtic extracted it in full measure. Willie Maley, as bad a loser as there ever has been, was keen to stop the Yankees 'crowing over their fluky win in Boston', and even the mild-mannered Jimmy McGrory noted tersely in his diary: 'This was a very important game, a game we had to win . . . We played our best game of the tour and whacked them 4–1; great scenes afterwards, nearly all our players were carried shoulder-high off the field.' It was a match in which right-half Peter Wilson underlined his claim to have been the 'Man of the Tour', at least in the eyes of Tom White, who described his contribution as 'magnificent', extolling 'his heady, moving forward play' as 'a sheer delight – hardly a ball has he wasted'.

The rather ad hoc arrangements of the tour were demonstrated for the last time with the tacking-on of a match at Baltimore (v. Baltimore Canton) on 30 June, again under floodlights, one in which the 'speed and accuracy of Celtic's passing bewildered an out-generalled home team', thus enabling the visitors to end on a high note their first visit to a country that in little more than a decade would shake off economic depression to become the world's superpower. However, its attractions had been lost on Willie Maley, judging by his final dispatch to the *Evening Times*:

> Out here we have been really yearning for Scotland. It has been pathetic, especially now we are going home, to meet our exiled pals and to feel how much they would like to be coming with us. Only necessity keeps the majority out here, as America, with all its charms, has no real grip on the Scot or Irishman with a love for his country.

He added that the only bright feature of the trip was the hospitality and enthusiasm extended to the tourists by these same expatriates. It was a mood that he carried aboard the RMS *Transylvania* on 1 July, when he talked to pressmen prior to the return home on the liner, a departure that was preceded by the Celtic players being showered with confetti and, poignantly, said Jimmy McGrory, just about everybody in the Celtic party being handed messages to take back to friends and relatives in Scotland. Maley dropped a broad hint that Celtic FC were unlikely to return to North America if he had anything to do with it. He was scathing about the standards of refereeing and the pitches and denounced the 'rough handling' of his players during matches, ending with a contemptuous dismissal of the administration of the sport on the Continent, rather unfairly so given the impact that the economic situation had had on a game striving to gain a foothold in a continent obsessed with the established sports of baseball, gridiron football and ice hockey. It did not go unnoticed that once the ship set sail Maley exuded bonhomie, in stark contrast to the outward journey. Celtic were welcomed home as as enthusiastically as they had been waved off, with groups of supporters taking up 'points to vantage' on the banks of the Clyde to wave at their heroes as the liner moved upriver to dock at Yorkhill Quay, where 'a special staff' of policemen had been drafted in to prevent the players being mobbed on their arrival in Glasgow. A famous face was missing as the party stepped ashore, for Jimmy McGrory had given his colleagues the slip early that morning, at around six o'clock, by disembarking in the customs officers' boat as the liner arrived off Moville, County Donegal, a prearranged stratagem devised to ensure that he could get married with the minimum of fuss a few hours later in the local St Michael's Church. Once back in Glasgow, Tom White, while expressing reservations about the conditions (the heat, travelling and other matters, but not the refereeing), was noticeably less acerbic in his judgement of the tour, stating that 'We have had a wonderful experience and enjoyed every minute of it,' and asserting that Celtic would be delighted to go back 'within the next year or two', sentiments that were endorsed by captain Jimmy McStay, who had won universal admiration for being the acme of diplomacy throughout the trip. As it happened, Celtic did not return until 1951.

That cleavage of opinion about the whole enterprise was reflected in two contentious newspaper articles. The *Daily Record and Mail* published an attack by an expatriate Scot based in New York on Celtic's 'rough tactics' and a 'lack of self-control', exemplified by his claim that at the end of the Hakoah game they had walked off the pitch instead of entertaining the notion, apparently suggested by the body language of their opponents and the match officials, of playing extra time to decide the custody of the cup put up by mayor Jimmy Walker. It would have been better, he added, if Celtic had not come at all. 'Man in the Know', who was dubious about the venture and the idea of Celtic going back to America, nevertheless reacted furiously in the *Glasgow Observer* of 25 July 1931 with a diatribe in his own inimitable style. After ascribing the accusations to 'a Rangers supporter whose Blue bias stuck out aggressively', he did not hold back:

> Experience has made us distrust American statements and to totally discount Light Blue propaganda. Anyone who believes an American must be a credulous simpleton. Anyone who believes a Rangers supporter must be and is a fool. The average Rangers fan, if he is not solid bone from the chin up, is probably a blithering half-wit and commonsense can never eat its way through the fatty deposit which clouds his brain.

All such exchanges were to be rendered meaningless a mere six weeks later . . .

* * *

POSTSCRIPT
Celtic's 1931 Tour Itinerary

23 May. Philadelphia 6–1 v. Pennsylvania All Stars (McGrory 2, R. Thomson, A. Thomson, Napier, o.g. by Smith of Penn. All Stars)

24 May. New York 3–2 v. New York Giants (McGrory 2, Napier)

30 May. Boston 3–4 v. New York Yankees (McGrory, A. Thomson, Scarff)

31 May. North Tiverton (Rhode Island), 0–1 v. Fall River FC

6 June. Pawtucket (Rhode Island), 1–3 v. Pawtucket Rangers (Napier)

7 June. Brooklyn 5–0 v. Brooklyn Wanderers (McGrory 2, R. Thomson, A. Thomson, Scarff)

13 June. Montreal 7–0 v. Carsteel (Scarff 5, Napier, Hughes)

14 June. New York 1–1 v. Hakoah All Stars (Napier)

21 June. Chicago 6–3 v. Bricklayers (Wilson 2, R. Thomson, Hughes, McGhee, Napier pen.)

25 June. Detroit 5–0 v. Michigan All Stars (Napier 2, McGrory, R. Thomson, McGhee)

27 June. Toronto 3–1 v. Ulster United (McGrory 2, A. Thomson)

The only match played on a ground reserved for football, according to Tom Maley in his October 1931 account of the tour in *The Journal of the RMS Transylvania*.

28 June. New York 4–1 v. New York Yankees (Napier 2, R. Thomson, A. Thomson)

30 June. Baltimore 4–1 v. Baltimore Canton (McGhee 2, Hughes, Whitelaw)

This match has been listed elsewhere as having taken place on 29 June, but the match report in the 1 July 1931 edition of the *Baltimore Sun* – headed 'Celtics [sic] Trim Canton 4 to 1' – refers to a 'splendid exhibition' at Homewood Field 'beneath the floodlights last night' by a team 'who sail for home at noon today from New York'.

Summary: Played 13 (won 9, lost 3, drew 1), with 48 goals for and 18 against

Goal-scorers: McGrory 10, Napier 10, Scarff 7, R. Thomson 5, A. Thomson 5, McGhee 4, Hughes 3, Wilson 2, Whitelaw and o.g. (Smith, Penn. All Stars)

CHAPTER 10

The Grim Reaper

We can confidently report that as we have a youthful side to which we can still keep adding, we may look forward with expectancy and hope to a continuance of successful seasons.

The Manager's Report, Celtic Football Guide, *summer 1931*

The winning of the Scottish Cup in 1931 was a very important success for Celtic. Not only did it get the 1930s off to a good start but it also put Celtic's name on a trophy at a time when Rangers were the dominant team in the land.

At that period, there were only two major domestic trophies, the League Championship and the Scottish Cup. Rangers had come into existence in 1872, some 15 years before Celtic, but right from the start of the league in season 1890–91, up until 1920, the Bhoys had proved the more successful side:

Decade	League Championship	Scottish Cup
1890–91 to 1899–00	Celtic 4 Rangers 3	Celtic 3 Rangers 3
1900–01 to 1909–10	Celtic 6 Rangers 2	Celtic 3 Rangers 1
1910–11 to 1919–20	Celtic 5 Rangers 5	Celtic 3 Rangers 0

That makes a total of fifteen league titles to Celtic and ten to Rangers; while, in the Scottish Cup, Celtic had won nine to Rangers' four. And if we include two other well-regarded local competitions of the time – the Glasgow Cup and the Charity Cup – Celtic again come out the better of the two sides. Over those same three decades, while Rangers won thirteen Glasgow Cups to Celtic's twelve, the latter's seventeen Charity Cup victories dwarfs the eight of the Light Blues.

However, once the 1920s were under way and Rangers came under new management (that of Bill Struth), that scenario changed during the decade. They might have been still having trouble getting their hands on the Scottish Cup but, in the league, the men from Ibrox dominated:

League Championship

Celtic 2 Rangers 8

Scottish Cup

Celtic 3 Rangers 2

And Rangers also took the honours in the lesser tournaments, five Glasgow Cup wins to Celtic's four; and six in the Charity Cup as opposed to Celtic's three. So, taking all the above into account, it might come as no surprise that Celtic fans around the world were quite delighted in April 1931 when news came through of their heroes' 4–2 victory over Motherwell in the replay of the Scottish Cup final.

Shortly afterwards, a Celtic party headed off to North America for the club's first tour across the Atlantic, a venture much enjoyed by player and fan alike (see Chapter 9). On their return, they all had a few weeks off before reporting in for pre-season training.

The Celtic side of the 1930–31 season had been remarkably settled, the same 11 names being on the team sheet for the majority of its matches. John Thomson was the goalkeeper; Willie Cook and Willie 'Peter' McGonagle the full-backs; Peter Wilson, Jimmy McStay and Chic Geatons made up the half-back line; with a forward five of Bertie Thomson, Alec Thomson, Jimmy McGrory, Peter Scarff and Charlie Napier. It was also a relatively young side, the average age just over 25.

The only other players involved were goalkeeper David Robertson (2 apps), the promising left-back John Morrison (5 apps), utility player Willie Hughes (8 apps), half-back Graham Robertson (8 apps), wing-half Bob Whitelaw (10 apps), inside-forward Hugh Smith (3 apps), outside-left Con Tierney (7 apps), outside-left Peter Kavanagh (5 apps) and centre-forward Joe Cowan (1 app).

The league season of 1931–32 got off to a good start, reinforcing the belief of Celtic fans that the future was rich in promise. Of the first seven matches, Celtic won five and drew two, scoring twenty-six goals and losing seven. On the other side of the city, Rangers had also started well, with new signing centre-forward Sam English – just in from Yoker Athletic – showing his goal-scoring prowess. So, as the sides ran out at Ibrox for their first league clash of the season, on 5 September 1931, both sets of fans were full of anticipation.

The events of that afternoon are so well documented that they only need a brief resumé in this book. A crowd of around 75,000 was present when the match kicked off at 3.15 p.m.; the weather was bright and sunny but the play in the first half was nervous, with too many errors and chances at goal were few. Five minutes into the second half, the Rangers half-backs broke up a Celtic attack and right-half Davie Meiklejohn passed the ball out to Jimmy Fleming, on the right wing. He evaded a tackle from Celtic's left-back Peter McGonagle, then, noticing that centre-half Jimmy McStay was caught out of position, sent a pass through the middle into the path of Sam English, who raced towards the Celtic goal.

John Thomson read the situation and knew he had a decision to make. Goalkeepers of that period were taught not to leave their goal unless in an emergency but he would also have realised that staying on his line would have given English a bigger target to aim for. He hesitated for only a few seconds then ran forward and, just as English was preparing to shoot, Thomson dived at the ball. His body duly blocked the shot but, as he came downwards, his head made contact with English's knee. The ball trickled past the post; English rose to his feet, limping; Thomson lay where he had fallen.

Rangers inside-left Bob McPhail, close to the action, later mentioned that Thomson's head was out of alignment and that blood was pouring down from his scalp onto the jersey he was wearing on the day. Both sets of players signalled frantically to the side of the pitch for help. Trainer Willie Quinn was quick to reach the stricken player, with Willie Maley not far behind. Rangers manager Bill Struth also arrived, all of them stunned by the severity of the accidental collision. A stretcher was called for and the unconscious player was taken off to the pavilion, where he was examined by the Celtic doctor, ex-player Willie Kivlichan, who diagnosed a depressed fracture of the skull and ordered that Thomson be immediately transferred to the Victoria Infirmary, on Glasgow's south side.

The players were muted as they watched him leave the field. Jimmy Marshall was in the Rangers team that day. A medical student at Glasgow University at the time, he feared the worst, as he later told a reporter: 'I knew within myself there was little hope. I couldn't say so of course for all of us know that where there's life there's hope but the game for me stopped at that awful moment.'

The incident had occurred at the Rangers end of Ibrox and their support, like fans everywhere, were not unhappy to see an opponent down and a section even cheered. Rangers captain Davie Meiklejohn was quick to approach them and gesture for silence; it was an effective appeal and Thomson was stretchered off in comparative silence. Chic Geatons, according to the local *Evening Times* 'Final Sport' edition report that evening, 'popped inside the red jersey after a delay of fully five minutes' before going into goal for Celtic (no substitutes were allowed then) but, frankly, the heart had gone out of the play and it petered out into a goalless draw. Some five hours later, Johnny Thomson died from his injuries; he was 22 years of age.

One must always be wary of over-emphasising the talent of a player who died so young and in such distressing circumstances. In the case of John Thomson, however, that wariness could never be applied. Ever since he made his debut for Celtic in February 1927, he had received the praise and admiration of Scotland's football public. This tribute, for instance, is taken from one of the pen pictures in the Glasgow newspaper *The Bulletin* prior to the Scotland–England encounter in March 1931:

John Thomson. The latest Celt to wear the Triple Crown of

internationalism [The 'Triple Crown of internationalism' meant playing for Scotland in matches against England, Wales and Ireland in the same season]. And it fits snugly on that so modern mop of hair. Can bend like a willow and flits from post to post with the elusiveness of a beam from a mirror on a sunny day. One hundred per cent confident about everything he does. Wellesley-born and Parkhead-reared. One of the few unspoilt by a football nation's platitudes.

In his book *I Saw Stars*, published in 1947, R.E. Kingsley (better known as 'Rex', the *Sunday Mail* sportswriter) was equally complimentary:

> But where was there a grander boy than Celtic's Johnny Thomson? Shy and self-effacing, pleased about the devotion so embarrassingly offered him by the Celtic fans but always quite certain it wasn't merited. I remember meeting him some days before his tragic death. He had started work as a salesman in a Glasgow gents' outfitters. We met outside the shop. As we talked, some passers-by hesitated, took a good look at him, then decided to stop indefinitely. In no time, we heard the murmur 'that's Johnny Thomson'. The admiring crowd grew. I could see Johnny getting redder and redder, till . . . 'You'll have to excuse me, Rex; I must get back in the shop,' he burst out, and vanished through the doorway. The crowd sighed and started to shuttle off. I overheard . . . 'Greatest goalkeeper in the country . . . he'll risk everything to save his goal . . . ' The world knows that on Saturday, 5 September 1931, he did . . . and lost his life thereby.

As can be imagined, Thomson's passing hit the Celtic community hard. Deaths in football are fortunately rare and for one to occur in such an iconic game was particularly hard to cope with. Celtic were due to play Airdrie on the following Wednesday (the day of the funeral) and that match was postponed by the Scottish League. Willie Maley, though, was apparently keen to get his troops back playing again, so the game against Queen's Park the next weekend went ahead. Celtic tried out a couple of goalkeepers – John Falconer and Joe Coen – over the next few weeks, then eventually brought over a young man who had impressed on the North American tour when playing for Fall River in Massachusetts. Thankfully, Joe Kennaway rose to the challenge and remained the club's keeper for the remainder of the 1930s. However, only a few months after losing John Thomson, Celtic Football Club was struck by another tragedy.

Peter Scarff had joined Celtic from juvenile club Linwood St Conval's in 1928, made his first-team debut against Arthurlie in the Scottish Cup in January 1929 and almost immediately became a regular at inside-left. Peter seems to have been a constant-running and tireless grafter, his capacity for hard work a real bonus to the team of the time.

On 23 September 1931, only two weeks after John Thomson's funeral, a Celtic side travelled down to Ayr to play the local team in a testimonial for their centre-forward Willie Fleming. Willie had spent one season at Parkhead – 1924–25 – scoring 10 goals in his 19 appearances, but, with his rival for the position, Jimmy McGrory, in such peerless form, he realised his chances were going to be few and moved to Ayr. At half-time in the match, Peter Scarff complained of a shortage of breath and was taken off as a precaution. It was assumed that he had some kind of mild chest infection.

Over the following two months, Peter kept his place in the side but there were signs that all was not well. The grafting required was becoming more difficult and the final whistle became a blessed relief. His last game for Celtic was on 19 December 1931 at Parkhead against Leith Athletic, when his after-match condition was so worrying that the club doctor arranged for further tests to be performed immediately. The diagnosis of pulmonary tuberculosis was quite clear and, on 12 January 1932, Peter Scarff was admitted to the Bridge of Weir sanatorium.

In 1860, Hermann Bremmer had opened a centre in Gabersdorf in Germany to try to cure – or more accurately ameliorate – tuberculosis by rest. He believed that fresh air and good food in an establishment more like a hotel than a hospital would benefit the patient. Such a place soon became known as a sanatorium. By the early 1930s, this was still regarded as the main remedy for the condition. Other treatments were in their infancy. Collapsing the affected lung had come into use but was not widespread; the Bacillus Calmette-Guerin (BCG) had first been used in humans in 1921 but had still not gained popularity; while the availability of penicillin – first cultured by Alexander Fleming in 1928 – would not be fully developed until the early 1940s.

In 1932, therefore, sufferers from tuberculosis were, if they could afford it, treated with isolation, plenty of fresh air, good food and the best of attention. It was a sympathetic form of treatment but not a particularly effective one for many people and Peter Scarff was one of them. The Celtic support was always keen to hear how he was doing and various bulletins came out from the hospital. Some of these were quite hopeful, as there were periods of remission that gave rise to hopes that he would pull through. Unfortunately, they proved false and a quick deterioration ensued. In July 1933, it was announced that Peter would never play again; and only five months later, in December 1933, his death was announced to a shocked football public. He was 25. On 12 December 1933, Peter Scarff was buried at Kilbarchan in Renfrewshire, Willie Maley draping a Celtic jersey over his coffin before the internment.

Of the team that won the Scottish Cup in 1931, there could be little doubt that outside-right Bertie Thomson was the most sociable. He was a fine singer and good fun at a party but, like many others with those particular attributes, he never knew when to draw the line. En route to Celtic's first-ever tour to North America, only weeks after the Scottish Cup win in 1931, there was a social evening aboard the SS *Caledonia* during which Bertie Thomson sang 'The Sangs My Mither Used to Sing' to an appreciative audience. It would also be true to say that he became increasingly fond of a drink while on board, although this might have proved more difficult once the side reached the USA, as prohibition was still the law. Still, a thirsty man would no doubt have found ways round the problem and Bertie Thomson was certainly that. His cheerful friendliness also made him a popular guy with the support, especially those who also enjoyed a wee dram, and one could just imagine Willie Maley's stern, disapproving gaze at this fine player's predilection for the bottle.

It obviously became a topic of some concern, as it was later learned from one of the crew that on the return journey, on board the RMS *Transylvania*, Willie Maley took steps to try to make sure that Bertie was refused alcohol – or at least his intake was reduced – for the duration of the voyage.

Every player was obviously badly affected by the death of John Thomson in September 1931 and possibly Bertie Thomson found some solace in drink. However, it apparently did not affect his form at that point, as he was capped for Scotland against Wales in Wrexham on the last day of October 1931, scoring his side's second goal in the 3–2 win. The following week, he played for the Scottish League against the English League at Parkhead, when the Scots won again, this time by 4–3.

Bertie had only missed one league match for Celtic in the first half of that season of 1931–32 but a broken bone in his right foot, received in the 0–1 loss to Hamilton on 23 January 1932, put him out of action for two months. This was the last thing a guy like Bertie Thomson needed; all that free time on his hands and those 'friends' to chat to. He did play a couple of matches before the end of the season but, by the following campaign, it was noticeable that Bertie, although still a regular in the side, was slightly off the pace, the talent still there but perhaps the enthusiasm – or, more probably, the fitness – not quite as fulsome as before. There was also a difficult period during September and October of 1932, when the relationship between Thomson and Willie Maley – always tenuous – erupted into open warfare after a 1–4 defeat by Queen's Park. Both parties seemed to over-react to the situation, Thomson was out of the team for nearly two months and the side suffered.

He did make the Scottish Cup final side of April 1933, when Celtic beat Motherwell again, this time by a solitary goal, but, after only two matches in the following season of 1933–34, Bertie Thomson was transferred to Blackpool. From then on, his career was in freefall. After just over a year down south, he came back to Motherwell, where he lasted 15 months, then moved to Ireland and a side called Brideville in Dublin.

Off the field, Bertie continued to live as though there was no tomorrow, his behaviour giving more and more cause for concern as his reliance on alcohol increased. In a small paragraph tucked away in an inside page of the *Daily Record and Mail* on 25 November 1936, a report read that Bertie Thomson, 'the ex-Celtic, Blackpool and Motherwell footballer', was fined £5 with the alternative of 30 days' imprisonment after being 'found guilty of having on 14 August 1936, in a house at 327 Argyle Street, Glasgow, assaulted Susan Conway, or Thomson, his wife, by stabbing her twice with a pair of nail scissors, and also striking her on the face with his fists. Thomson was allowed two months in which to pay the fine.' One year after that court case, on 17 September 1937, Bertie Thomson died from heart trouble at the age of thirty.

John Thomson's father (also named John) surely articulated the grief that enveloped the relatives of the three players struck down in their prime when, on the eve of his son's funeral, he told a friend, Bill Paterson (himself a goalkeeper), that 'We were at his bedside for only two minutes and saw our bairn, for he was still the bairn to Ma and me, being taken away from us.' The losses were of such numbing frequency within such a short time period as to bring to mind the Border lament that recorded the Scottish defeat at the Battle of Flodden in 1513–'The Floo'ers of the Forest are a' wede awa'.'

* * *

With the loss of three of their colleagues within little more than six years, the other stars from the 1931 Scottish Cup final team must have been a little reflective on their own future. In the event, they would have little reason to worry, as most reached a fair age. The appearances below refer only to major competitions.

Right-back Willie Cook – after 110 games for Celtic, the Northern Ireland international moved to Everton, with whom he won an FA Cup medal in 1933. He also played against his former club in the final of the Empire Exhibition Trophy in 1938. Willie then went on to have a career in coaching and management, covering England, Wales, Northern Ireland, Norway, Peru and Iraq. He died in 1992 at the age of 82.

Left-back Willie McGonagle – usually known as 'Peter' (after his father of that name, a player with Hamilton), Willie spent 10 years at Parkhead, making 325 appearances, before joining Cheltenham Town. He died at the age of 52 in 1956.

Right-half Peter Wilson – made 395 appearances for Celtic between 1923 and 1934. He then played for Hibs and had a spell as player-manager with Dunfermline Athletic before joining the Royal Navy for the duration of the Second World War. Peter was an Ayrshire lad, born in Beith and died in that same town in 1983, aged 77.

Centre-half Jimmy McStay – the younger of the two McStay brothers of that era, Jimmy's 472-match career covered the years 1920 to 1934. He was then freed and played for Hamilton for a year before taking over as manager of Alloa. In 1940, Jimmy became Celtic's second-ever manager, replacing Willie Maley. However, the war years proved a difficult time for Celtic in general and Jimmy was given little help or money to maintain or improve the side. Eventually, in 1945, he was replaced by Jimmy McGrory. Jimmy McStay died in 1974, aged 78.

Left-half Chic Geatons – a Lochgelly boy, Chic played over 340 times for Celtic between 1927 and 1941. In 1945, he became a coach at Celtic Park, holding the position until 1950. He died in 1970, at the age of 62.

Inside-right Alec Thomson – another Fifer, this one from Buckhaven. Alec had a 12-year, 451-match career at Celtic Park before moving to Dunfermline Athletic for another 3-year spell. He retired in 1937 and died in 1975, aged 74.

Centre-forward Jimmy McGrory – Jimmy's career as player and manager is so well documented that it hardly needs recalling here. He died in 1982 at the age of 78.

Outside-left Charlie Napier – nicknamed 'Happy Feet', Charlie spent seven years at Parkhead before moving south to Derby County and then Sheffield Wednesday. He died in Falkirk in 1973, aged 62.

* * *

POSTSCRIPT

Fortunately, deaths on the field of play in football are relatively rare, yet almost unbelievably, within a year of the demise of John Thomson, another goalkeeper – admittedly in the junior grade – suffered an eerily similar fate. These words are from the *Daily Record and Mail* of 13 June 1932:

> For the second time within nine months, Scottish football has been marred by tragedy. On Saturday, Alexander Cruikshank, goalkeeper of the Glasgow junior club, Strathclyde, was fatally injured trying to save his goal during the replayed Eastern Charity final between Strathclyde and Rutherglen Glencairn at Barrowfield Park.
>
> He sustained a fracture of the skull and died last evening in Glasgow Royal Infirmary.

The *Glasgow Eastern Standard* of 18 June 1932 gave further details:

> The young man sustained his fatal injuries by an accidental kick, in full view of his father, mother and sweetheart, who were spectators at the Glencairn game at Barrowfield.
>
> No one suspected the injuries to be fatal. He was unconscious when carried off, but recovered in the pavilion, and as his teammates went out for the second half said, 'Good luck, boys; see and win.' He became critically ill on Sunday. An operation showed his case was hopeless. Death occurred about 6 p.m., similar, almost to a detail, to the fate of the late John Thomson.

By an astonishing coincidence, on the day of John Thomson's death, Bill Paterson (a fellow goalkeeper and a partner with Thomson in an abortive linen business in Fife) was concussed while playing for Airdrieonians against Falkirk at Brockville Park. He had thrown himself at the ball in an attempt to thwart a scoring attempt by Gall, the home side's outside-left. Stretchered off, Paterson's concussion was such that it was only after three days that he learned of his friend's death. In the interval, his wife had tried to apprise him of the tragic event but it was only when he was in a position to read the newspapers that he learned the grim news (as recounted by Bill Paterson in the *Sporting Post*, Dundee, 23 May 1953)

CHAPTER 11

War and Peace

At midnight hundreds of ships (warships, merchant ships, tugs, steamers, motorboats) opened up on the Firth of Clyde to create the most tremendous victory din. For miles around and far inland, the noise was heard and people on the coast, excited by the din and the spirit behind it, suddenly defied the coast black-out ban and allowed their lights to blaze out onto the streets. Glasgow became a city of revelry last night. Crowds packed the main streets, dancing and singing to the accompaniment of guitars, mouth organs and other instruments. The night sky all over the city was aglow with the light from hundreds of bonfires. Late-night transport could not cope with the homeward-bound crowds . . . [The following night] Garlanded with twinkly, coloured fairy lights, George Square was packed with crowds such as it has never seen before. Nearly 100,000 people jostled, sang, danced, whistled, shouted, leapt on to passing buses, taxicabs, tramcars, and formed 'human chains' to guide them through the milling throng. Tramcars and buses were jammed. There were only inches to move around in as men, women and children went delirious with pent-up VE-night delight.

The Daily Record and Mail *of 8 and 9 May 1945 reflects the celebrations that followed the 7 May unconditional surrender of the Germans. 8 May was officially declared 'Victory in Europe Day'.*

Hibs and Hearts are playing their Rosebery Charity Cup final at Easter Road as a 'VE Day plus 1' attraction for Edinburgh. And it is rather appropriate that inside-left Bobby Combe will be in the Hibs side. Bobby was a prisoner of war in the notorious San Bostel Camp in Germany, where, he says, they were virtually starved. He was released recently and is gradually getting back some of his lost weight. The crowd will give Bobby a special welcome.

Extract from Scottish Daily Express, *8 May 1945*

For all its impressive regeneration in recent decades, Glasgow has never quite shaken off the 'tough' image that grew up during the inter-war period and lasted into the post-war era, fostered in large part by the rather lurid image projected in the bestselling 1935 novel *No Mean City*, and that despite earning the reputation of being the most hospitable large town in Great Britain during the Second World War, when its status as an important gateway to the Atlantic made it a host to innumerable servicemen from all quarters of the globe. The journalist Gordon Irving, proud though he was of the role of his city at war, was all too aware of its contradictions when he described it as follows in January 1945:

City of war-time lights and good restaurants, city of slow but all-night transport, of first-class shops and third-class houses. Dirty, grimy, damp but warm-hearted. Packed with hard-toiling men and women. Home town of brave fighting warriors from Bastogne to Burma, of warm-hearted, kindly households, of wives who love to shop and men to smoke, of bowler-hatted business-men and brightly dressed women. City of hardship and harmony, of engineering and shipbuilding, of an accent you can spot anywhere on earth.

None of his readers would have been in any doubt as to the district most associated with 'third-class' housing, and that would have been a generous tag when associated with the state of the majority of the dwellings in an area located just south of the city centre from which it was separated (as the 'new' Gorbals now is) by the River Clyde. In an article titled 'The Forgotten Gorbals' published in the populist, campaigning 'photojournalistic' weekly magazine *Picture Post* in January 1948, A.L. ('Bert') Lloyd was intent on stirring the national conscience with his depiction of a community of 40,000 'shockingly housed' people huddled together (often several to a single room) in squalor and poverty in 252 acres comprising largely decaying tenements rented out by absentee landlords, 'private people in London, Sydney, Shanghai and elsewhere' and even Glasgow Corporation, the municipal authority. From the mid-nineteenth century onwards, the Gorbals had become the home of thousands of labourers (and their descendants) who came to work on the railways and the docks: 'They came for higher wages, for fuller plates, for what they conceived to be a better way of life than was possible in starving Erin and the wasted Scottish Highlands.' The portrait of this 'rough' area that emerged from Lloyd's typewriter was a compassionate one of 'Britain's most abandoned slum', a depiction of a monument to civic neglect. He made no attempt to gloss over the fact that it had its share of drunkenness and violence, but dispelled the myths perpetuated by 'sensation-mongers' who made it sound like hell on earth: 'The population is not composed of criminals . . . murder is rare in the district.' He focused on what was remarkable about a section of the population living on the margins, 'kind, friendly folk with a strong feeling for social justice' striving to bring up families in the most unpropitious of circumstances, as illustrated starkly by the caption to the photograph taken in her Commercial Road home (by the famous Bert Hardy) of a Mrs Greenan: 'Borne thirteen children, lost seven from pneumonia.' It was high time for change, Bert Lloyd concluded, while noting that the inhabitants, who believed that the area was 'ready for dynamiting', were sceptical of any remedy from a Corporation they no longer regarded as 'shockable' and which, indeed, took another 20 years before it finally stirred itself into action. It was a fatalism of sorts, and it elicited from Lloyd an acute observation:

As is usual where people find circumstance a hard thing to grapple with, the Gorbals is a great place for pipe-dreams: a place where folk think passionately of sudden fortune. Street bookies do a roaring trade round the ramshackle back-courts; and in many tenements the dream-book is the only literature. Football takes on the proportion of a mythology, and players are seen as heroes of a fantasy world. In the bars and on the street corners you run into men with, you would think, small capacity for academic learning, but with such knowledge of the intricate history of professional football as would earn them a professorship in any other field. It used to be said, 'Every man has two capital cities: his own and Paris.' In the Gorbals, every man has two football teams: his own and Celtic. The local team is Clyde. But the dream team is the one in green and white hoops. Inside Gorbals houses the commonest pictures are of 'The Sacred Heart' and the Celtic team. You see few likenesses of the Saints but many of Johnny Thomson, the Celtic goalkeeper accidentally killed on 5 September 1931, in a game against the Rangers, and now spoken of reverently as a popular martyr and a bright hero brought down by misfortune.

The Gorbals itself had a local hero, a supporter of the 'dream team' who had emerged from that Celtic stronghold to earn a VC, which his widow collected from King George VI at Buckingham Palace. It was perhaps appropriate, given his praise of Glasgow's military fame, that it was Gordon Irving's newspaper, the *Daily Record and Mail*, which would highlight the extraordinary valour recently displayed by 30-year-old James Stokes. A former pupil of St Luke's RC school in Ballater Street and a labourer who lived with his wife Janet and their child in a single-apartment flat in what was described as 'a rundown tenement' in Clyde Street at the time he joined the Army, Stokes was described by a neighbour as 'not a very big chap [actually he was 5 ft 4 in. tall], but there was nothing he would not face'. In its edition of 18 April 1945, the paper described the private's decisive interventions when his King's Shropshire Light Infantry platoon was held up in its attack on German positions during its push towards the Rhine. Twice 'he went into enemy strongpoints alone, without waiting for orders, and silenced the intense fire'. On the first occasion, he came back with 12 prisoners but refused to go to the regimental aid post for attention to a severe wound. On the second, he was seen to fall as he approached a farmhouse, 'firing from the hip', but he got up, lifted his rifle and went on into the building, from which he emerged shortly afterwards with five more prisoners in tow after the firing inside had ceased. Stokes, though 'terribly wounded', was with the platoon as it formed up for its assault on its final objective when, suddenly, he dashed forward alone, intent on reaching a strongpoint 60 yards away, but fell mortally wounded when only 20 yards short of his target. It was said that his final utterance as he raised his hands to his comrades was 'Good-bye, boys.' No wonder that one later account of his deeds was headed 'The soldier who would not give up!' His widow received a letter from his commanding officer that read: 'Your husband was a very brave and gallant man. These are no vain and empty words.' After revealing that its account of Stokes's deeds and the plight of a widow and a five-year-old son having to rely on an army allowance had 'touched the heart of a nation', the newspaper launched the 'Stokes Hero Fund'. It stated that 'many people feel that young Jim should get a better chance than his dad' and that his 'over-wrought' widow was not only in need of a holiday but also 'anxious to move to another neighbourhood where little Jim can thrive in more congenial surroundings'. By the time the fund closed around the end of May 1945, the public subscriptions, boosted by the newspaper's donation of one hundred guineas and the proceeds of a packed matinee show hosted by the legendary Sir Harry Lauder at the local Metropole Theatre, had amassed a sum exceeding £1,600, a substantial total in a period of wartime austerity.

James Stokes, whose memory lives in the James Stokes VC Celtic Supporters Club, died shortly before the cessation of hostilities in Europe provided his favourite club with an opportunity to put a better gloss, however slight, on their dismal wartime record. Only two days before the ceasefire announcement, a victory over Partick Thistle (by 1 goal, 9 corners to 1 goal, 2 corners) qualified them to play Rangers in the Glasgow Charity Cup final, a bit of spice being added by the much-anticipated contest between the great rivals being billed as a 'rubber' match, both clubs having won the trophy 24 times. Up to then, season 1944–45 had threatened to be just another one of those, like the previous five (Glasgow Cup win in

1940 and Charity Cup triumph in 1943 notwithstanding), that had left the club and its long-suffering supporters with few happy memories. It had started promisingly enough, with three successive Southern League victories before the wheels came off with a 2–6 humiliation at Hamilton that prompted one Willie Fanning of Caroline Street, Parkhead (the proverbial stone's throw from Celtic Park), to set in motion the founding of the Celtic FC Supporters Association. The autumn period was characterised by the mediocrity that was all too often the manifestation of the club's lukewarm attitude to wartime football, with fourteen matches resulting in only four wins and nine defeats, including two losses to Rangers. Predictably, press reaction was scathing. 'Rex' of the *Sunday Mail* was dismissive of the eleven that was thrashed 0–4 by 'a far from brilliant' Rangers in a league match at Celtic Park in early September 1944 – 'Too many players who can show their ball-control only when the game was played at half-speed . . . the half-back line moved like a bulldozer' – and described the forward line in the 2–3 Glasgow Cup final defeat by the same side four weeks later as looking 'as if it had come out of a hat', an oblique reference to the widely held belief that manager Jimmy McStay was not in sole control of team matters. Remarkably, the onset of winter coincided with a transformation, for Celtic went undefeated in the championship from the first Saturday in December 1944 to the end of the league season, a fifteen-match sequence that brought fourteen victories and one draw, enabling them to finish as runners-up, albeit seven points behind Rangers. The turnaround was gradual rather than spectacular, with early December references to the side 'still lacking in cohesion' and being 'laborious and lopsided' even in victory turning to praise for the 'confidence and poise' displayed in a 3–0 Yuletide victory over Clyde at Shawfield. The change in fortune confounded even the club's most fervent admirers, as the 1945–46 edition of the *Celtic Football Guide* admitted in its review of the previous season, though not without displaying a touch of disingenuousness about what had gone before:

Surprise and jubilation. Those same players who had been in the habit of leaving the field at the end of the game on the losing side although they had performed as well, if not better than, their opponents, suddenly rocketed their club from a singularly low rung on the Southern League ladder to second position from the top, which they maintained to the end of the season.

It was, said the annual publication, 'a triumph for youth', singling out for particular attention the Ne'erday 1945 league clash at Ibrox Park, albeit the goal-scorer was the veteran wing-half George Paterson, home on leave from the RAF: 'Only one goal separated the teams but it was a game Rangers never looked like winning and Celtic were their masters.' The writer exulted in the promise of the likes of 21-year-old Willie Miller ('fast developing into one of the finest goalkeepers in the game'), the 18-year-old Jimmy Mallan (possessor of 'a well-developed positional sense and the right temperament'), who had been plucked from reserve football to fill the centre-half berth, the 'singularly clever' 22-year-old half-back-cum-inside-forward John McPhail and the 21-year-old Johnny Paton, 'equally at home on either wing'. And the club could still rely on the old faithfuls, namely Malcolm MacDonald, 'the finest footballer in the country'; the versatile Matt Lynch, 'our most consistent performer' that season; the stalwart full-back Bobby Hogg; and the evergreen 'Jack-in-the-box' forward Jimmy Delaney. But Delaney's relationship with the club entered the early stages of an eventually irretrievable breakdown after he found himself excluded from the side when restored to fitness after pulling a muscle in a Southern League sectional defeat at Falkirk in late March 1945 that damaged fatally their chances of advancing in the competition. He claimed that he was being victimised by the directors because he had 'applied to the club for a benefit', a request that was rejected. It was due to the intervention of a third party, the newly formed Celtic FC Supporters Association, that what turned out to be a temporary, uneasy truce was brokered in time for Delaney to play in the Summer Cup in June.

It meant, however, that he would miss out on the Victory in Europe Cup match that evolved from the controversy that enveloped the Old Firm Charity Cup final, a debacle that resulted from the hurried necessity of the football authorities to mark the cessation of hostilities in Europe. On Sunday, 6 May 1945, the day after the semi-finals of the competition, George (later Sir George) Graham, secretary of the SFA and also honorary secretary of the Glasgow Charity Cup Committee, tried to contact – unsuccessfully – Rangers manager Bill Struth with a view to having the Charity Cup final played on 'VE day plus 1', which Graham thought, like others it must be said, would be on Tuesday, 8 May. When he finally spoke to Struth the following day (Monday, 7 May), he appears to have been given short shrift by a manager who thought he was being presented with a fait accompli. Rangers' stance on the matter of their 'non-participation' was outlined in a club statement that appeared in the *Daily Record and Mail* the next day (8 May), by which time it had been announced by the government that 'VE day plus 1' would be Wednesday, 9 May, declared as a national holiday. In this opening, acrimonious (and publicised) exchange of letters, Rangers stated their case, perhaps out of an awareness that they had effectively conceded the moral high ground to Celtic, who had agreed to Graham's proposal:

> We would point out that the decision to transfer this game was taken without consultation with the Rangers Football Club, or, as far as we know, without consultation with the Glasgow Charity Cup Committee. The first notification we had was in its appearance in the Press. The following excerpt from one of the evening papers, 'Rangers state that, owing to the fact that they have to meet Motherwell in the [Southern] League Cup final on Saturday [12 May], and, in addition, have a couple of injured players, they are unwilling to play the match,' is without foundation.

After George Graham's reply ended with the observation that he 'expected any club invited to take part in a match on such an historic occasion would have been proud of the honour and the privilege', a wounded Rangers issued an immediate riposte that condemned Mr Graham's 'gross presumption' in the matter of 'the invitation, if it can be called such', and asserted that 'the Rangers club can be rightly proud of its efforts for charity, which are not exceeded by any other club in Scotland'. The upshot was that, after the Charity Cup final was finally played on 21 May (Rangers beat Celtic 2–1), the beneficiaries had enjoyed a bonus, for George Graham had arranged to fill the vacuum caused by Rangers' 'withdrawal' from the earlier, proposed date by asking Celtic and Queen's Park to take part in a 'VE Cup' match at Hampden Park on the afternoon of Wednesday, 9 May, an event intended, said one newspaper, as 'one of commemoration and thanksgiving'. Both clubs 'readily agreed' to a contest that would be played under Glasgow Charity Cup rules – no extra time, corners to count to decide the outcome, failing which the toss of a coin would decide the destination of a specially commissioned trophy. The players on the winning side would collect not only the Victory in Europe Cup, but also four War Savings Certificates each (the losers got two each). The proceeds were to swell the Charity Cup's funds, which would benefit from a 29,000 crowd to the tune of an estimated £3,500. The amateur club Queen's Park, Celtic's opponents in this match, would be no pushover, having acquitted themselves well that season. They had finished in a respectable mid-table position, recovering from an indifferent start to remain undefeated in 14 matches in the Southern League and Southern League Cup from Ne'erday to Easter Monday 1945, when Celtic beat them 3–0 in the League at Parkhead. Rangers, who dominated wartime football in Scotland, put paid to 'The Spiders'' Southern League Cup hopes by defeating them by the same margin in the semi-final in front of 87,000 at Hampden Park. It is a measure of Queen's Park's playing strength at the time that the club could supply two players (goalkeeper Bobby Brown and centre-forward J. 'Tony' Harris) to the Scotland side that played England at Hampden Park in April 1945. Scotland experienced another of its wartime hammerings (1–6) at the hands of the old enemy, but both performed well as individuals. Only Willie Waddell of Rangers represented the 'Old Firm' clubs.

At 2.45 p.m. on Wednesday, 9 May 1945, the teams and the match officials lined up at a sun-dappled Hampden Park to join the 'reverent' crowd in listening to a thanksgiving service for which the Govan Burgh Band was in attendance to play musical accompaniment to the speaking and other roles carried out by the Rev. D. Langland Seath (Eaglesham), SFA president Douglas Bowie and well-known 'radio and concert' artiste Elliot Dobie. A time, no doubt, for those present to reflect on six momentous and trying years in the nation's history, with thoughts especially for those who would never return.

Celtic: Miller; Hogg and P. McDonald; Lynch, Mallan and McPhail; Paton, M. MacDonald, Gallacher, Evans and McLaughlin.

Queen's Park: Hamilton; J. McColl and Galbraith; I. McColl, Whigham and Cross; Lister, MacAulay, J. ('Tony') Harris, Dixon and Aitkenhead.

Referee: R. Calder (Rutherglen).

That note of respectfulness was carried forward into the match itself, with 'Alan Breck' of the city's *Evening Times* commenting that the play was 'so wholesome . . . the players obviously enjoyed themselves, and there were few, if any, examples of those petty incidents associated with other occasions'. As a result, the crowd were treated to a 'keen, clean and interesting' game whose outcome was in doubt right to the end. Queen's Park opened the scoring in the 25th minute through 'excellent work' by 'Tony' Harris and Johnny Aitkenhead that was finished off by Arthur Dixon, much to the approval of the watching Rangers trainer, his father. Celtic hit back only two minutes later when Johnny Paton netted after the opposition defence failed to cut out a cross from the left wing. Celtic went into the second half leading by a corner. 'Alan Breck', who said that the match 'was an occasion I would not have missed', summed up the spirit in which the match was played when he described its decisive moment: 'Nine minutes from the end Paton forced the corner off Cross which gave Celtic the Cup. Queen's Park did not agree it was a corner, but they did not cry about it.' Apparently, the referee awarded a bye-kick, but reversed his decision after a signal from the linesman. Celtic had secured a historic memento, another of the 'one-off' trophies in which they have specialised down through the years, albeit one attained by the narrowest of margins: one goal and three corners to one goal and two corners. 'Alan Breck' thought that 'the tradition of Celtic never to frown on good causes' made them appropriate winners, and so it was fitting that the Celtic captain Malcolm MacDonald, adjudged by many to have been the most accomplished performer on the pitch, should be the personification of dignity afterwards: 'We are all very proud to have been asked to play in this match.' MacDonald had featured in what 'Alan Breck' described as the most eye-catching and memorable bit of play in the match. During the first half, the gifted and versatile Celt, a quick thinker playing at inside-right, 'drew the entire defence away from him to the left and then turned the ball over to the completely unmarked Paton, who seemed too surprised to do anything about it'. In his summary for the rival *Evening News*, Harry Miller stated that full justice had been done to the event, the whole atmosphere being 'impressively delightful' and 'the game voted the keenest and most exhilarating in a long time'.

A couple of hours after the final whistle blew, another match took place at the same venue, one apparently also scheduled in the same commemorative vein. In goal for a Glasgow schools select that totally outclassed their Lanarkshire counterparts was a 14 year old from the local King's Park Secondary whose father had been a centre-half for both Rangers and Scotland. He 'kept a good goal', said one report, though he had little to do. A few weeks later, due to the unavailability of regular goalkeepers, and only after seeking his father's permission, that 'slim, lithe youth' would line up behind eight of the aforementioned Queen's Park players when – after playing for his school side in the morning (at the insistence of a headmaster who took great pride in the team) – he played in goal in the afternoon for that club in a Summer Cup tie at Hampden Park against Clyde, becoming probably the youngest-ever player to make a senior competitive debut in Scotland, at the age of 14 years and 234 days. One spectator present would later recall that the boy did well, 'but really there was not much in that first game to suggest that he might not be merely a nine-day wonder'. In August 1945, he was in the side that, in a league match brought forward to mark the surrender of Japan, took its revenge (2–0 at Hampden Park) on Celtic for that Victory in Europe match defeat. Fast-forward 22 years and there he was, aged 36 years and 196 days, becoming the oldest player to make his international debut for his country, and at Wembley no less in a famous Scottish victory, an achievement to be followed nearly six weeks later by him standing under a crossbar at time-up in a Lisbon stadium shedding tears of joy after becoming the oldest man to have kept goal for a side that had won the Continent's most prestigious club competition. For both him and Celtic, victory in Europe seems to have had a special resonance bordering on destiny. His teammates affectionately called Ronnie Simpson 'Faither', but, come to think of it, 'The History Man' would have been just as appropriate.

CHAPTER 12

The Great Escape

1948: The Year in Headlines

January: Mahatma Gandhi, the 'Great teacher', advocate of non-violent protest and leading Indian nationalist, is assassinated in Delhi.

April: The Marshall Plan, a six-billion-dollar package of economic and military aid for Europe, is launched in Washington as the 'Cold War' takes a firm hold on the Continent.

July: The National Health Service comes into operation in the United Kingdom.

August: Fanny Blankers-Koen, a Dutch housewife, achieves the feat of winning four of the nine gold medals available to women competitors at the Olympic Games in London.

December: Seven Japanese officials convicted of war crimes, among them former premiers Hideki Tojo and Koki Hirota.

Celtic FC did not have its troubles or sorrows to seek in the late 1940s, a bleak period for the club illustrated in the following extracts from an official annual publication:

'Celtic were in danger of relegation' was the sensational cry in the early stages of the Scottish League last season. After nine games they stood ingloriously at the bottom of the table with one win. Indeed, they occupied second last place after 13 matches, with only four wins to their credit. All the more reason for admiring the pluck

139

with which they climbed out of danger and finished the season in the upper half of the table, with nine clubs below them.

'An Observer', Celtic Football Guide, *summer 1947*

Season 1946–47 will go down as a black one for this grand old club. Another season and no honours at Celtic Park, and to add to our sorrows we have lost our chairman, Mr Tom White, who died 4 March 1947, and one of our old directors and dear friend, Mr Tom Colgan, who died 13 November 1946. RIP.

Jimmy McGrory (manager), Celtic Football Guide, *summer 1947*

The first proper post-war season of 1946–47 had seen the introduction of a new trophy, the Scottish League Cup. Older Celtic fans were greatly pleased; in the years between the wars, they could recall that the team's style of play had been more suited to the winning of cups rather than leagues, so the advent of another cup competition should really have suited Celtic.

They were also buoyed up by other factors. The biggest pool of players for some time – 35 in all – was available to manager Jimmy McGrory. The entire terracing at Celtic Park had been tidied up and strengthened with concrete edging; and basic ticket prices would remain the same: 40 shillings (£2) for the Stand, 24 shillings and 8 pence (£1.25) for the enclosure and 17 shillings and 4 pence (87p) for the ground.*

Unfortunately, though, the manager's optimism was not reflected in the performances of the team. That season of 1946–47 and the following one were among the worst in Celtic's history.

During the 1946–47 season, only goalkeeper Willie Miller seemed sure of his place. Some positions were staffed by a few names, others by many. For instance, while three right-backs (Hogg, Lamb and McDonald) and three left-backs (Milne, McDonald and Mallan) were tried out, no fewer than nine names were listed at outside-right (Sirrel, Cantwell, Hazlett, Rae, Bogan, Evans, Jordan, Docherty, F. Quinn). Few were truly successful, with the result that in the league

---

* Sums in brackets reflect decimal currency equivalent today, though not the monetary equivalent/worth in 2013.

campaign only 53 goals were scored as 55 were conceded. Six defeats and two draws in the first eight matches meant that Celtic were always chasing the rest.

Celtic's Season 1946–47

P	W	D	L	F	A	Pts	Pos.
30	13	6	11	53	55	32	7th

The cup competitions proved no more successful:

League Cup: failed to qualify for next stage from section matches
Scottish Cup: Celtic 1 Dundee 2 (1st round)
Glasgow Cup: Celtic 0 Clyde 2 (1st round)
Charity Cup: Celtic 0 Rangers 1 (final)

In the following season of 1947–48, the performance in the cups was equally disappointing:

League Cup: failed to qualify for next stage from section matches
Scottish Cup: Celtic 0 Morton 1 (semi-final, a.e.t.)
Glasgow Cup: Celtic 1 Third Lanark 3 (semi-final)
Charity Cup: Celtic 0 Rangers 2 (final)

Hardly inspiring results but, even worse, the players seemed to save their poorest performances for the league campaign. They started badly, losing six of their first nine matches and a further collapse occurred after going down 0–4 in the New Year fixture against Rangers, Celtic losing seven and drawing two of the next twelve games. Particularly damaging was the run in late March/early April – a 1–5 thrashing by Third Lanark at Cathkin, a 2–4 loss to Hibs at Parkhead (after being 2–1 ahead at the interval) and a 1–3 defeat again by Third Lanark, this time at Celtic Park in the penultimate match of the league season, when 'during only two brief spasms did the forwards get the goal into focus – and then Petrie [the Thirds keeper] filled the picture' (*Scottish Sunday Express,* 11 April 1948).

The club was in desperate trouble and the reports in the national press reflected this. 'Never have Celts sunk so low' was the headline in the *Scottish Sunday Express* the day after that home defeat by Third Lanark. In his report, John McShane said of Celtic that 'to describe their play as amateurish is no compliment to the unpaid'. One day later, on 12 April 1948, in the *Evening Times*, 'Alan Breck' commented that 'what has long been considered impossible − and silly to contemplate − was now a distinct possibility, namely, that the Celtic club, renowned abroad, are just about toppling into the Second Division'.

To any Celtic fan of the period, that quote might have been well nigh unbearable. It was bad enough having to come to terms with the unpalatable truth that, since the end of the war, it had been Hibernian who were vying for supremacy with Rangers, that Celtic were in danger of becoming 'just another club', but now the unthinkable might just be about to happen. In truth, disappointment and frustration had been the lot of the Celtic supporter for the decade or so that followed the Empire Exhibition triumph in 1938. That litany of a forward line − Delaney, MacDonald, Crum, Divers and Murphy − was now fading from memory, and their successors were regularly being dubbed 'the Five Sorrowful Mysteries'.

Some form of change had been needed and the Board had duly obliged. Centre-forward Jock Weir, who had only moved from Hibs to Blackburn Rovers the previous year for £10,000, was brought in to Parkhead for the sum of £7,000, making his League debut against Falkirk at Brockville on 28 February 1948. Celtic won 1−0 thanks to an 89th-minute Willie Corbett penalty, but ex-Ranger Andy Cunningham, writing in the *Scottish Sunday Express* the following day, was not impressed by their play:

> If the Celts had one forward with the most elementary idea of goal-scoring the result should have been in no doubt at half-time. Jock Weir may be the fastest centre in Scotland but all his speed and upsetting sprints out to the wings will not be productive to Celtic until they have a co-ordinated forward line with constructive ideas . . . Paton and Bogan spent most of their time taking corners. They

had dozens of them, all well taken, be it noted, but never the suggestion of a goal.

With one match left after the home defeat by Third Lanark, Celtic were fourth from bottom of the league, in a very precarious position. With two points available for a win in a thirty-match division, Queen's Park were already relegated, leaving one other club to join them in 'B' division:

	Played	Points
Morton	27	23
Hearts	27	23
Celtic	29	23
Queen of the South	29	23
Airdrie	27	20
Queen's Park	28	17

Only victory at Dundee would remove the spectre of relegation from Celtic, whose goal average was much superior to Queen of the South.

In his opinion column in the 12 April *Evening Times*, two days after Scotland had lost 0–2 to England at Hampden Park, 'Alan Breck' noted:

> The talk one heard an hour or two after Hampden had been left behind was not so much of the Scotland v. England international which had just taken place there or of the upcoming Morton v. Rangers Scottish Cup final; what seemed to hit every other one with shattering urgency was the grim position of Celtic in the league . . . a First Division without Celtic is strange to contemplate. No more 'Old Firm' games on New Year's Day and no more ground-filling visits by the Parkhead club all over the country.

Contrary to popular mythology, there was a large measure of

sympathy for Celtic's plight – as the use of the word 'shattering' in that quote suggests – in the rather more sober press coverage of the time, which, despite the paper rationing in force, did nevertheless not fall short, and rightly so, in highlighting the mediocrity that had brought the club to its present sorry state.

'Waverley' summed up the relegation struggle in the *Daily Record* of 12 April 1948: 'Celtic, I believe, reached a new low against Third Lanark, and if they fail to win their last game against Dundee, they are in the unenviable position of waiting anxiously for the remaining results of Airdrieonians and Queen of the South.'

The fans themselves were horrified at the plight of their beloved club. The prospect of relegation was just too much for them to take in. Their feelings were clear: a club of Celtic's traditions should be in the running for the title, not scrapping around in the relegation zone. Within the club, the players were also disappointed with the position the club was in but were clear about the lack of unanimity in direction from above, as would be illustrated by the confusion surrounding team selection for the upcoming final league match on 17 April at Dundee, where victory would end Celtic's relegation worries.

Inside-forward Jimmy Sirrel, later to have successful managerial careers at Notts County and Sheffield United, remembered the period well: 'You'd come in at two o'clock and you don't know whether you're playing or not and at half-past two they would tell you the team. I was due to play that game. To all intents and purposes, I was playing. So when he read out the team I wasn't playing.'

Centre-forward Frank Walsh, Scotland's leading goal-scorer with 23 when with Kilmarnock in season 1945–46, joined Celtic in November 1947. He had strong feelings about the chairman of the time:

But Bob Kelly, I don't know. It's just a feeling I've always carried. He had lost faith in me. As far as he was concerned, as chairman, he wanted no more to do with me . . . there was a very important match coming up at Dundee and McGrory on the Tuesday had told

Cigarette cards issued in late nineteenth/ early twentieth century depicting eight stalwarts who helped to build Celtic's reputation as one of Britain's greatest football clubs:

Sandy McMahon (versatile forward), Davie Hamilton (winger), Davy Adams (goalkeeper), Peter Somers (inside-forward), James Hay (defender), Jimmy Quinn (centre-forward), Alec McNair (full-back) and 'Sunny Jim' Young (defender).

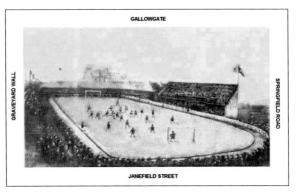

The first Celtic Park. This photo, believed to be the first illustration of the club's first ground to be published in a book, is taken from the Glasgow Evening Times of 20 August 1974 and is of an 1890 painting by J. Nicol. Street names etc. have been added around the rim of this reproduction in order to pinpoint the location of a stadium whose pitch ran north to south. Dalmarnock Street became Springfield Road in the 1930s. The authors are indebted to Jamie Fox for adding the street names, etc.

RIGHT: This is believed to be a photo taken during the Scotland v. England international match at Celtic Park in 1894. Note the pavilion in the background.

BELOW: The team that achieved Celtic's record victory in a competitive match: 11–0 in a League match against Dundee in October 1895.

Standing (back): Tom Maguire (trainer), James Kelly (captain), Allan Martin, Dan Doyle, Barney Battles and Willie Ferguson. **Seated** (middle): Johnny Madden, Sandy McMahon, Peter Meechan and Willie Maley. **Sitting** (flanking Glasgow Cup): James Blessington and Dan McArthur.

The 'Sarsfield Brake Club' about to set off from the Gorbals area of Glasgow for a Celtic match during the early twentieth century. These brake clubs were essentially carts drawn by horses, each club having a banner bearing a colourful portrait of a favourite player.

Pictured in early 1900s, this famous duo of Jimmy McMenemy (left) and Alec Bennett were two members of a Celtic forward line during a highly successful era for the club: Bennett, McMenemy, Quinn, Somers and Hamilton.

MEMORIAL CARD

Benny Lynch
World Flyweight Champ.

John Thomson
Scotland's Goalkeeper

Patsy Gallacher, pictured in an alternative strip (all-green jersey), in action against Queen's Park at Celtic Park, c. 1920, with the 'Grant' Stand in the background.

Benny Lynch and John Thomson memorial card. Gorbals-born Benny Lynch was flyweight champion of the world from the mid to late 1930s, but died aged only 33 in August 1946 after being dogged by health and personal problems. A well-known supporter of the club, Benny was a favourite with the Celtic fans, as was goalkeeper John Thomson, whose tragic, accidental death (aged only 22) at Ibrox Park in September 1931 was also still fresh in the memory of supporters at the time these cards went on sale in the late 1940s.

RIGHT: Celtic FC,
Scottish Champions, 1922.

The Celtic squad that toured North America and Canada in 1931.

Top row: Chic Geatons, Peter Wilson,, John Thomson, Robert Whitelaw, Willie Hughes and
Willie ('Peter') McGonagle. **Middle**: Bertie Thomson, Alec Thomson, Jimmy McGrory,
Jimmy McStay (captain), Peter Scarff, Charlie Napier and Will Quinn (trainer).
Bottom: John Morrison, Willie Cook, Hugh Smith, Joe McGhee and Denis Currie.

Within little more than six years of this photo being taken, three of the players would be dead –
John Thomson, Peter Scarff and Bertie Thomson.

(Photo, thought to be the only one in existence of the touring squad wearing their strips, courtesy
of Gary Martin)

ABOVE: 'Victory in Europe' Cup match, 9 May 1945. Players of Celtic and Queen's Park line up to listen to the pre-match thanksgiving speech. Although the Celtic players have their backs to the camera, three of them can be identified, all standing next to each other from the left: Malcolm MacDonald (captain), Willie Miller (goalkeeper) and Bobby Hogg (full-back).

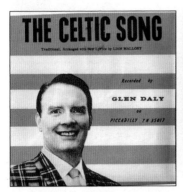

Sheet-music cover for the 1961 song that has been heard in all corners of the globe.

Pre-season preparation at Celtic Park, July 1955 – before Jock Stein revolutionised training methods after his arrival in March 1965. Prominent in this photo is Charlie Tully (wearing cap), just behind Neilly Mochan.

ABOVE: Photo of 'Possibles' (reserve) team taken before Celtic pre-season public trial match, August 1958.
Standing: Duncan MacKay, Billy McNeill, Pat Crerand, Dick Beattie (goalkeeper), Steve Lynch and John Divers.
Seated: Bobby Carroll, Mike Jackson, Eric Smith, Jim Conway and Bertie Auld.

RIGHT: The young Bobby Evans, c.1950. He was described by a Celtic teammate as 'the perfect professional footballer'.

BELOW: Bobby Murdoch, wearing an all-green strip, netting his first (and Celtic's second) goal in the 3–0 home European Cup-Winners' Cup quarter-final first-leg victory over Dynamo Kiev in January 1966.

LEFT: Cartoon published in French newspaper *Nice-Matin*, 25 May 1967. Helenio Herrera, the Inter Milan coach, is seen trying to reassure four of his players – Facchetti, Corso, Mazzola and Burgnich – that 'these tales of Scottish monsters are just cock-and-bull stories'. A large number of publications were unaware that a new trophy would be presented to the European Cup final winners.

RIGHT: Number 12 of a series of cigar bands commemorating the first 17 European Cup finals (1956–72 inclusive) that was produced by the Dutch company Schimmelpenninck. Celtic v. Inter Milan was the 12th final.

LEFT: These inflatable footballers (often called 'Jimmy Johnstones', being clearly modelled on the famous Celt) were a feature on the terracings at Celtic matches during the 1970s.

RIGHT: Celts for Change was a highly effective pressure group in the early 1990s. The message above, brandished on the Parkhead terracings, came to pass in March 1994 with the dissolution of the family dynasties that had controlled the club for many decades.

Black humour has long pervaded one of the bitterest rivalries in world sport. This photo, taken by a Celtic fan at a home League match against Rangers won 3–0 by his favourites on 29 April 2012, shows fellow supporters taunting rival fans with a 'Four horsemen of the Apocalypse' banner shortly after the Ibrox club went into administration as a result of a financial collapse. The figures depicted on the banner are, left to right: Neil Lennon (Celtic manager), 'Hector the taxman' (cartoon figure used in Inland Revenue adverts), the 'Grim Reaper' and Craig Whyte (controversial Rangers owner).

Celtic, the team of his heart and soul: Rod Stewart at Celtic Park in November 2012, shortly after the event whose brochure he is displaying. (Photo courtesy of Anthony Brawley / Celtic Graves Society.)

me, 'You're playing on Saturday at Dundee.' When Saturday came, it was Weir outside-right, Dan Lavery centre-forward. They changed their mind and played the Irish boy. I always felt I would have loved to have played with Weir on the wing. That was the type of player I liked playing with, a fast-raiding winger and me, a fast-raiding centre. I would have done well with a player like Weir.

One of the regulars in the side at that time was John McPhail, who, in an interview I (Jim Craig) recorded with him in the summer of 1997, was quite blunt about this particular period in the club's history.

Q John, there were some terrible years for Celtic at that time. Why was that? I mean, there were some good players available.

A There were several good players. You couldn't put your finger on anything in particular. However, I must be honest and say that there were also some very poor players. As a Celtic fan, I was weaned on the Exhibition team and the side of the '30s, so when I went there, and walked in among players who were, let's say, non-Celtic class players, then that was disappointing. So, while we had some really good players, there were many of the other type as well.

Q There were stories at that time about Jimmy McGrory not picking the team and Bob Kelly being the man controlling everything. Was that true?

A Just about that period, I think Jimmy let go of the reins himself. He felt he hadn't been making good choices. I liked the old chap enormously but he wasn't a dominant figure and quietly, without any great fuss or announcement, Bob Kelly gradually took control.

The Celtic board held their regular Thursday evening meeting on 15 April, two days before the match that might prove so crucial to the future of the club. They delayed naming the team because 'several minor injuries were being attended to' and trainer Alec

Dowdells 'is to be given every opportunity of having his men fit on time'. McGrory would only say that there would be as few changes as possible, since 'that is only fair to the boys', but the local *Evening Times* had picked up a whisper, accurate as it turned out, that Dan Lavery would be at centre-forward and Jock Weir on the right wing.

The Celtic players trained at Parkhead on the morning of Friday, 16 April, before heading over to Perth, where they used the Royal George Hotel as a base. On arrival, they were allocated rooms and then had an early dinner. And after that, well, let's hear from John McPhail again:

> Bob Kelly said, 'I don't know what to do with you, so just go out and relax.' Now had that been modern times, with events as they are, we would have been better watched. But we all felt a devotion to the club, so we went out and merely had a beer or two, something like that, and went to bed.

Just as well they had a devotion to the club! What might they have got up to if they weren't taking it seriously?

Sunshine was beginning to dispel the early-morning frost as Dundee awoke the following day to news on the wireless of a train crash. Twenty-two people (including three children) had lost their lives and thirty were injured when a Glasgow to London mail train ploughed into the rear of a passenger train that had stopped outside Winsford Station near Crewe during the night, a tragedy that rather put events in the 'Jute City' into perspective.

However, there was some respite from that terrible news that morning – and from a weekend bus strike in Dundee – when the streets of the city centre were filled with the sights and sounds of students wearing fancy dress costumes intent on 'tapping' every potential donor as part of their charity drive on behalf of the St John Ambulance Association, their activity even spreading up to the Hilltown district and Dens Park, the venue of the Dundee v. Celtic league match scheduled to kick off at 3.15 that afternoon.

The *Dundee Courier and Advertiser* had set the scene that very morning of 17 April 1948: 'The Scottish Cup may be today's glamour event but for drama one must turn to Dens Park. Celtic are at the cross-roads. They will face up to Dundee realising that they must play the game of their lives to secure precious points.'

Celtic's line-up, when finally revealed, had several changes from the previous week's home defeat by Third Lanark. Leaving aside injuries, the selection must have struck Celtic's followers as smacking more of desperation than inspiration. There were three changes in personnel, but also no fewer than eight positional changes. Out went half-back Joe Baillie and the two wingers, Tommy Bogan and Konrad Kapler. To replace these, Jock Weir was moved to the right wing and Johnny Paton took over on the left. The other changes came at right-back, where Bobby Hogg (in his 17th season) returned after three months out, and the fielding for the first time at right-half of Bobby Evans, set to play in a position he would make his own with great distinction over the next decade. The teams were:

Celtic: Miller, Hogg, Mallan, Evans, Corbett, McAuley, Weir, McPhail, Lavery, W. Gallacher, Paton.

Dundee: Brown, Follon, Irvine, Gallacher, Gray, Boyd, Gunn, Patillo, Stewart, Ewen, Mackay.

The opening stages of the match were packed with thrills and excitement for the 31,000 crowd. The *Edinburgh Evening News* sports edition observed that 'Celtic were playing grand, aggressive football and the Dundee defence had an exceedingly hot time.' Quickly sensing the weakness on the left-hand side of the home defence, where, according to one account, 'Boyd was strangely off-colour and Irvine evidently not 100 per cent fit,' Celtic kept plying the zestful Jock Weir with the ball. He seemed to relish his new position and tormented his opponents with his speed, strength, craft and sheer determination. As the *Scottish Sunday Express* noted: 'The Parkhead side had pace and power on the wings and the effervescent Weir set the tempo of enthusiasm and dash which marked their play in the first half.'

Celtic's adventurous play might have come as a surprise to those who thought the pressure might prove too much for a side that had been performing so poorly of late, but it was as if the 'all or nothing' outlook so necessary in their situation played in their favour, acting as a form of release from any inhibitions. That might account for the recollections of chairman Bob Kelly, who was experiencing a baptism of fire in his first season in that role: 'There were few instances of desperation by the team, that is the real measure of how well they played in the most testing of circumstances.' A brief resumé of the important moments would include:

6th minute The way the match was unfolding made it inevitable that goals would be forthcoming, and Celtic thought they had made the breakthrough in the 6th minute, only for Dan Lavery's effort to be disallowed by the referee, Mr Scott of Paisley, apparently for a foul on keeper Brown.

14th minute Celtic got their deserved goal as the result of a goalmouth scramble in which it seems that three goal-bound shots were blocked by Dundee defenders before Weir squeezed the ball home. 1–0.

16th minute John McPhail had the ball in the net but the referee ruled that the goalkeeper had been fouled.

25th minute According to the *Edinburgh Evening News* report, 'Celtic and their fans thought they had scored again when the home goal had an amazing escape when a perfect cross by McPhail seemed to go into the net and back out again.'

44th minute There was a shock in store for Celtic's system when Ewen netted the equaliser with a 15-yarder at a psychologically damaging time for Celtic. 1–1.

The *Courier and Advertiser* reported that the footballing antics (shooting-in, etc.) of the local charity-minded students were a 'mirth-provoker and money-getter' during the interval but one wonders how much the

Celtic fans joined in the merriment, given the tension of the occasion, which was only heightened with the resumption of play.

50th minute Stewart should have put Dundee ahead 'when he robbed Miller, who had a problem in clutching a cross, but he shot wide past an open goal'.

60th minute George Mackay brought the spectre of relegation closer to Celtic with a thunderbolt of a shot. 1–2.

It was like a blow to the solar plexus and many Celtic supporters present must have feared there and then that the game was up for their favourites. However, according to the *Courier and Advertiser*, at this crucial juncture of the match, when Celtic 'seemed to lose heart', Dundee, instead of pressing their advantage 'lay back, with fatal results'. Nevertheless, the Celtic fans must have been close to despair when Lavery's net-bound drive was saved by Brown, who dived to push it round the post. However, they knew the way to help the side and their increasing vocal support was soon rewarded.

78th minute A McPhail header was dropped by Brown on the goal line and Weir was on hand to 'shoot the ball out of the keeper's hands into the net' before the latter could retrieve the ball. 2–2.

88th minute Weir got the winner for Celtic when he rounded off a move engineered by John McPhail (who had been at the heart of much of Celtic's bright, attacking play) by fending off Gray, Irvine and the goalkeeper Brown before netting as right-back Follon desperately attempted to tackle him. 3–2.

The Celtic support went into raptures when that goal went in and the noise level only increased when the referee blew the final whistle.

Weir's hat-trick was the first – and only – one scored by a Celtic player that season and he had amply repaid the fee paid for him only two months earlier. Doubly ironic, therefore, was that the selling club, Blackburn Rovers, should be relegated from the First Division at the end of that season and that, on the very day of Weir's feat, the *Sporting Post*, which had the ear of both the Dundee clubs, should reveal that, before they secured his services, Celtic had approached Stirling Albion for centre-forward George Henderson, who by then (April 1948) had joined Dundee United.

Reflections by former players can vary considerably in their composition and many years had passed since that eventful day when I asked two stalwarts of the side for their memories in the summer of 1997. I suspect that John McPhail's recollections of the game might be more to the liking of Celtic fans. Don't forget, the opening sentence follows his aforementioned reference to the 'one or two beers' the night before:

> The next day, we all went on to that park brand new, fit as fiddles. We scored first through wee Jock Weir and they equalised just before half-time. Wee Jock was right on form. They had made me captain that day and I was getting on to the wee man all the time to do something for us. Then Dundee went 2–1 ahead, but in the last ten minutes, marvellous, two hoaching great goals by Jock, 3–2, and that saved us. As it worked out, we finished fifth from bottom. Supposing that we had been beaten in that game, we would still have been safe. But that didn't matter, we just knew we had to win that particular match and we did it.

I also interviewed the talented Willie Miller, goalkeeping stalwart of the war and post-war years: 'Another match I will always remember is the one at Dundee in 1947–48 when we were in danger of relegation. There were some nerves before the game and some celebration afterwards – thanks to three goals by Jock Weir *whom I never thought was a very good player.*'

Celtic had done all that was required of them, two points in their final match. In the end, Celtic finished fifth from bottom, certainly a safe position but one hardly to the liking of the dedicated support.

		Played	Points
12th	Celtic	30	25
13th	Queen of the South	30	25
14th	Morton	30	24
15th	Airdrie	30	21 (Relegated)
16th	Queen's Park	30	20 (Relegated)

One spectator that day at Dens Park had been placed in a difficult position. According to the local *Courier and Advertiser*, the great ex-Celt Patsy Gallacher had a 'three-fold interest' in the game, namely his former club and his sons playing in direct opposition to each other, Tommy of Dundee and Willie of Celtic: 'I really don't know which son I wanted to see on the winning side. Maybe a draw would have pleased me and yet I must say I'm glad Celtic won and so avoided relegation.'

Not so happy was Jimmy McGrory when, some years later, he was told by one of the Dundee players that the team had been offered their 'biggest-ever' bonus to beat Celtic that day. McGrory, whose job as manager had been on the line at Dens Park, did not identify the player concerned in his 1975 autobiography written in conjunction with journalist Gerry McNee, but such was his anger (and it took a lot to get McGrory riled) that his initial inclination was to write a strongly worded letter to Dundee FC, though it is difficult to see what effect such a belated missive would have had.

McGrory was all too aware that, had matters not turned out as they did, he would have been obliged to submit his resignation to his chairman, Bob (later Sir Robert) Kelly, who – shortly before he died in 1971 – stated that the drama at Dens Park represented 'the greatest ordeal I experienced in watching football', adding that 'of one thing I was positive, we would never again, whatever the circumstances, reach the depths of 1948'.

Sir Robert, as he would only have been too happy to acknowledge, had been spared the embarrassment and irritation that he related Willie Maley had suffered when one of his customers at The Bank restaurant, with feigned innocuousness, asked the former Celtic manager if he recalled being in charge of the club when it suffered its record defeat (0–8 at Motherwell in April 1937). An enraged Maley had replied, 'As long as there are bastards like you around, I'll never be allowed to forget it!'

* * *

The season just passed, 1947–48, does not provide any pleasant reading to our faithful followers, and if anybody deserves a good team at the Paradise, it is our supporters. They have firmly stood by us through what was probably the worst season in the history of our grand old club . . . Their patience and understanding sustained us and inspired us to do our very utmost to achieve some improvement . . . I would like to take this opportunity to thank every one of you for the grand support and encouragement you gave the players all through a very trying season. A worrying chapter is closed and we hope and trust we will never have a repeat.

Jimmy McGrory, manager's report, Celtic Football Guide, summer 1948

CHAPTER 13

A Mountain to Climb

This Ross seems to be a sturdy fellow. Rumour has it that he attends to training to a ridiculous degree. A run in early morn is good for any man, Ross, but practising 'charging' against railway trucks is completely out of it.

Scottish Athletic Journal, 20 October 1882

Physical fitness has always been an essential requirement for footballers. No matter how talented the performer or how great his range of skills, they must be accompanied by a considerable degree of running power to put them into operation.

Through the years, various methods have been employed. Back in 1882, one young man from Ayrshire had his own, rather idiosyncratic way of keeping fit, as can be seen from the report in the *Scottish Athletic Journal* shown above.

Most other players, though, did not have that same degree of fanaticism, relying on running to maintain fitness. Right up to the 1960s, few Scottish – and British – clubs did much work with a ball during training. Running was the standard way of keeping fit, long runs to build up stamina followed by sprints to aid sharpness.

* * *

When I, Jim Craig, signed for Celtic in January 1965, I was fairly appalled by the methods of training. I had been playing for Glasgow University, where the sessions had been taken by guys who were usually graduates of Physical Education from Jordanhill College. The various runs were timed and/or measured, our pulse rates were taken after runs, we were given advice on diet plus general health and we always played small-sided games towards the conclusion of the session.

When I arrived at Parkhead as a part-timer, in the middle of winter, expecting a really professional attitude towards training, I discovered that we only did running . . . and plenty of it! Out on the track that surrounded the pitch in those days, with the only illumination coming from some lights suspended from the main stand, we always completed the same routine. Run 2 laps (880 yards), walk a lap; run 1 lap (440 yards), walk a lap; 4 x 220 yards, walk the other 220: 8 x 100 yards sprints, walk the bends of the track in between; then finish with 4 laps of running 50 yards then walking 50 yards. As the far side of the track was in complete darkness and the trainer was standing at the foot of the tunnel, we were always quicker down the home straight. And when we pleaded our case with the coach – 'Any chance of a ball, please?' – we received the stock answer, 'Och, you'll get plenty of that on a Saturday!'

When I went full-time just about 18 months later, at least there were the sessions at Barrowfield – our training ground just further east along London Road from Celtic Park – to look forward to. By that time, under Jock Stein, most of the training was centred round ball work and was usually tough and interesting. Unfortunately, the main pitch at Barrowfield was prone to flooding after a spell of prolonged rain and when that occurred – a not infrequent event – we had to go elsewhere. And one vivid memory of that situation remains with me, when all the players – kitted out in training gear – would be going through a session of callisthenics in the main foyer of Celtic Park while the Boss got on the phone to find us somewhere to train. Mount Vernon Dog Track was very good in helping us out, which led to a very unusual situation where the team that had just won the European Cup trained on the football pitch in the middle, while outside the wire fence the dogs were exercised round the track!

* * *

Apart from the occasional unusual venue, the training once Jock Stein had arrived was well organised and tough. I must stress, though, that, up till that time, running was the main feature of the training sessions of most football clubs. The only time in the history of Celtic to that point when training regimes like that were not the norm was in the late 1940s, when a truly remarkable man was brought in to oversee the coaching. Jimmy Hogan had been born in Nelson, Lancashire, in 1882 and went on to have a fine career as an inside-forward with various clubs between 1902 and 1913. A visit to Holland with Bolton in 1910 inspired him to become a coach and, while still playing, he took on that role with several clubs on the Continent.

When the First World War began, Hogan was manager of Austria Vienna. Unfortunately, this put him in the category of 'enemy' so he was allowed to go to Hungary where he worked with MTK Budapest, leading them to consecutive league titles in 1917 and 1918. He brought a new professionalism to the game, combining higher levels of fitness with technical coaching, laying the groundwork for the development of the great Hungarian side of the early 1950s.

Hogan took the Swiss national team to the final of the 1924 Olympics; joined forces in the early 1930s with Hugo Meisl to create the Austrian national side known as the 'Wunderteam'; then returned to England at the end of the 1930s to work with Aston Villa and Fulham. Wherever he went, he emphasised better conditioning, greater ball control, quick passing, flowing play and creative flair. Those who worked with Hogan had nothing but praise for a man recognised as a true visionary of the sport . . . or, as his time at Celtic Park might suggest, most of them did!

Jimmy Hogan joined Celtic in the summer of 1948, shortly after Celtic had come uncomfortably close to relegation, as full-time coach to manager Jimmy McGrory. It was a revolutionary move for a Scottish club and caused much surprise in the sporting press. For a player's viewpoint, though, let's hear the thoughts of Tommy Docherty, who at that time had just come out of the Army after his National Service and reported to Celtic for pre-season training:

It was in the great days of Charlie Tully and players like that and they looked upon coaching as a bit of a joke . . . there were headlines saying they had signed this magnificent man who had coached the Austrian 'Wunderteam' and the Hungarians. All of them had been raving about him but the Scottish players' attitude was: 'Who's this fellow then?' I took to him very quickly, so did several of the other young players at Celtic Park at the time, but on the day of the first home game, when he sat us in the dressing-room and said, 'This is the day the good ship Celtic will be launched,' one of the players said, 'You'll find a few passengers.'

He was a lovely man. He seemed dour but had a lovely sense of humour. And he was a very religious Roman Catholic. He never swore or used any bad language at all. You could not possibly point a wrong word at him. That didn't go down well at Celtic Park with some of the players. These days we see players huddled together – bonding they call it – in the middle of the field before the game; well, Jimmy used to have them do that in the dressing-room before we went out so it didn't cause any embarrassment out on the pitch. One or two of the older players looked at him as if to say, 'What's this about?' but some of the younger ones like myself were all for it. We thought it was great.

In his autobiography, Docherty also recalled:

The best thing that happened to me at Celtic was the arrival of Jimmy Hogan to take over the side. This man was a wonder with the youngsters. It's a bitter joke now but the established stars would have nothing to do with him. Yet this was a man who went to the Continent and laid the foundation of the Austrians' and Hungarians' football. How blind can you be? But whatever the attitude of the 'big boys', I have never regretted that I took in every word that Jimmy Hogan said. I reckon that I received my basic coaching from one of the greatest coaches the world has ever seen.

Praise indeed, and from such a distinguished source. However, while Tommy – and a few others – obviously listened, the majority did not respond and, once Jimmy Hogan left, the old ways returned, as exemplified by one notable episode. After completing a very successful season in 1953–54 when the league title and the Scottish Cup had both been won, a Celtic party comprising manager Jimmy McGrory, a few backroom staff, a couple of directors and a squad of players had travelled to Switzerland for the World Cup finals. In his book *Passed to You*, Charlie Tully gave us his version of the trip and its repercussions.

We players sure paid in full for that wonderful trip to Switzerland and the World Cup. Scotland's terrible tanning by Uruguay (who beat the Scots 7–0), a country hitherto thought of as being filled with mud huts and peasants, had shaken everyone. Especially the proud Scots. Hadn't they, asked the proud ones, taught the world the art of ball control? Hadn't they pointed out that the air was for the birds and the ground was where one played football? Everyone more or less agreed with them, because, as everyone knows, the Jock is the greatest guy in the world except when someone suggests he can't play football. Then it came out in the newspapers that not only had Uruguay beaten Scotland's best in all the arts but it was obvious to one and all that they had been fitter and faster. The damage was done . . . and the players were in trouble.

When we returned to Glasgow and our loved ones, that holiday became a memory. For it was obvious that Celtic meant to exonerate themselves from any claim, continental or otherwise, that they were not the fittest club in the business. That first morning back at training, some of the boys were late. Jimmy McGrory got slightly annoyed. 'The prestige of this club is, as always, at stake. We've had some good players at Parkhead, probably a lot better than some of you will ever be, but they had to abide by the rules and so will you.' He then dropped a bombshell . . . 'As part of our early training we are going to run up Ben Lomond.' The idea originated in Switzerland, when the club secretary Desmond White, who had been well-known with pre-war Queen's Park [as a goalkeeper], asked the lads to climb a mountain near Interlaken. Dessie, who is an enthusiastic climber, took Doc Fitzsimmons and Sean Fallon up with him 'on trial' and to our astonishment all returned safely.

But this Ben Lomond business . . . it was going to be different.

On Tuesday, 20 July 1954, the Celtic party travelled from Parkhead to the Trossachs by bus to start the climb. Joining them on the day was a young journalist from the *Daily Record* called James Sanderson, who in the 1970s and early 1980s would become a mainstay of phone-in programmes for Radio Clyde. The following words are taken from his Wednesday, 21 July 1954 report of the venture:

I called Celtic the Tensings of Parkhead. I wish I hadn't. Yesterday they made me eat my words on a gruelling, mud-splattered rock-strewn 'assault' on Ben Lomond. They took the 3,192 feet in their stride; I took the 3,000 feet . . . and left it at that . . .

I've got to hand it to them. Picnic parties stopped to stare. Hikers wouldn't believe it . . . and the sure-footed Celts went on to paint the Ben green-and-white. It was muddy . . . and it was murder. Every foot was done at the double. In some places the run slowed down to a mud-bogged crawl. They sweated, groaned and mumbled but on and up they went. The field began to string out but up and on they came, jogging, running, walking and crawling over the worst bits. 'How far in front is Zatopek?' Bertie Peacock asked. And there all the time was coach George Paterson. He coaxed, cajoled and shouted. 'Get up that mountain' . . . and how the Celts went to it.

Then only a few hundred feet to go. Into the lead went Bobby Evans, Sean Fallon, Hugh Fletcher and Bobby Collins. I was well behind. I would have cheered them on . . . but I didn't have the breath. Out in front, by a short mountain head, went Collins. He was first to the top . . . and won the Desmond White prize for being the Tensing of Ben Lomond. Close behind were the three weary musketeers of Fallon, Fletcher and Evans . . . twelve finished in a bunch – and the Ben was well beaten.

And that was it. The Celts had painted the Ben green-and-white . . . and they did it in an hour and a half. An hour and a half of training that would make even a Hungarian blush!

* * *

The run up Ben Lomond was certainly an innovative form of training but did it help to bring Celtic success in the season that followed?

Celtic's League Cup

Section Games	Home	Away
Dundee	0–1	1–3
Falkirk	3–0	2–2
Hearts	1–1	2–3

PL	W	D	L	F	A	Pts	Pos.
6	1	1	4	9	11	3	3rd

Celtic failed to qualify for the knockout stage.

Scottish League Division One

	PL	W	D	L	F	A	Pts	Pos.
Aberdeen	30	24	1	5	73	26	49	1st
Celtic	30	19	8	3	76	37	46	2nd

Scottish Cup final: replay, Celtic 0 Clyde 1

Perhaps the season could be summed up by the expression 'so near yet so far'!

But let's leave the last words to Charlie Tully: 'I don't know what was proved by our challenge to Ben Lomond. But I do know that if the Celtic management asked us to climb Mount Everest, we'd have had a go. Moaning like hell, of course.'

* * *

Charlie Tully assumed legendary status within months of his arrival in Glasgow in 1948. His Northern Ireland international colleague Danny Blanchflower, in his *Sunday Express* profile of Charlie published shortly after Charlie's death in July 1971, described him as 'Celtic's great star at a time in their history when they were a poor second to Rangers . . . In his prime, Charlie was like one of those magical figures from a schoolboy magazine.' Tully's impact can be judged by Blanchflower's recollection of sitting beside a swimming pool in Rhodesia where the talk turned to football:

> I mentioned Charlie Tully. Immediately a man in the company stood to attention. He had been a bus driver in Edinburgh and he loved Glasgow Celtic. He used to visit a family in Glasgow, all of them big six footers, when he went to the matches. Tully was worshipped in that household. At the mention of his name everyone had to stand to attention.

Blanchflower and Tully had known each other since they were teenagers in Belfast, when Tully's work for a firm that installed fire sprinklers took him to Gallaher's tobacco factory, where Blanchflower was employed. At the time, they also played against each other – Tully was 'a bundle of tricks, quicksilver, lithe and graceful with a beautiful style . . . fun to watch with a ball at his feet', said Blanchflower, a wing-half for Glentoran, of his immediate Belfast Celtic opponent.

CHAPTER 14

The Changing of the Guard

In one street in the East End of Glasgow, the Gallowgate, there are
66 pubs. Many of the people who lived round the Gallowgate are
now living in newly built Glasgow suburbs which have no pubs at
all. At present the majority of the men who have 'flitted' to a new
suburb and who like a drink travel to their former neighbourhoods
and use the pubs with which they are familiar. There are strict rules
in Glasgow pubs against singing, music (apart from that provided
by a radio set), and any other game but dominoes and draughts.
These restrictions, plus 'Temperance' propaganda, have given rise to
the prevalent idea that most Glasgow pubs are mere 'drinking dens'
and have no social function. Whilst this is true of a small proportion
of Glasgow clubs (and particularly the 'wine shops'), the amount of
social activity in pubs used by working-class men is considerable.
Many of these men do regard the pub as a club.

Jack House, in a chapter on community life in the city in The Third Statistical
Account of Scotland: Glasgow, *published in 1958. Note the absence of
any reference to women, whose presence in those pubs was frowned upon then.*

*The 'suburbs' he refers to were in fact the new, peripheral housing schemes
built in the 1950s – Barlanark, Easterhouse, Castlemilk and Drumchapel.*

The first quarter of the game proved embarrassing. Scotland were
quite unprepared for the South Americans' fleetness of foot and
wholehearted – sometimes excessive – determination. The Scottish
half-back line, composed entirely of over-thirties, had not been

exposed by Yugoslavia's slower style. But their current opponents, with an average age of twenty-three, were treating them with the disrespect which youthful hooligans might employ on ageing school janitors.

Clive Leatherdale, in his Scotland's Quest for the World Cup, *1986. Paraguay won this match 3–2. Scotland, with only one point from three matches, finished at the bottom of their group – behind France, Yugoslavia and Paraguay – in the 1958 World Cup finals held in Sweden. France and Yugoslavia advanced to the next stage.*

There is an old saying, 'If you sup with the devil you need a long spoon,' one that a famous sportsman of the 1950s would have done well to heed. In the STV studio in October 1957, Bobby Evans did not pause for thought when asked by Arthur Montford, the presenter of the fledgling *Scotsport* programme, what advice he would give to young players, replying, 'I'd advise them not to read the papers – the Scottish press particularly.' Evans admitted on more than one occasion that football journalists, whom he pilloried for a tendency towards 'unbalanced criticism', were a 'favourite hobby horse' of his, which many might find surprising in view of the fact that in the latter part of the decade he ran a newsagent's business close to Queen Street Station in Glasgow. Nevertheless, it was a statement that would come back to haunt him.

At the time of its utterance, however, he was at the top of the football tree, only days away from being a standout in a 7–1 League Cup final rout of Rangers that is still a cherished part of Celtic folklore. This performance underlined his status as 'the sheet-anchor not only of Parkhead's green and white but also of Scotland's dark blue', a reputation that had been richly earned over the 13 years since the 'rufus-locked laddie' had made an immediate impact in his first appearance in a Celtic jersey during the club's pre-season public trial in August 1944. As 'Nelidon' of the *Glasgow Observer and Scottish Catholic Herald* observed: 'The 17-year-old Evans from the junior St Anthony's [where he had earned the princely sum of 6s 6d per match], a close-season signing, sparkled in the Green and White front rank, his smartly taken goal drawing a big hand from the fans.' Two weeks later, he would be making his debut in the first team proper in the wartime Southern League match against Albion Rovers at Coatbridge (19 August), in a forward line that just managed (1–0) to get the better of a stubborn home defence whose centre-half was a miner cum part-time footballer called Jock Stein. Evans earned plaudits from Glasgow's *Evening Times* – 'The new Parkhead left winger, Evans, did well' – and the *Sunday Post* – 'This red-head has all the makings'. Even an early realisation of a depressing reality, namely that he was learning his trade in a Celtic side that had been struggling for several years to recover its former glories, could not deter the youngster. His boundless energy and an all-consuming love of the game gave him the resilience to overcome such setbacks as being a member, three weeks later, of an eleven in which he found himself starved of service as his teammates strove hopelessly to contain a rampant Rangers as they ran out 4–0 winners at Parkhead, with one report noting that 'Little Evans had promise but no ball.' He was soon able to shrug off the misgivings of a father who was concerned about 'the rude remarks from the terracings' that his Protestant son might receive after signing for a Catholic club, one where Evans came to admit that 'my opposite faith never made any difference'. Ironically, he could have been a Rangers player after being spotted playing for Glasgow junior club St Anthony's at their Moore Park ground, only a stone's throw from Ibrox Park, by two famous Light Blue players, namely Willie Waddell and Willie Woodburn. They told their manager, Bill Struth, what an asset Evans would be, but there was no follow-up for some reason. Thus it was that one abiding early image of Evans as a Celt is the recollection of one sportswriter of 'a young carpenter who used to race to Parkhead in his overalls, covered with sawdust', anxious not to miss a minute's training in the light nights. Throughout his career, Evans would be dedicated to fitness. Bertie Auld remembers being a youngster at Celtic Park in the mid- to late 1950s when Evans, who acted as a mentor to the younger players, would do extra laps round the track at training, which was anathema to some, who, as Bertie recalls wryly, 'were always looking for a way out and often nipped into the "Jungle" enclosure for a fag'. Indeed, so obsessive a trainer was Evans, a lifelong abstainer from cigarettes and alcohol, that at one stage early in his Celtic career the management became so concerned that he was punishing himself as he tried to recapture his form that they insisted that he have a complete rest from football for one month, during which period, according to a member of the backroom staff, Evans 'went about like a bear with a sore head'. It was symptomatic of the pressure that Evans felt (perhaps even put) himself under as he made a determined push to establish himself in the Celtic first team. He featured in several positions (outside-left, outside-right, inside-left, inside-right, centre-forward) before he found his true niche when he was fielded at right-half – almost as a gamble, one suspects – on one of the most fraught days in the club's history, that Saturday in April 1948 when a 'last-gasp' 3–2 victory over Dundee at Dens Park finally removed the spectre of relegation.

Evans never looked back. Within six months, he would earn international recognition in the position he had by then made his own, becoming a member of the Scottish side that in quick succession beat Wales 3–1 at Cardiff and Ireland 3–2 at Hampden Park before achieving a sort of immortality with a 3–1 victory, very much against the odds, over England at Wembley in April 1949. That meteoric rise to fame, however, came at a price, with the first manifestation of what his critics discerned as a tendency towards impetuosity and 'thin-skinned prickliness'. Irked at being omitted from the World Cup qualifier against England at Hampden Park the following year – the result he clearly felt, like many Celtic fans it should be said, of a press campaign to write him down and to write up the Rangers player (Ian McColl) who took his place – he wrote to the SFA (against the advice of Celtic chairman Bob Kelly) to say that he would prefer not to be chosen for his country. Fortunately for the national side the selectors took greater note of his other statement in the same missive, namely that he would continue to give of his best if selected. Commenting on the controversy, one Celtic fan said that 'every supporter of the club knows that Bobby has had the best season he has ever had with Celtic, in some matches appearing to be doing three men's work'.

In May 1957, the former Celtic trainer Alex Dowdells paid Evans a back-handed compliment when he said, 'I don't think Bobby even began to appreciate until a season or two back that the willing horse always gets the biggest load to carry.' That theme of Celtic being a sort of one-man band in many games, with Evans carrying the team on his back, would become a recurring one as the 1950s progressed with him stamping his mark on the game as an all-time Celtic (and Scotland) great. Evans the idol of those schoolboys whose fathers used to take them down to the front of the Parkhead terracings to get a better view, Evans the player you wanted to imitate in the kickabout games with your pals in the schoolyard or back court, Evans the man whose brilliant and inspiring consistency earned him such nicknames as 'Mr Dynamo', 'The Fighting Redhead' and 'Mr Perpetual Motion'. Indeed, the respected football correspondent of the staid and venerable *Glasgow Herald*, Cyril Horne, a man not given to lavishing praise, elevated Evans to a Celtic pantheon occupied already in his opinion by the likes of Quinn, Gallacher, McGrory and Delaney in terms of embodying the spirit of the club, even going so far as to say in his March 1953 profile of the player that, 'though no one doubts the tremendous influence these men brought to bear on their teammates, it is equally true that none spared himself less for the club than their present right half, Evans'. Writing at a time when Celtic were mired in mid-table, and only weeks before Celtic annexed the Coronation Cup – an unexpected triumph – Horne pointed out that Evans had yet to play in a great Celtic side, which made it 'a matter of weekly wonderment not only from what reserve he produces his tremendous stamina but why he does not show signs of being disheartened as his efforts continue to bring meagre reward'. It was, said Horne, 'the athlete's pride in his physical fitness coupled with the blessing bestowed on him of being possessed of more grit than the average footballer that explains the ability of Evans to finish a game as strongly as he starts it.' And who could fail to be impressed by the genuine modesty of a player who claimed that he never took selection in the team for granted, that his 'biggest kick' was seeing his name on the team sheet every week? The major honours piled up after the 'breakthrough' Scottish Cup victory in 1951 that ended nearly 15 years in the wilderness: the Coronation Cup in 1953, the League and Scottish Cup 'double' in 1954, the League Cup in 1956 and 1957. And in the vanguard of these triumphs ('here, there and everywhere') was the unstintingly tenacious, whole-hearted and resolute Bobby Evans. At international level, he acquired such stature as would make one writer exclaim, 'A Scottish team without Evans is unthinkable.' The correspondent for *The Times* of London endorsed that verdict in his coverage of the Scotland v. England clashes at Hampden Park in 1956 and 1958, describing Evans in the former as 'the best player afield, a redheaded terrier of a wing half always in the thick of the fight' and in the latter as a 'stocky, gallant player making a stand at the heart of an overworked defence' in a home side hopelessly outgunned by England. You could almost imagine Evans being present at the Alamo or Custer's Last Stand.

It seemed somehow only fitting that he should be the man to make a piece of Celtic history when he became the first captain of the club to lift the League Cup aloft when it was finally won in October 1956, after ten years of trying, with a 3–0 victory over Partick Thistle in a replayed final. Sadly the first rift in the lute of his relationship with the club meant that he was deprived of the opportunity of repeating that pleasant task when the trophy was retained the following season. In May 1957, after representing his country in a World Cup qualifier in Madrid, he touched down at Prestwick Airport en route to joining the Celtic touring party in St Louis, USA, and learned from a conversation with his wife Rene and a waiting journalist during the stopover that – for reasons that are still obscure – he had lost the club captaincy to Bertie Peacock. This was a 'bitter disappointment' of which he would be reminded when he thumbed through the next edition of the *Celtic Football Guide* only to see a photograph of the new captain being congratulated by his teammates after the appointment was made on board the transatlantic liner *Mauretania*. Evans seemed to get over this perceived (and surely undeserved) slight as he maintained his customary high level of performance during a season that culminated in his being made captain of Scotland during the World Cup finals in Sweden in the summer of 1958. The previously tactless *Guide* paid him the compliment of having been 'the outstanding success of the Scottish side' in the competition, which may have come as scant consolation for a snub that rankled to the end of his days at Parkhead. That parting of the ways would hover into prospect sooner than he could have anticipated, with an incipient changing of the guard coming about during a match that ended in bizarre circumstances. Celtic's opening league match of the following season, against Clyde at Shawfield Stadium on 20 August 1958, was barely 20 minutes old when Bobby, who by now had moved to centre-half in the wake of Jock Stein's enforced retirement through injury, jumped for the ball along with his direct opponent, Johnny Coyle, and then suddenly went down in a crumpled heap on the turf. He came back onto the field a few minutes later after treatment, but lasted only another ten minutes before being led off for good 'like a man suffering an acute and sudden attack of lumbago'. Celtic were now left, in those pre-substitution days, to carry on with ten men, but the irrepressible Bertie Auld put them in front on the hour mark with a 20-yarder that 'hardly rose a foot' as it flew past McCulloch. Ten-man Celtic held on valiantly to their lead against the Scottish Cup holders and their resistance was only broken in the final five minutes by an incredible blunder that, temporarily, overshadowed Evans' misfortune. The home side's inside-right, Dan Currie, had just 'niblicked' the ball over the bar from only a few yards out when Celtic goalkeeper Dick Beattie took the resultant goal kick, tapping the ball to right-back Duncan MacKay with the apparent intent of collecting the return pass and punting the ball as far upfield as possible. Unaccountably, however, Beattie 'fumbled' the 'tap back' and, while he was still groping for the ball, in came the alert Coyle to rob him of it, poke it through the hapless keeper's legs, then run round him to touch the ball into the empty net. To rub salt into the wounds, Currie headed the winner for Clyde (2–1) 30 seconds later.

Clyde: McCulloch; Murphy and Haddock; Walters, Finlay and White; Herd, Currie, Coyle, Robertson and Ring.

Celtic: Beattie; MacKay and Mochan; Fernie, Evans and Peacock; Tully, Collins, Byrne, Wilson and Auld.

Referee: J. Mowat (Rutherglen).

Celtic had been plunged into a personnel crisis before this match, with two members of the '7–1' team, Sean Fallon and Billy McPhail, having been forced to quit football because of injuries they had sustained before the official start of the season. With Evans now sidelined for four months with what was diagnosed as 'a racked back' and the other recognised centre-half, John Jack, also unavailable due to injury, Celtic turned to a 6 ft 1 in. 18 year old whom the *Evening Times* (Glasgow) writer called 'Willie McNeill', a youngster who Celtic 'had chucked in where the water is deep and they have complete faith that he will swim strongly against the Clyde'. He had been called 'Willie' by his family and at school, and it took the use of 'Billy' by a writer covering junior football, Allan Herron, in a few paragraphs about the Blantyre Victoria centre-half, for that forename to stick. Doubtless, the *Evening Times* writer would have delighted in coining that metaphor, given that the youngster would be making his first-team competitive debut in a League Cup sectional match against the same club that had defeated Celtic three days earlier. Unconsciously, perhaps, he put his finger on the 'survival of the fittest' nature of the youth policy on which Celtic were now embarking. 'This is the Teen Age in football', exclaimed Jim Rodger in the *Daily Record* of 4 August 1959, and indeed youth was all the rage. Youth culture in all its aspects was in the ascendancy in the late 1950s, with Britain emerging from post-war austerity. Teenagers (as they were now called) seemed to be acquiring a brash self-confidence to go along with their new-found economic clout in terms of disposable income, much of which was invested in clothing and 'pop' music, as represented in the record sales for the likes of the 'King of Rock 'n' Roll', Elvis Presley, and, in purely British terms, the 'King of Skiffle', the Glasgow-born (Bridgeton no less, close to Celtic Park) Lonnie Donegan. Youth's time had well and truly arrived, and in football terms this was amply demonstrated by the way the nation had taken to their hearts the ill-fated 'Busby Babes' of Manchester United. The Celtic equivalent would be dubbed 'The Kelly Kids', after the club's chairman, but his 'brainchild' would soon be called into question, as illustrated by the aftermath of the August 1959 public trials. In those days, Celtic used to hold two of these, spaced over a few days with the proceeds going to charity, and the ex-Celt John McPhail, now writing for the *Daily Record*, hailed the performance of three youngsters in the first of these: 'Dan O'Hara, Malcolm Slater, Jim Conway – mark these names, Celtic fans, for these are the names I say will make an impact on the Parkhead terracings this season.' Tommy Mackle, a recent acquisition from junior club Johnstone Burgh, impressed in both trial matches and was promptly inserted into the first-team line-up for the opening match of the season, the left-winger netting Celtic's only goal in a 1–2 League Cup defeat by Raith Rovers at Kirkcaldy. He played another five games (netting once) before disappearing from the first-team set-up by the end of September and being freed at the end of the season. Dan O'Hara, an inside-forward from Fauldhouse United whose shooting power 'from all angles' allied to 'impressive mobility, positional sense and footwork' dazzled McPhail, would manage eight games (netting once) in a first-team spell that ended in February 1960, while Malcolm Slater would amass a total of five first-team appearances (also netting once) before being freed at the end of that season. Jim Conway fared rather better, scoring 13 times in a total of 43 first-team outings before his transfer to Norwich City in April 1961. 'Rex' was scathing of this hit-and-miss, quasi-lottery approach in his *Sunday Mail* judgement of 10 April 1960, stating that it was Celtic's 'tragedy' that 'so many young men are pitchforked into the side at the same time, learning little from each other since all are at the same learning stage'. No one, though, in the 40,000 present to witness Billy McNeill's debut on 23 August 1958 in the aforementioned League Cup match at Celtic Park could have been left in any doubt that they had just watched a Celtic star of the future as 'he soon tumbled to the Coyle tricks to sew up the middle'. He deployed the same self-assurance in an interview with Jack Harkness in the *Sunday Post* the following weekend: '"I hope

Bobby is soon fit enough to come back to the team," says the delightfully modest youngster, "I want to go back and pick up some more experience in the reserves."' He would get his wish soon enough, but he was laying down a marker for the future, both on and off the field. He had done nothing to dispel the impression that had been growing since April 1957, when Jock Stein (then the reserve-team coach) had first spotted him playing in a secondary schools international at Celtic Park, that this 'tall, gangly boy' from a military background (his father was a regular soldier turned army PT instructor) was 'officer material'. It was fortunate for McNeill's development that Stein, already ambitious to prove himself in management, was only dissuaded by a talk with chairman Bob Kelly and manager Jimmy McGrory from taking up the offer of the manager-coach post at Cowdenbeath in April 1958, the *Daily Record* reporting that 'the officials told him that he is playing a vital part in the Celtic club as coach to the Celtic reserves'.

Evans' restoration to the centre-half berth came in early December 1958, on a bone-hard pitch in a home league match against Motherwell that was abandoned seven minutes from time with Celtic leading 2–0. His return 'gladdened many a heart', a reflection of the affection in which the now 31 year old was held. Although his playing career was now winding down, the general feeling was that he would end it in a Celtic jersey and then perhaps remain at the club in a coaching or scouting capacity, but it was not to be. According to Evans, in his *Scottish Daily Express* series published only a few days after his transfer to Chelsea in May 1960, the writing was on the wall in the summer of 1959 when, before the start of the season, he was taken aside by 'Mr Kelly, the undisputed boss at Parkhead' and sounded out about the possibility of moving to the right-back position. Evans obviously suspected that chairman Bob Kelly, whose influence in team matters was indeed paramount, was keen to see the centre-half position occupied by Billy McNeill, who in the interim had gained further first-team experience as a wing-half and would start the new (1959–60) season at right-back. Evans, who would also have been concerned at the implications of such a positional change for his place in the international team that he now captained, bridled at a suggestion that caused him to 'reach the conclusion that my days as a top man at Parkhead were numbered' in either position: 'I had Billy [McNeill] breathing down my neck at centre half, and he was obviously very much in favour with the men who mattered. [Duncan] MacKay was going to provide hot opposition at right back.' His uncertainty about the future not having been removed after further talks with Bob Kelly and Desmond White, another director, he made a verbal request for a transfer in the autumn of 1959. Celtic, he said, turned it down, leaving him 'bewildered and bitterly disappointed'. He added that he felt so 'completely let down by the club that I no longer had any heart to stay with them' and, although at the time the troubles were smoothed over, 'the let-down feeling never left me'. It would not be unreasonable to speculate that this inner turmoil could have been a factor in the erratic nature of his performances in the closing months of his career at Parkhead, despite at least one writer's claim that he was playing as well as he ever had done. Look at the evidence. On 13 February 1960, during the first half of a Scottish Cup tie at Paisley against the holders St Mirren on a 'snow-dappled and sanded pitch', Evans jumped up to grasp the ball with both hands to prevent a lob reaching the 'greased-lightning' home centre-forward Gerry Baker, who was giving the veteran 'a hectic time'. Three days later, there appeared the following in the sports pages (more specifically in the 'I stick out my neck' readers' letters section) of Glasgow's *Evening Citizen*:

> I left the St. Mirren–Celtic cup-tie at Love Street with a firm opinion on one aspect of our future international sides – Bobby Evans is no longer the man to fill Scotland's centre-half jersey. I have long been an admirer of Bobby Evans, both as a footballer who never gave up trying and as a sportsman. It may have been a good tactic to jump into the air and catch the ball like a goalkeeper (as he did on Saturday) but it was a surprisingly graceless act from a no.1 player. Bobby, slow on the turn these days, has been relying on his positional sense. Now, it seems, even that is suspect.

Imagine, then, the surprise of a Mr Mackenzie of the Gallowhill district of Paisley to find himself being confronted that same evening on his doorstep by an irate Bobby Evans. (The newspaper had a practice of printing the letter writers' addresses.) Significantly, Evans's main bone of contention with the letter writer was the alleged lack of sportsmanship – his action, said Evans, being preferable to kicking his opponent's feet from under him after he had gathered the ball – and not the assertion that his playing powers were in decline. At the very least, the player's extraordinary reaction hinted at a certain, subconscious perhaps, insecurity about his current standing both in the game and at Celtic Park. Perhaps, too, Mr Mackenzie's observation about his decreasing mobility chimed with the suspicion held by his critics that Evans had not quite been the same player since his back injury.

Certainly, that observation was given short shrift by press reports of his performance in the home Scottish Cup quarter-final 2–0 victory over Partick Thistle in March 1960, with Evans being described as 'immaculate' and 'as solid as the Rock of Gibraltar'. He was also eulogised as 'the very spirit of Scotland' after his display for the Scottish League against the Football League at Highbury later that month, a paean of praise that was followed up in early April with further plaudits after he kept in check the much-touted Joe Baker, brother of Gerry, in Scotland's 1–1 draw with England at Hampden Park ('what a player – and what a captain!' enthused one writer). And yet it was becoming increasingly difficult to reconcile such endorsements with definite signs of fallibility. A week after magisterial powers of timing and interception were on view in that match against Partick Thistle, an astonishing lapse of concentration in the first ten seconds at East End Park ('Evans completely missed the ball') enabled Charlie Dickson to net the first goal of Jock Stein's managerial reign at Dunfermline and help them to stave off the threat of relegation with a 3–2 victory. Worse was to come in two Scottish Cup semi-final matches against Rangers in early April, when the bustling Jimmy Millar once again proved to be Evans's 'bogey man'. Tommy Muirhead, writing in the *Scottish Daily Express* on the way that Millar had harassed the Celt in the first (drawn) match, said that he had 'never seen Evans left floundering so often out of position', but the most damning verdict was that of 'Waverley' of the *Daily Record* in his account of Rangers' 4–1 rout of Celtic in a replay that brought out fervent choruses of 'God Save the Queen' from the Rangers end of Hampden Park at the final whistle: 'Once again Scotland's centre half looked a puzzled and anxious man when faced with Millar's liveliness and enterprise. Never once did Evans settle. Result was the loss of balance of Celtic's whole defensive system . . . Bobby Evans was far removed from the crafty, cool and rock-like centre half of Europe-wide reputation.' And all the while Billy McNeill was being seen as the coming man, the 'superb headwork' of the tall, lanky youngster drawing plaudits while playing at right-half alongside the medium-sized, stockier Evans. When given an opportunity to deputise for Evans at Motherwell in late March, while the latter was on duty for the Scottish League in London, his commanding performance at the heart of the defence prompted one writer to assert that McNeill was 'ready to step into Bobby Evans's shoes at any time'. McNeill was given two more chances to stake his claim to the centre-half position, the most significant of which came when, not for the first time in the pre-substitution era, Bobby Evans went into goal, this time at Dens Park in mid-April as a result of goalkeeper Frank Haffey being unable to resume after the interval due to a groin injury sustained during a first half in which Dundee took a 2–0 lead. Evans kept a clean sheet during a tamer second half, one in which he was not often called into action, his only real threat coming from an Alan Cousin shot that he dived to save, prompting the *Sunday Post* reporter to observe that 'on this display the evergreen red-head looked a better keeper than a pivot, for Alan Gilzean had Bobby on a string in the first half . . . [After the break] McNeill blocked the middle better than Evans had done.' The rapid progress of McNeill must surely have been a factor in Celtic's rather philosophical reaction, despite public protestations of surprise and disappointment, when Evans refused to re-sign and was transferred to Chelsea in late May 1960; hints would emerge later that there were other issues involved in the rupture. Immediately after his transfer request was granted,

Evans was dropped from the side for the remaining matches of the season, and was thus deprived of the opportunity of making a bit of Celtic history. It would be Billy McNeill who wore the number 5 on his pants when Celtic ended their 'no-numbers' policy on 14 May 1960 in a friendly match against Sparta Rotterdam, organised as part of 'Dutch Week' in Glasgow, a match also notable for the home side putting five goals (5–1) past a bespectacled goalie, Muhring, and the bemusement of spectators when a dozen or so pretty Dutch girls scattered tulips among the crowd.

As for Evans, he had well and truly burnt his boats with the club, and not least with its supporters, when he signed up for his surely ill-judged series in the *Scottish Daily Express* after his move was completed, not the least of his unflattering observations being the parting shot that he had 'joined a greater and better club'. He was repaid in kind, and more. Six years earlier, the *Celtic FC Supporters Association Handbook* had rounded off their praise of him by expressing the hope that 'long may he continue to grace the football arena playing for his club and country'. In the 1960–61 edition, the editor, George Marshall, deplored the 'unpleasant taste' of 'the post-transfer publicity' engendered by Evans's outpourings, while the general secretary of the organisation, Hugh Delaney, could not forbear to put the knife in when mentioning recent departures from Parkhead. After honourable mentions for Charlie Tully, Jock Stein and Eric Smith, he went on: 'And, oh dear, who was the other fellow? His name escapes me at the moment. Who cares anyway? He couldn't have been so important.' It was no way to treat a legend.

CHAPTER 15

'Une Tornade Nommée Celtic'*

Martin Samuel, in his 26 May 2011 article in the *Daily Mail*, revealed that, when his club played in Lisbon in 2007, Manchester United manager Sir Alex Ferguson (a Rangers man both as supporter and player) had commandeered a film crew from in-house broadcaster MUTV and took them out to the Estádio Nacional, where he had the crew film him 'walking out on to the pitch and at various points around the stadium'. The footage was never broadcast, being intended for Ferguson's personal collection of memorabilia. 'To this day,' said Samuel, 'Ferguson remains in awe of Jock Stein, the manager, and his Lisbon Lions', the first British team to lift the European Cup.

Inter in their pomp, Inter '*Gli invincibili*'. A Sunday afternoon at a sun-dappled Stadio San Siro, 2 April 1967. Some 85,000 spectators watch table-toppers Internazionale demolish their local rivals AC Milan 4–0 with such style, goal-scoring precision and sheer all-round authority in the 'Derby della Madonnina' (so named after the statue of the Virgin Mary atop the Duomo) that few present would have any reason to doubt the growing conviction, bordering on certainty, on the Continent that they would become the first Italian club to

---

* This chapter has drawn heavily on research at the Bibliothèque Nationale in Paris, which has a magnificent collection of newspapers from virtually every city and major town on the continent of Europe, to bring a fresh perceptive on the most famous and significant match in the history of Celtic FC – Pat Woods.

attain a much-coveted treble: the *Scudetto* (league championship), the *Coppa Italia* and the European Cup. Indeed, after watching Inter eliminate Real Madrid in the quarter-finals of the most prestigious competition in club football, beating the holders home and away in a tie widely regarded as 'the final before the final', Roger Macdonald of *World Soccer* had been so taken by Inter's aura of invincibility that he averred in the April edition of the magazine that here was a team 'which no one can now prevent winning their third European Cup', that 'soccer is said to be unpredictable, but Inter, with their ruthless, relentless tactical system have reduced uncertainty to complete insignificance'. The *nerazzurri* (literally 'the blacks and blues'), it seemed, were masters of all they surveyed in that early spring of 1967. This, after all, was a club that had recently achieved the feat of winning both the European Cup and the 'World Club Championship' in successive years, the first to do so (in 1964 and 1965), a team that still positively reeked of class. It was a side built around four players of unquestioned international stature: Giacinto Facchetti had virtually revolutionised the role of the full-back after Inter's legendary coach Helenio Herrera had harnessed the player's athleticism to a capacity for incisive, precisely timed and highly productive overlapping; Luis Suárez, imported from Barcelona, was a playmaker of exceptional vision and positional sense; Sandro Mazzola overcame the difficulties in following in the steps of a famous father, Valentino (captain of both the national side and of *Il Grande Torino* side that perished in the 1949 Superga aircraft disaster), to become a forward whose superb close control, tremendous pace and finishing power made him an invaluable contributor to the creation of a football dynasty that rivalled that of his father's club; and the ever-dependable, resolute 'sweeper' and club captain Armando Picchi marshalled the fort-like defensive system that underpinned Herrera's counter-attacking strategy. And thus there was every reason for the unmistakable air of self-satisfaction that Herrera exuded in the early months of that year when he confided scornfully to Macdonald that his major *Scudetto* rivals, Juventus, had more chance of winning the national lottery than the league title and when he seemed to be paying little more than lip service to the threat posed by the team he publicly identified, after Inter's victory over Real in Madrid, as the only remaining obstacle to his winning the European Cup: 'I doubt whether they would beat us in [the final in] Lisbon. After all, we would need only one goal to win. Their only hope, as I see it, would be to play us at home first in the semi-final, and make us score twice or more to win on aggregate.' He was obviously not privy to a conversation that the manager of the team Herrera referred to – Celtic – had already had with the football correspondent of *The Times*, Geoffrey Green, who quoted Jock Stein's words as follows: 'I would like to meet Inter just once, on a neutral ground. They can shut up the game for twenty minutes and then turn on the tap to suit themselves. But we will make them work for every minute and I would like to see their answer.'

In fact, the laudatory words had barely flowed from Macdonald's typewriter when questions were suddenly being asked about the impregnability of Inter. Four successive draws in the second half of April stalled their apparent procession to their League Championship crowning and also forced them into a play-off against CSKA Sofia in the European Cup semi-finals. Self-doubt began to creep into their displays, a corrosion that not even *Il Mago* ('The Magician'), as Herrera was described, could dispel. Indeed, it is difficult to avoid the conclusion that his handling of the pressure being heaped upon them undermined the efforts of his players to keep Inter at the top and, in the process, inflicted severe damage on the reputation of a revolutionary coach who had not only revived an ailing Inter at a time when Juventus and AC Milan were the dominant forces, but also virtually single-handedly transformed the role of the coach in Italian domestic football and, arguably, beyond, creating the cult of the manager as we know it today in the process. Before his arrival on the scene, one writer observed, the focus had been on the players, but Herrera 'placed the coach in a new light where it seemed that the personal charisma and character of the man in charge were responsible for the quality of his side's performances', being reputedly a man who could change a game 'with a snap of his fingers and dictate tactics from the dugout with mysterious signals'. An obsessive and a perfectionist who reputedly kept a miniature football pitch (model) and, intriguingly, a Bible by his bedside, he undoubtedly brought a new dimension to the mental, physical, technical and motivational preparation of teams, but there was an element of the cold-hearted technician about the total control he exerted on his players both on and off the field, not least in the monitoring of their private lives. As Inter's season began to fall apart in April and May 1967 under Juventus's relentless closing of the points gap in the title race, his methods and personality laid Herrera open to the charge of being ill-equipped to measure up to the challenge. Piqued by critics beginning to write off Inter as a spent force and by suggestions that a tired-looking side in need of freshening up was the result of his not deploying his squad to best advantage and of his ill-judged transfer dealings, the coach responded – it was alleged – by 'excessive training', in effect overworking his players ('putting lead into the delicate mechanisms of robots', observed drily Giuseppe Signori of the Rome-based weekly magazine *Vie Nuove*). These players were, in any case, by now fed up of the endless *ritiri* – the preparing in seclusion for matches, away from families and friends – that were insisted upon by the highest-paid coach in world football, one who also, it was rumoured, fuelled resentment by earning twice the amount of winning bonuses enjoyed by his players for their European Cup exploits. All was not well behind the scenes, and Herrera did not help the situation in which Inter found themselves by his continual alienation of the rest of Italian football with what the aforementioned Signori characterised as *l'urlante burbanza* (roughly, an overweening arrogance tinged with gruffness), a trait that induced him to direct a barrage of invective in a 'disquieting and offensive' fashion to rival coaches such as Luis Carniglia of Bologna and Oronzo Pugliese of Roma that earned him a fine from the Italian football federation and only underlined the club's unpopularity in Italy outwith their own band of supporters. This hostility towards Inter even reared its head in Scotland, as revealed by Celtic captain Billy McNeill in his *Evening Citizen* (Glasgow) Saturday column just days before the European Cup final. McNeill told of his being startled by an Italian

TV man covering the team's preparations down on the Ayrshire coast who said, 'I hope you beat Inter, and there are others in Italy, too, who want to see you win.' The weekly magazine *L'Espresso* singled out one particular individual for the resentment shown towards the Milanese team for its wealth, ruthless determination to win and perceived favours from officialdom – 'Dislike is centred on their coach Herrera, who is said to be arrogant, provocative and ungracious to opponents'. But the real victims of this disdain for Inter were the players and, in the most personal and scandalous terms in respect of manifestations of hostility, the 'petrol millionaire' and club president Angelo Moratti, who bore the brunt of this resentment in the form of coins being thrown in his direction into the *tribuna* (the Italian equivalent of the British directors' box) during away matches as a 'reminder' of Inter's alleged 'buying' of referees, the vandalising of his car and his being targeted for 'jostling' by fans of rival clubs, and – after the defeat by Mantova that cost Inter the 1966–67 league title – his home becoming the target of noisy and unpleasant chanting by jeering fans of AC Milan and Juventus; little wonder that there was speculation that Moratti, tiring of all this, was considering resignation in order to devote more time to his oil business. Herrera, himself being linked with a move to Real Madrid, may have shrugged all this off by stating that 'If Inter win in Lisbon we win for all, but if we lose we lose for ourselves', but the perspective that Sandro Mazzola provided to the BBC TV commentator Kenneth Wolstenholme some months later was more graphic and pertinent: 'The pressures got so great on us that we started to be frightened of losing. This had never happened before, and when it started we knew it was fatal . . . There was nothing we could do when the pressure got on top of us.' Nothing, indeed, for the stubborn Herrera turned a deaf ear to the pleas relayed on his teammates' behalf by his captain Armando Picchi about the enhanced training, a major factor – according to one biographer – in the captain concluding that Herrera was 'losing the plot' to the extent that the team could end up 'losing the lot'. Picchi confided to an incredulous journalist on the journey to Lisbon his premonition that Inter would lose both there and at Mantova seven days later on the decisive last day of a domestic championship in which their advantage had been whittled down to a solitary point.

This feeling that Inter was a club in meltdown was reinforced on the eve of the European Cup final by the bluntness of Louis Naville when commenting in *Paris-Normandie* on reports of concern on the part of their fans about speculation in the Italian press regarding the possible departure of the twin architects of *La Grande Inter*. President Angelo Moratti's retirement and coach Helenio Herrera's switch to Napoli were both being mooted, causing a sense of alarm that was exacerbated by the 'perceptible signs' of decline being exhibited on the field of play: 'The Spaniard Suárez, the playmaker of the team, is a mere shadow of the player he was; the Brazilian Jair [a winger] has lost his "punch" and the remarkably gifted Corso [a midfielder-cum-winger] has become progressively slower. In brief, new blood is needed if Inter's reign is not to come to an end.' So much for the claims of Herrera in particular that the absence of both Suárez and Jair through injury was a huge contributory factor to defeat in Lisbon . . . That same day, the Milan-based *Corriere della Sera* identified several reasons as to why the Portuguese were leaning towards Celtic, a prospect that had prompted president Moratti the previous day (Tuesday, 23 May) to try to turn round a losing public relations battle by handing out match tickets and Inter scarves, badges, etc. in the airport lounge after the club's chartered aircraft touched down in Lisbon. As the newspaper pointed out, at least one recent Italian TV programme had not painted an entirely flattering picture of the Iberian nation, reports of which probably had a counter-productive effect when Herrera popped up on Portuguese TV to ask for the 'Latin brotherhood' to support Inter. Cited too was the fact that the Benfica fans still nursed their resentment at their favourites being obliged to play against Inter (the winners) in a European Cup final on the latter's own ground two years earlier, not to mention the undercurrent of envy in regards to both Milanese clubs having supplanted their club at the summit of European football. This sense of anger and frustration was compounded by Herrera saying that he would buy Eusebio, their star player, 'even if it took all the *lire* in the world', though it should be said that the authoritative French sports daily *L'Équipe* claimed that the player himself had telephoned Herrera to express his interest in just such a move. It hardly helped, either, when it became known locally that, in a rather high-handed fashion, Herrera had demanded complete privacy for himself, his players and his backroom staff, forcing the manager of their Muxito hotel on the outskirts of Lisbon to cancel a large number of reservations. Ironically, this proved to be as counter-productive as his TV appeal, since the hotel turned into a virtual prison camp for the players. Once again, Herrera had ignored a plea from Armando Picchi, who pointed out that being cooped up was affecting the morale of the team. Thus, apart from their fans (outnumbered at least three to one by the Celtic hordes, according to some estimates), Inter, it seems, were virtually friendless in the Portuguese capital, as Alex Cameron hinted in his *Scottish Daily Mail* match-day piece on the extent of the club's unpopularity: 'The journalistic corps reporting here could scarcely be described as Milan admirers . . . Herrera is not liked by the international press because he says the opposite to what he intends to do. He does the reporters the injustice of thinking they don't realise this.' By contrast, his counterpart – Jock Stein – gave a masterclass in preparation, most notably in the arts of setting the tone for his players and of projecting the image of a club that was making its debut on the international stage in terms of being the cynosure of European attention, with millions the length and breadth of the Continent, not just back home, watching live TV transmission of the match, not to mention radio, newspaper and magazine coverage. Billy McNeill, his captain, says that his manager got his approach 'just right', enabling his players to fly out to Portugal 'totally relaxed', with the feeling that 'we were setting out for a big adventure'. The canny Stein, however, made sure that there would be no opportunity for any 'holiday' mentality or sloppiness to creep in by holding back his squad while the directors, press and the guests of the club disembarked at their destination, in order that he could check that the players were wearing their Celtic uniforms smartly, and that their ties were straight, before they faced the waiting reporters and TV cameras. Gair Henderson, looking back on the first anniversary of the final in Glasgow's *Evening Times*, recalled Celtic's arrival in Lisbon, a revealing illustration of Stein's highly developed sense of occasion and his awareness that big matches are won just as much off the field as on it:

> The Italians arrived in Lisbon first. They gave the Portuguese football writers a shoulder cold as frozen lamb and schoolboy autograph hunters were rudely pushed aside – and Inter hid themselves away in the hinterland of hills away on the other side of the River Tagus. Then came Celtic – different as night from day. From the moment they stepped off the aircraft, and by calculated design, they set out to win friends. At the airport itself Jock held court to newspaper men from all over Europe. He laughed and he made jokes – and he made everybody welcome. The players – I suspect under careful instruction – signed autograph books until they had writer's cramp. Photographers and TV cameramen were given the impression that Celtic would pose for pictures from dawn to dusk if need be.

Celtic based themselves at the more accessible Estoril, on the shores of the Atlantic Ocean, where they did not shut themselves off from visitors, be they pressmen or well-wishing fans. All was geared towards the 'goodwill' factor.

Nothing was to be left to chance if Stein's unbounded ambition for the club was to be realised. Celtic FC had reached a fork in the road before deciding to appoint him as manager 30 months earlier. Had a notoriously conservative chairman, Bob Kelly, opted for the status quo at a club going nowhere and mired in mediocrity, with its despairing support melting away, it could have resulted in a venerable institution being headed for oblivion, but now – remarkably – here it was, mingling with the aristocracy of European football and being presented with a golden opportunity to shake off the bonds of parochialism and make a name for itself globally: the much-trumpeted Celtic 'brand' would have its real origins in Lisbon. Even Hans Christian Andersen would have been hard put to come up with such a fairytale. There is an eerie undertone of destiny in Stein's interview with Ken Gallacher in the *Daily Record* of 9 May

1966 in which the manager, than whom no one was ever more conscious of the value and importance of tradition to a club such as Celtic, said – just two days after the club had clinched its first league title in twelve years – that it was up to everyone at Parkhead to 'build up our own legends' and 'not to live with history', but also to be fully aware of the fact that 'the greatness of a club in modern football will be judged in performances in Europe'. When he then refers to his confidence that 'we have nothing to be afraid of in the European Cup', it is impossible to escape the feeling that, even months before they kicked a ball in the competition for which they had just qualified for the first time, he had sufficient confidence in the depth and quality of his squad to consider them as potential winners of the Holy Grail of club football that had eluded British clubs, eight of whose attempts had foundered at the semi-final stage. Bertie Auld, whose midfield partnership with Bobby Murdoch had been hugely instrumental in enabling the manager to fulfil his dream of participating in the showpiece of the European game, once said of Jock Stein that he 'gave you that fantastic inner strength, like you could achieve anything'. For his part, Stein's belief and pride in his squad was beyond measure, as he articulated in the days leading up to the final: 'Cups are not won by individuals. They are won by men in a team, men who put their club before personal prestige. I am lucky – I have the players who do just that for Celtic.' Lucky, too, that he had players who were both fearless and unpretentious, and possessed of a fair degree of that self-confidence which is termed in the Glasgow vernacular 'gallusness', a characteristic that both baffled and charmed Continental observers during the club's halcyon years in Europe. Messrs Jean Clerfeuille (president) and Albert Heil (secretary) of Nantes FC, officials of a club who were guests in Lisbon of a Celtic FC impressed by French hospitality during an earlier round in the competition, were astounded by what they witnessed on the bus to the Estádio Nacional on the afternoon of 25 May 1967, despite the delay in getting there caused by a driver who had lost his way. The former told Jacques Ferran of *L'Équipe:* 'The players never stopped singing and bantering. You would never have believed that they were about to take part in a European Cup final!' In truth, the latter prospect was not one calculated to daunt a bunch of lads who came from a part of the world where streets and pieces of waste ground had acted as their academies of football. When he interviewed Bertie Auld for an *Evening Times* (Glasgow) profile in June 1972, the sportswriter Malcolm Munro, a fellow native of the city's Maryhill district, joked that Panmure Street had 'so many holes and ruts in it that when they started a five-a-side game they usually ended up looking for players who had fallen into the holes'. The irrepressible Bertie himself chipped in: 'By the time you'd dribbled round the holes you then had to beat the man. We played at any time, with anything. Usually a tennis ball we'd pinched – for even a tanner ba' was outwith our finances. Sometimes Panmure Street was playable. My old man was a brickie's labourer and he'd try to level off the patch.' That he was in charge of such a happy-go-lucky squad only underlined Jock Stein's contention that teamwork was the essence of Celtic, a constant refrain of his in the build-up to that final which acted as a powerful counter to Herrera's rather bombastic declaration that Inter had more class than Celtic, that, 'Man for man, we have the edge in individual skills', and to his dismissal of the Scots as 'These men from the north who run as if they want to be the first men on the moon.' Deftly, after learning of Herrera's harping on about the loss of Suárez and Jair, Stein told the Turin-based *Tuttosport* that 'real teams' were made up of fifteen, sixteen or seventeen players and that the absence of his top scorer Joe McBride (out through injury for the past five months) was a 'severe blow', but nevertheless 'if Celtic lose we will have no excuses'. Even more significant was the chord he struck with the Portuguese public by underlining Celtic's philosophy of an obligation to entertain, with statements of intent such as 'We play to score goals, Inter not to concede them' and his determination to get across the message, as he told Hugh McIlvanney of *The Observer*, that Celtic did not just want to win the Cup, but also to win it playing good football, 'to make neutrals glad we've won it, glad to remember how we did it'.

Jock Stein's personality dominated this final, his imprint all-pervasive, despite the strain that he willingly shouldered to ensure that his team would be in a position to perform at its highest level in the most important match in the club's history. The final training sessions held by both squads at the Estádio Nacional on the morning of 24 May 1967, the day before the final, both highlighted the differing approaches of the men in charge and, perhaps, provided a clue to the more perceptive observers as to the mood in the respective camps: Herrera the disciplinarian and ring-master, blowing on his whistle and shouting instructions, whereas Stein joked with his players throughout and yelled for joy when he scored a goal during a light-hearted practice match. The watching *Liverpool Echo* correspondent was one of those who came away with the belief that the Scots had a great chance of success on the basis that 'Celtic looked physically fitter and much faster than the Italians'. It was probably Stein's last chance for a moment of light relief before the serious business began. He was all too aware that Herrera, a man steeped in the background manoeuvring that surrounds such occasions, would employ various ploys to try to unsettle Celtic with a war of nerves. Sure enough, barely had Celtic arrived – belatedly, as has already been noted – at the stadium when the old master of gamesmanship arranged for one of his reserves to spread rumours that Suárez was actually in Lisbon and ready to play (he was at home in Italy), a strategy he followed up by trying, again unsuccessfully, to withhold Inter's team lines from Stein, who, in his *Sunday Mirror* column three days later, was still bristling with anger when recalling that he told the referee in no uncertain terms that his team would not leave their dressing-room until he saw them, as was his right. There was, then, a touch of desperation in Herrera's last-gasp ploy, a formal protest made minutes before kick-off to UEFA delegates about the Celtic players wearing numbers on the sides of their pants and not on the backs of their jerseys. The timing was not accidental, for Herrera, a meticulous preparer of dossiers on potential future opponents, had seen Celtic play in such numbered pants at Zurich in an earlier round – a match, incidentally, watched by UEFA officials, whose HQ was in Berne, just sixty miles away, and who obviously had seen nothing wrong with the numbering – and at Ibrox in the title decider against Rangers three weeks before the European Cup final. The delegates, who clearly saw the protest for what it was, dismissed it. As it happens, Herrera had a point, albeit for a more practical reason than that he intended, since the relative smallness of the numbers on the pants and the unfamiliarity of most of the foreign press with the Celtic players in an era when there was little coverage of football on television and no facilities at hand immediately in the stadium for 'playbacks', resulted in John Clark, Tommy Gemmell and Billy McNeill (and not Jim Craig, the real 'culprit') being variously identified in a number of Continental newspapers with bringing down Cappellini for Inter's penalty award and for Bobby Murdoch, Bertie Auld and Willie Wallace (not the real scorer, Steve Chalmers) being similarly credited with Celtic's winner. Nevertheless, Herrera had picked the wrong man on whom to practise his dark arts, for Stein not only proved himself a match for Herrera's cunning and attempts to play hardball ('Herrera thought he could push us around, but he found out otherwise,' he told Alex Cameron), but he also had an ace or two up his sleeve. He had the advantage of having taken the measure of Herrera himself when he went to study Inter Milan's methods in the autumn of 1963 at the invitation of the *Scottish Daily Express*, a venture in which he was accompanied by the manager of Kilmarnock, the famous ex-Ranger Willie Waddell who, in his later, journalistic capacity for that newspaper, recalled in a 19 May 1967 article the fresh perspective on both the game and the art of football management that Stein had acquired from this 'learning' trip: 'He saw a man [Herrera] absolutely dedicated to the game, with the singlemindedness and driving urge to get the best out of the players at his disposal. Stein saw new horizons to football, the application [needed] of the man in charge and the same approach from the fellows playing the game. Stein saw the benefits of *living* football.' It should come as no surprise, then, that Stein's insatiable quest for football knowledge would enable him to hoover up insights into Inter Milan's methods and style of play that would prove invaluable far sooner than he could have anticipated. After his brief stint as part-time manager of Scotland ended with a 0–3 defeat in a World Cup qualifying play-off against Italy in Naples in December 1965, he persuaded the Internazionale and Italy full-back Giacinto Facchetti, a player he much admired, to adjourn with him to the hotel bar after the post-match banquet for a chat. Much of this was devoted to Stein quizzing Facchetti about his club and his role in the Inter team in such an easy, relaxed manner that the latter, as he admitted in an interview with the distinguished football writer Gabriele Marcotti published in *Celtic View* in May 2001, was never made to feel that it was some sort of interrogation, albeit napkins and pieces of paper were used for diagrams and formations. A long-time observer of Stein, Rodger Baillie, writing in the first (1969) edition of his annual *Playing for Celtic*, captured the public face that masked the manager's cunning: 'The average fan on the terracing might spot him ducking into a dug-out, sometimes see a gloved hand shooting out waving instructions, or if he is on the pitch at a bad injury . . . but that is the only public glimpse they get during a game.' Few people, if indeed anyone, in the game got really close to the formidable personality that was 'The Big Man'. Few, if any, matched his attention to detail.

The scene was set for a final that could be categorised as a tale of two cities, a match between two teams with nothing in common. Internazionale represented prosperous Milan, the symbol of the post-war Italian 'economic miracle', the home of elegant arcades and world-famous brands such as Alfa Romeo, Pirelli and Zanussi, a rival to Paris in the world of fashion and a passion for the arts (the La Scala opera house apart, it had no fewer than 121 cinemas). On the other hand, Celtic came from distinctly unglamorous Glasgow, then associated with industrial decline and a place in the throes of redevelopment as its slums came tumbling down, its character described in unflattering terms by a visiting Swiss journalist in late 1966 as 'grey, dirty and foggy, with long rows of black tenements' and as 'not a city where one thinks of amusement, it is a city of work'. It was a difference reflected in the status of the clubs themselves at the time. Inter were regarded as a football machine, a team of unquestionable pedigree, famed for their achievements in the international sphere and replete with acknowledged world-class players. Celtic were comparatively inexperienced at the highest level of the European game, an outfit more renowned for their exuberant play and exceptional fitness than for performers of the highest class, albeit some Continental scribes were already elevating Jimmy Johnstone to a pedestal occupied by the likes of Matthews and Garrincha. The disparity in wealth was underlined graphically in a comparison between the training facilities of both clubs: Celtic, albeit one of the two biggest and richest clubs in Scotland, made do with modest, cramped and 'basic' Barrowfield close to their stadium in the poorest part of Glasgow, while Inter, a club at which no expense was spared to ensure that it remained at the top, boasted several football pitches, tennis courts and a 'magnificent' swimming pool, in addition to the best available medical equipment and changing cabins, at the state-of-the-art Centro Sportivo di Appiano Gentile complex located in a secluded, wooded area near Como, thirty miles north-west of Milan. Nevertheless, in his brief managerial time at Celtic, an undaunted Stein had assembled a side that did not know the meaning of the word 'defeat' and he had prepared them with such thoroughness that they arrived at the Estádio Nacional radiating fitness, verve, an unshakeable belief in their own ability, and a hunger for a triumph such as they and the club had never known, a team determined – in Stein's own words – 'to prove their calibre to themselves as well as to the rest of the football world', an eleven sent into battle with his invocation that they play 'as if there are no more tomorrows'. These were the priceless assets and qualities that enabled them to emerge with stunning immediacy from a desperate moment psychologically to secure a foothold in the game after a potentially dream-shattering penalty award. Here was the stuff of human drama to be shared by people separated by some 600 miles but brought together by the 'little box in the corner', which had only recently become an essential, affordable component of daily life in European households, a window to the world that was transforming the vista of sport, not least football, its most popular attraction. Thus it was that when Inter Milan took the lead via the penalty spot in that sudden, early moment when Celtic's Jim Craig was adjudged to have fouled Renato Cappellini, the full-back's mother – on hearing the news from another son (Denis) of Jim's misfortune while she was weeding the garden, unable to bear watching the proceedings on television – dropped to her knees uttering the words 'Jesus, Mary and Joseph!' as she took out her rosary beads, while in the stadium itself her husband turned to his brother-in-law Philip and said, 'I've come all this bloody way to see that!'. Meanwhile, in a café in far-off Le Mans, a city in north-western France, viewers were not put off by the variable quality of the images on the screen (the result of violent thunderstorms which hit the country that afternoon), so enthralled were they by the spectacle that was unfolding in the Portuguese capital, as one of them, Thierry Pilette, wrote to *Miroir du Football*: 'Most of us, including myself and my factory workmates, thought that Inter's sickening defensive tactics would prevail after being awarded a dubious penalty, then the equaliser prompted an eruption of joy from everyone in the room. Celtic's attacking approach had won everyone over. Real football was the victor in Lisbon.' Indeed, instead of 'tensing up' (as many must have feared) in the face of seasoned campaigners with two European Cups already under their belt, the men in green and white channelled the pent-up energy that had marked the early minutes of their participation into steeling themselves to the task of overcoming a formidable (some thought insurmountable) hurdle. Celtic may have been intent on not giving the Italians a moment's peace to indulge their controlled style of play at their own pace, but, for all the Italian team's reported vulnerability in recent matches, on the face of it, Inter's situation seemed tailor-made for a side of their expertise and calculated approach, given the stubbornness and resourcefulness of their organisation at the back. As Bryon Butler of the *Daily Telegraph* explained: 'Inter's defence is no ordinary one. It employs up to ten men, and is a devious, complex, immensely physical thing in which everything is sacrificed to survival.' But, he added, they failed this time to ensnare a team in its web because 'they could do nothing to relieve the pressure and because in Celtic they had opponents who more than matched them for class, and strength, and persistence', an analysis that gives the lie to the simplistic notion that Celtic just ran Inter off their feet. As John Rafferty of *The Scotsman* noted, the central thrust of Stein's philosophy of making his men play for, and believe in, each other lay in impressing upon them not only 'the virtues of speed, backing-up, and shooting on sight', but also the absolute necessity of the creation of space by movement, of his players 'moving around' their markers to make room for their colleagues to push right up on top of – and around – opposing defences. In a profile of Inter's captain Armando Picchi written shortly after the final, the BBC TV commentator in Lisbon, Kenneth Wolstenholme, outlined the effectiveness of this focus:

> For the first time a team refused to play Inter's game. Celtic would not pump long passes into the heart of the Inter defence, or sling across high centres. They knew that Picchi would pick off every one of them. Celtic tried it the other way. They attacked in small packs with short, accurate passing. They used the individual skills of players like Johnstone to take on the Inter defenders one by one. They shot into the packed defence. And they played quickly across the field to get the defence on the wrong foot before coming through to strike. For the first time the defence began to creak. Picchi swept up like a hero, but he had so much to sweep up. The line of four backs, behind which he was supposed to operate, was pushed back until it was on its toes, cramping his style. And before the end, the rout was complete. Inter Milan were defending simply by weight of numbers. Tactics had flown out of the window.

The Inter 'stopper', Aristide Guarneri, confirmed the eventual disintegration of Inter's rearguard as Celtic laid siege to Sarti's goal, lamenting after the match that 'There seemed to be twenty-two Scots, shooting from every direction.' It would have been all the more galling had he known that the player widely credited by pressmen across the length and breadth of Europe with being Inter's tormenter-in-chief as a result of his rampaging down the left flank, namely the buccaneering Tommy Gemmell (memorably described by Geoffrey Green as 'a big blond cat set among the Italian pigeons'), had been following a blueprint that was a product of Jock Stein's chat with the full-back's more famous counterpart some 18 months earlier. Celtic's adaptability and improvisation in this final dispelled the long-held Continental belief that the British had little or no talent for tactical adjustment in adversity. Jock Stein, who always maintained that 'The team who can overcome best the unexpected happenings during a game will be the winners', summed up the achievement in typically concise fashion in a post-match interview with Alex Cameron in which he revealed how and why Celtic made a subtle change at half-time: 'Inter play in a diamond formation and they try to bring the opposition into the apex and stop them there. We decided to go round about. We achieved this by overlapping our backs. This had the effect of pulling defenders out of the penalty box.' Indeed, so obsessive had been Herrera's belief that Celtic's only threat came from their fitness, pace and strength, and so disorientated did he become by the fury of the Scots' reaction to an early setback, that he failed to counter a deadly threat that was ultimately his team's undoing. Two days after the final, the Turin-based *La Stampa* newspaper reported that the Inter forward Angelo Domenghini became so alarmed by Gemmell's marauding down the Italian side's right flank that he suggested to Herrera that he should try to block the incursions, only to be informed that he should stick to his task of attempting to keep the Celtic defence 'on the hop', an assignment that he found increasingly futile as the result of a lack of service from a beleaguered midfield and rearguard.

There was no mistaking the note of lingering bewilderment in Giacinto Facchetti's voice when he recalled, 34 years after the event, the confusion that Celtic had sown in the Inter ranks by their refusal to be fazed by their seventh-minute setback: 'Their heads did not go down. Losing 1–0 did not demoralise them, they simply fought even harder. It was incredible. They just kept coming and coming . . . When Tommy Gemmell equalised we were shocked. This was not supposed to happen. Maybe that's where we lost it altogether. Celtic weren't following the script, and we weren't sure how to react.' Celtic, he added, 'wanted it more, they deserved the crown'. Jock Stein surely put his finger on the source of Facchetti and company's ordeal (the term *un calvario* in Italian match reports could hardly be more expressive) when he told the annual gathering of Scottish referees at Gorebridge in June 1967 that Inter had been faced with a situation beyond their control: 'I don't think Inter Milan ever met a team like Celtic.' He would have got no argument about that from Armando Picchi, whose exertions in trying to contain the Celtic tide that warm afternoon had left him so exhausted by the interval that on reaching the dressing-room he grabbed a stool, placed it under a shower and sat there under the flowing water trying to cool down. He was quoted as telling close friends afterwards that if the contest had been a boxing match it would 'have been stopped after five minutes [a pardonable exaggeration], but instead we had to go on to the very end . . . I gave my all, but Chalmers's [winning] goal brought a sense of relief, for extra time would have brought a drubbing'. He would pay a heavy price for such frankness and for what Herrera regarded as his insubordination in questioning his boss's methods. He was made a scapegoat for the club's demise, being transferred to Varese at the end of the season. He observed wryly on his departure that 'When things go right it is always Herrera's brilliant planning; when things go wrong it is always the players to blame.' And it had gone very wrong for Herrera in Lisbon, so much so that, as the second half wore on, the coach, who during the first half had irritated reporters sitting a few yards behind him in the specially erected press stand with the stridency of his instructions to his players as he pleaded with them in vain – and in a manner bordering on apoplexy – to 'Keep the ball! Keep the ball! Don't give it away!' in the face of Celtic's relentless pressure, was to be seen holding his head in his hands, resigned to defeat. There would be no sympathy for him or for a team whose negativity had completely lost them any chance of backing from the neutrals in the crowd; little sympathy (or indeed credibility) either when claims emerged over the years that, injured players apart, Inter's players had been affected by food poisoning at their pre-match hotel or by a cold shower taken before kick-off that had left them 'done in and dizzy' in the heat. It was noted how the white-clad ball-boys had jumped for joy at Gemmell's equaliser and that when Chalmers netted the winner a Portuguese policeman had sprinted 20 yards down the touchline to congratulate Jock Stein, whose pre-match promise to the locals had been utterly vindicated. The Celtic striker's nifty deflection of Murdoch's shot enabled Jean Eskenazi of *France-Soir* (Paris) to breathe a huge sigh of relief that a 'terrible injustice' had been averted, that the self-belief, persistence in adversity and 'impeccable team spirit' of the 'brave hearts' (*coeurs vaillants*) from Scotland had prevented 'a baleful influence on football' from triumphing in the most memorable – at least in terms of 'dramatic intensity' – final of all 12 he had covered from the competition's inception. Pierre Lagoutte of *Le Parisien Libéré* captured the extraordinary impact of Celtic's victory when he said that 'Never in the history of the competition has there been such an explosion of joy and popular delight as manifested itself at the final whistle'. The *Gazette de Lausanne* correspondent went into raptures when singling out one particular player as a symbol of his assertion that Celtic had rehabilitated the honour and image of football when he described Tommy Gemmell wandering about the pitch at the end of this 'memorable triumph' beaming with delight and draped like a victorious warrior with the 'flag' of his opponent [i.e. Sandro Mazzola's 'swap' jersey]: 'His smile was the smile on the face of the whole of football, that of real attacking football in all that world-conquering passion and conviction which we have come to love so much.' Several of his teammates were seen to be weeping tears of joy as they struggled to make the safety of the dressing-room amid the chaotic post-match scenes on the pitch and even the normally dour Jock Stein was caught up in the tide of emotion, telling Douglas Ritchie of *The Sun* (Scottish edition): 'I just can't find the words. The team did everything and they are the greatest bunch of boys I have ever met. They did it for the club. High praise? After tonight's game no praise can be too high.' Here was ample vindication, too, of the faith in the virtues of the British game that Stein had articulated when telling the Milanese newspaper *La Notte* before the match that the Latin style which had dominated European competition 'had had its day' and would give way in Lisbon to the more athletic style and brisker tempo of what one French newspaper called *les insulaires* (the islanders), a word that carries overtones of the supposed insularity from football ideas that the Continentals believed had proved to be a handicap to teams from across the Channel challenging the hegemony of the Italian and Iberian clubs who had turned the European Cup into their private property before Celtic brought it to northern Europe for the first time. Alan Hubbard of the *Sheffield Morning Telegraph* highlighted the perception that British football had been sneered at before the triumph of the Scottish side (whom he hailed as 'Britain's club of this and any other year') when he suggested that Celtic had not only won the Cup but also hurdled a barrier that was at once mental, tactical and quasi-political, claiming that there was a bias against British competitors by 'European' sports officialdom: 'I have seen it often in boxing and tennis, as well as football.'

For Herrera and Inter, the agony was not over. It was bad enough that, in the hours immediately following the final, gloating fans of AC Milan should have staged a mock funeral for their rivals in the streets of that city, but there was further torment in store for their fans when Inter lost the league title seven days later at Mantova as a result of a horrendous error by Giuliano Sarti, the goalkeeper credited by Jock Stein with preventing humiliation for his team in Lisbon (it could have been 6–1, said the Celtic manager). Six days after that championship debacle, Inter were eliminated from the *Coppa Italia* at the semi-final stage by lower-division Padova. The dream of the 'treble' was in ruins, and the personal trauma of it all was laid bare in a bizarre interview Herrera granted that summer to a famous Italian journalist, Oriana Fallaci, in the magazine *L'Europeo*. She had been dismayed on returning from a recent assignment in New York to find a nation gripped by the unfolding drama of the Inter–Juventus title race at a time when the Middle East was on the brink of Arab–Israeli conflict (the Six-Day War). Despite her self-confessed dislike and ignorance of football, the serious-minded Fallaci, a youthful member of the Italian Resistance in the Second World War and a specialist in politics and world affairs, shrugged off any reservations she may have had, understandably, about the comparatively trifling topic of sport to elicit some frank thoughts from a far from chastened (outwardly at least) Herrera. After denying reports that he had been in an emotional state at Mantova ('no tears, no shame, no embarrassment' was his verdict on the result), he preferred to concentrate on what he described as 'a fabulous season'. In an obvious reference to the European Cup, he spoke in glowing terms of the victories over Russian champions Moscow Torpedo, Hungarian champions Vasas Budapest, Spanish giants Real Madrid and Bulgarian champions CSKA Bulgaria, but – oddly, and revealingly – he made no mention whatsoever of the final itself or, indeed, of the name of Celtic anywhere in the interview. It was as if he was determined to expunge his club's defeat, and his conquerors, from his memory by simply wiping it from history. One could not have imagined a sportswriter letting him away with such an omission. Celtic, meanwhile, were still basking in the rapturous praise accorded to their achievement, plaudits that would have been all the more gratifying for coming from a nation that Jock Stein believed had largely rather underplayed his club's chances of even reaching the final. Peter Lorenzo of *The Sun*, accompanying the English national side to Vienna for a friendly against Austria, reported the 'roar of delight' at the final whistle from the players, manager Sir Alf Ramsey and his backroom staff crowded around the TV set in their hotel: 'Immediately the television transmission ended the England party sent a cable of congratulations to the Celtic conquerors in Lisbon.' Desmond Hackett, once described as 'the last man in England to wear a brown bowler', stated in his *Daily Express* match report that 'won' was a tame description of the victory: 'Glasgow Celtic, super, superb Celtic marched proudly into soccer history tonight when they became the first British team to win the European Cup . . . They shattered Inter Milan and the 2–1 score was an affront to the magnificence of Celtic. They were *demanding* the Cup from the first moments of the final in the golden mould of the National Stadium.' His compatriot Brian James, who characterised Celtic's display as one in which 'every man was an attacker by impulse, a defender by occasional necessity', was no less effusive in the *Daily Mail*:

> Celtic won more than a trophy. They won the acclaim of all those who love soccer and believe the game must be entertaining as well as intelligent. Inter, twice holders of the trophy, attempted to tear

the living spirit out of this match with their tactics. Given that one goal they sought to do no more, and suffer [i.e. permit] their opposition to do nothing either . . . Celtic played with the skill all Scotland knows they possess. They played with the persistence Stein had promised. Above all, they played with the patience of men whose belief in themselves is absolute and with the passion of men who knew their cause to be just.

Jock Stein would have lapped all this up, but he took his greatest satisfaction in silencing the doubters, as he wrote in the 1968 edition of the annual *International Football Book*:

> I know we were shock winners. I heard the rumblings before we faced Vojvodina (Yugoslavia) and Dukla (Prague) and then the fabulous Inter Milan from Italy in the final. Comments like, 'Celtic will never do it, they're not in the same class.' It was suggested that we were incapable of getting even to the quarter-finals, never heed the final. But we *did* get through to the final, we *did* win . . . and in the humblest way I think we did it well. No matter what lies ahead, or what went before, Celtic won the European Champions Cup for Scotland and for Britain. Not even the cynics can scrub that feat from the record books.

He could just as easily (and perhaps more accurately) have described it as a victory for a Glasgow and District XI, as Hugh McIlvanney has characterised the players born within a thirty-to forty-mile radius of the city and who had set off on a Tuesday morning as a bunch of local lads largely unknown to the wider world and returned home three days later having already acquired legendary status. No team drawn entirely from such a narrow geographical area had – or has since – won the most coveted club trophy of them all. 'The whirlwind named Celtic', as *L'Équipe*'s 50th-anniversary chronicle of the European Cup described '*Les lions de Lisbonne*', had made an indelible mark on the history of a competition that the Paris-based newspaper had pioneered, the Scots' performance having injected new life into a tournament that was widely perceived to be stagnating (weighed down by what one writer called 'barren pragmatism') after its early flourishing during the reign of the glittering Real Madrid and Benfica. '*I leoni di Lisbona*'/'*Die Lissabonner Löwen*'/'*Los leones de Lisboa*', as they have also been called in various Continental publications down the years, carved out for themselves a very special place not only in the hearts of Celtic supporters but also in the annals of football, their achievement so unique that, come to think of it, what other team that has won the European Cup/Champions League has been assigned a nickname? And trust a French writer to encapsulate the significance and romance of it all in a memorable phrase: *Pour l'éternité. Bien sûr.*

* * *

Celtic: Simpson, Craig, Gemmell, Murdoch, McNeill, Clark, Johnstone, Wallace, Chalmers, Auld and Lennox.

Inter Milan: Sarti, Burgnich, Facchetti, Bedin, Guarneri, Picchi, Domenghini, Mazzola, Cappellini, Bicicli, Corso.

Substitutes: only goalkeeping substitutions were allowed at the time, and only in case of injury. Neither John Fallon (Celtic) nor Ferdinando Miniussi (Inter) was called upon in the final.

Referee: Kurt Tschenscher (West Germany).

Attendance: variously cited as 45,000, 52,000 and 55,000.

	CELTIC	INTER
Goal attempts	43	3
Corners	11	0
Free kicks	21	21
Offside	7	1
Goal kicks	2	28

Statistics from The Sun, *26 May 1967*

Celtic were widely hailed as the rehabilitators of attacking football. Here is a sample of what was said.

Harry Andrew (*Scottish Sunday Express*):

No team has shown such courage in adversity, for almost every break went against them in the final. Justice would have given them at least a three-goal margin in their favour. They made hacks of a side that was good enough to win the World Club Championship twice. They played glorious attacking football from the start. They won every neutral to their side. I saw even French, German and Brazilian journalists rising to their feet to cheer when they scored.

Giuseppe Prisco, vice-president of Inter Milan, typified the gracious acceptance of defeat on the part of the club's directorate, stating immediately after the match that his team would have conceded 'a wagonload of goals' had the final gone into extra time, adding that any other outcome would have been 'mortifying for the game of football'.

Sam Leitch (*Sunday Mirror*), probably translating from a Continental source, quoted the Inter coach Helenio Herrera as describing Celtic as: 'The most complete football outfit I have ever seen, a side with so many variations in attack it was impossible to legislate their downfall.'

Roger De Somer (*La Dernière Heure*, Brussels):

You had to have mingled with the Celtic camp and the club's followers to appreciate fully how, on the banks of the Tagus, these men from Clydeside brought a breath of fresh air to football itself, as reflected in the fact that after only a few minutes 50,000 supposedly neutral spectators were rooting for the Scots on an unforgettable afternoon during the course of which football with a smile on its face was reinstated.

Victor Railton (*Evening News*, London):

For too long the dead hand of defensive soccer has done its best to ruin the game as a spectacle. And nowhere has this disease been more apparent than in the top European competitions. Helenio Herrera, manager of 2–1 losers Internazionale of Milan and hailed as a genius in Italy, has not been concerned with entertainment by his teams . . . Now his boring, irritating, defence-minded plans have been shown up. Inter's negative play was torn to shreds by the all-out attack and vigour of Celtic.

O Seculo Ilustrado, Lisbon-based magazine, 27 May 1967: 'The European Cup passes from the Latin orb to the Anglo-Saxon [!!] one. It is in good hands, ideally so, since we do not think there is any other team (be they Portuguese, Spanish, Italian or French) that plays football like Celtic.'

It is appropriate that we conclude this chapter with extracts from a *Scottish Daily Express*, May 24th 1967 interview conducted by ex-Rangers player Willie Waddell, footballer turned journalist, in which Celtic manager Jock Stein is quoted as follows: 'Win or lose on Thursday we have created a fine image of Celtic and Scotland in the football world. I have worked around the clock for my club since the day I joined them because I believe they are one of the greatest in the world, and deserve nothing but the highest honours . . . It is true that I do not sleep much. There are days I feel the lack of it. But they are few. When I do I steel myself against it. I have to be at my sharpest when I meet the players. I ask so much mental alertness and fitness of them I must set an example. There are days when driving to Celtic Park in the morning I feel a sag. But as soon as I get among the lads I perk up. When one is at the top there is not time for rest or relaxation. Not for a second.' Stein', said Waddell, 'thrives on activity, on ideas, on success, on guiding and forming the careers of his Celtic family' and 'is a born leader – a great deal more than just a football expert.'

CHAPTER 16

Ole! Ole! Ole!

I had just moved to Dunfermline and got two tickets for the stand and was really looking forward to the game. We were all wanting to see the deep-lying centre-forward. We knew that Di Stefano was a great player and he could score goals but we wondered how it all happened and we saw it unfurl before our own eyes.

He was a player, that was the important thing. He wasn't a centre-forward or a midfield player, he was just a player who played where his team wanted him and set up the play. He could take the ball from the back men and give it to the front men or he could score goals himself. I think that was the thing we found impressive in a player of his standard. An outstanding feature of his game was that he left the impression that we would never see a better player than him and I think that still holds true for many of us.

Jock Stein talking about Alfredo Di Stefano's performance in the Real Madrid v. Eintracht Frankfurt European Cup final at Hampden in 1960

Whenever and wherever Celtic fans are gathered to watch the draws for the European trophies, the prospect of their club being drawn against Real Madrid is always high in their expectations. The Spanish club is certainly one of the biggest names in the game, with a long history of success. They have won La Liga 32 times, the Copa del Rey 18 times and the European Cup/ Champions League on 9 occasions, the vast majority of the successes coming after the Second World War, by which time Santiago Bernabéu had become the club's president.

Bernabéu had joined Real as a fourteen-year-old junior player in 1909, only seven years after it was founded, helping to paint the fence round its first stadium, the 'Campo de O'Donnell' (previously the team had played on vacant ground adjoining a bullring). He rose to become the club's president in the mid-1940s and, as one of football's few recognised visionaries, set out on his ambition to make Real Madrid the greatest club side in the world. First, he instigated plans for the building of an impressive new stadium (opened in 1947 and later named in his honour shortly after the initial capacity of 75,000 was expanded to 125,000 in the mid-1950s) and then ensured that he had the players to fill it.

The cornerstone of his team – and the one player he was determined to bring in – would be Alfredo Di Stefano, who had started his career with River Plate in Argentina in 1944 as an 18 year old. In 1949, when players in the Argentinean leagues went on strike over pay and conditions, the clubs locked them out and used amateur players instead. Meanwhile, the star players had been lured away to join a pirate league that had been set up in Colombia, which, at that time, was not a member of FIFA. Di Stefano joined Millonarios of Bogotá, the so-called *Blue Ballet*. When Colombia eventually joined the international association, Millonarios went on one last world tour, where the quality of Di Stefano was spotted . . . and Real Madrid pounced!

Santiago Bernabéu lived modestly, his other passions being for fishing and cigars, and he never drank alcohol. Indeed, no drinks, even coffee, were provided in the presidential box on match days, given his belief that people should be there to watch football, not to drink. It was his contention that, if they had even a cup of coffee during the interval, 'they would start arguing and miss the second half'. He is regarded by some observers as *the* driving force behind the inauguration of the European Cup, a competition that the Spanish side dominated from its inception in 1955–56, winning the trophy for five consecutive seasons. The timing of its introduction was highly fortuitous, given the advent of TV throughout Europe.

Real Madrid, with their all-white strip filled by the likes of Di Stefano, Puskás and Gento complementing their dazzling football, were made for the new medium. It was said that Di Stefano made Real Madrid, a club struggling before his arrival, and that Real Madrid made the European Cup. The last of those first five finals, at Hampden Park on 18 May 1960, certainly left an indelible impression on the minds of the supporters who turned up for the occasion. A crowd of 127,641 were packed in – including yours truly (Jim Craig) in the schoolboys' enclosure – and we all witnessed a thrilling encounter between Real and Eintracht Frankfurt, which the Spaniards won 7–3. The West Germans were excellent on the night but unfortunately were up against a wonderful Madrid side whose pace, cohesion and goal-scoring prowess were awe-inspiring. Few of the crowd left before the end and I can still recall the applause from the huge gathering as the Real players held up the cup for our inspection. Little did I realise that, only seven years hence, I would not only see such a trophy at much closer quarters – not the same one, that having been given to Real Madrid after their sixth triumph – but hold it as well! The crowd's appreciation of Real Madrid brought tears to the eyes of Bernabéu, who said at the time that all European Cup finals should be played at Hampden Park, adding that 'this was the most wonderful crowd ever to pack a stadium, this was Real Madrid's greatest game'.

Celtic and Real Madrid have met on six occasions. The first was at Celtic Park on 10 September 1962, a charity match to benefit the Jewish National Fund Charitable Trust, the proceeds of which went to help the rehabilitation of refugee women and children from Europe and North Africa. The match was the brainchild of a Glasgow businessman called Max Benjamin and had been organised by the Glasgow Blue-and-White committee, the name inspired by the colours of the Israeli national flag.

As was their custom for such matches in aid of charity, Real Madrid cut their fee from £14,000 to £10,000; the referee, Leo Horn from Holland, and his linesmen, Tiny Wharton and Bobby Davidson, both from the West of Scotland, all gave their services free; and a crowd of 72,000 (only six days after an estimated 250,000 had gathered in the city centre to say goodbye to Glasgow's beloved trams) arrived to see big names like Puskás, Gento and Alfredo Di Stefano. Behind the scenes, two strong club presidents, Santiago Bernabéu and Bob Kelly, would have been brought together again, their first meeting having probably come at that European Cup final at Hampden, when Bob Kelly was president of the SFA. They had much in common; both came from comfortably off middle-class families and had long associations with their clubs. (Bob Kelly had been a Celtic director for 30 years, succeeding his father James Kelly in 1932. James Kelly was the club's first captain in 1888 and he went on to become a director from 1897 until his death, including a period as Chairman from 1909 to 1914.)

On the night, Real proved too strong for Celtic. By the interval, they had a two-goal lead thanks to Puskás and Amancio. Gento made it 3–0 on the hour mark, then Steve Chalmers made it 3–1 one minute later. Encouraged by the goal, Celtic moved up a gear and took the game to the visitors, who suddenly found themselves hanging on to their lead. When the whistle for full-time came, however, it was still 3–1 in Real's favour and the crowd gave them a rousing reception, well aware that they had witnessed a great team in action. Real Madrid left behind some great memories and a lot of goodwill, as the sum of £10,000 (a large figure in 1962) went to the charity. A crowd of some 72,000 had turned up for the occasion, matching the one that had gathered at the same venue only two days before when, thanks to goalkeeper Billy Ritchie saving a Pat Crerand penalty and a late goal by Willie Henderson, Rangers had picked up a 1–0 league victory.

The Celtic support, though, had been delighted with the performance of their own side on that Monday evening. The fans refused to leave until their heroes came back out for a lap of honour, a request the players were happy to accede to, even though by that time some were in bare feet and others in socks. This was probably the first such lap of honour in the club's history and was much appreciated by the team. Later in the evening, the supporters gathered again outside the post-match reception in the Central Hotel and chanted the names of the players involved in the game.

Celtic's team on that special evening was: Frank Haffey, Duncan MacKay, Jim Kennedy, Pat Crerand, Billy McNeill, Billy Price, Bobby Lennox (Steve Chalmers), Charlie Gallagher, John Hughes (Bobby Carroll), Mike Jackson and Frank Brogan (Alec Byrne).

Ferenc Puskás described Pat Crerand as a 'potentially world-class player' and Billy McNeill as 'easily the best centre-half for his age he'd ever played against'. Di Stefano singled out Crerand, McNeill and goalkeeper Haffey ('a personality, every team needs one') for praise but his comments underlined that this was a Celtic team still feeling its way to the top: 'Your team is very fast and make plenty of chances but they don't shoot enough!' It was a problem he could have helped to address had he chosen to join Celtic instead of Espanyol in August 1964 but it appears that the rain which had greeted the team's arrival in Glasgow that September in 1962 acted as a deterrent.

In the 1963–64 edition of the *Celtic FC Supporters Association Handbook*, the general secretary Hugh Delaney put the performance into perspective – 'Celtic were beaten but made many friends among the neutral onlookers by their spirited, polished second-half display. That our boys could put up such a magnificent show against such opposition makes me wonder why they should become mediocre performers in other important games during the season.'

Twenty-eight years later, in season 1979–80, Celtic were paired with Real Madrid in the quarter-final stages of the European Cup. The first leg took place on 5 March 1980 at Celtic Park, when goals by George McCluskey (52 mins) and Johnny Doyle (74) sent the crowd of 67,000 home in ecstatic mood. Unfortunately, two weeks later, in the Bernabéu Stadium in Madrid, Celtic crashed out to the superior skills of the Spaniards, Santillana making the overall score 2–1 just before the interval, with further goals by Stielike (56) and Juanito (83), sending Real Madrid through to the semi-finals on a 3–2 aggregate. A crowd of 110,000 watched the action and the Celtic team was: Peter Latchford, Alan Sneddon, Tom McAdam, Roddy MacDonald, Danny McGrain, Davie Provan, Roy Aitken, Johnny Doyle, Murdo MacLeod, George McCluskey and Bobby Lennox.

In 1995, on 28 February, Celtic again played Real Madrid, this time at Estadio La Rosaleda at Malaga in a friendly. Under new manager Tommy Burns, Celtic were having a difficult time in the league (P26, W6, D16, L4) and the general consensus of reports of this match suggested they also struggled against Real Madrid in front of a crowd of 40,000, losing 0–2, the goals coming from Alfonso (18) and Butragueno (pen. 24). The Celtic side that day was: Pat Bonner (Gordon Marshall), Tom Boyd, Tosh McKinlay (Stuart Gray), Brian O'Neil, Tony Mowbray, Peter Grant, Charlie Nicholas (John Collins), Paul McStay, Pierre van Hooijdonk, Andy Walker (Willie Falconer), Phil O'Donnell (Brian McLaughlin).

And a similar scoreline resulted when the sides met on Lincoln Financial Field in Philadelphia on 11 August 2012, as part of the Herbalife World Football Challenge 2012, when goals by Callejon (21) and Benzema (67) gave Real Madrid victory. The Celtic starting 11 was: Lucasz Zaluska, Adam Matthews, Kelvin Wilson, Thomas Rogne, Emilio Izaguirre, Dylan McGeouch, Beram Kayal, Joe Ledley, Charlie Mulgrew, Kris Commons and Darryl Murphy.

Probably, though, the most memorable meeting of these teams was in another friendly, this time in Celtic's special year of 1967. On the afternoon of 25 May, shortly after the Celtic players and management had boarded the bus due to carry the Celtic travelling party from the Hotel Palacio in Estoril to the Estádio Nacional for the European Cup final, we noticed the figure of Alfredo Di Stefano standing just inside the doorway. Rumours abound in football and the players had heard about his forthcoming testimonial and the possibility that we would be the opposition. This now seemed to give us a further clue but more definite news was published in the press the following day, in both Scotland and Spain.

In Glasgow, in the *Evening Times*, under the heading 'Now for Real', Gair Henderson wrote: 'Real were so keen to play Celtic that they sent Di Stefano all the way from Madrid to Estoril yesterday to plead with Celtic to accept the invitation. Before the Scottish Champions, now the European Champions, went out to beat Inter Milan, they had accepted the invitation.'

In in Madrid, *El Alcazar* stated:

OLE! OLE! OLE!

In Lisbon yesterday a contract was signed for Glasgow Celtic, the new European champions (also winners of the Scottish League and Cup) to play Real Madrid in the testimonial match for Alfredo Di Stefano on 7 June in the Bernabéu Stadium. The signatories were Antonio Calderon, General Secretary, on behalf of Real Madrid, and Mr Stein, manager, on behalf of Celtic.

From what we learned later, it would appear that this agreement was signed during the pre-final hours when the players were taking an afternoon nap, although I must stress that we were not officially told of the details till later. (See below.)

The Celtic travelling party returned from Lisbon on Friday evening, 26 May, and was met at the airport by John Lawrence, the Chairman of Rangers, whose own club would play in the final of the Cup-Winners' Cup the following week. There had been no inkling of this gesture beforehand and it was much appreciated by the Celtic hierarchy and management; unfortunately, in the way such matters are regarded in Glasgow, the welcome did not please every Rangers fan. Frankly, we were staggered to see so many people lining the streets from the airport to the ground. Some have suggested that the highlight of the trip was passing Ibrox while holding up the European Cup. However, this is pure fiction, as the route recommended by the police took us through the Clyde Tunnel and along the north side of the Clyde. Once we reached Celtic Park, our eyes opened even wider. There were thousands waiting outside the ground and then, when we walked down the tunnel and on to the specially prepared vehicle for our journey round the pitch, we were astonished to find that the ground was packed with fans, all keen to see the European Cup and the boys who brought it back from Lisbon. From that point, the celebrations just went on . . . and on . . . and on . . .

By the following Monday, though, we were back at Celtic Park, where the Boss started proceedings by doing a little analysis of the final, merely pointing out things that we could have done better or incidents that might have been better handled. Needless to say, the penalty decision against me that resulted in Mazzola scoring Inter's goal did receive some coverage! He then informed us that we would be travelling again soon, heading for Madrid to play in a testimonial for Alfredo Di Stefano.

In the light of the outcome, you might think that everyone would have been delighted. That was far from the case. A few thought it was ridiculous to put our newly acquired status of European Champions to the test against obviously talented Spanish title winners. Others considered that the win in Lisbon was – and should remain so – the perfect way to end a memorable season; while the reluctant fliers, and there were a few, did not fancy the idea of further plane journeys.

There were some mutterings but the Boss was adamant. We were going, so, to keep our fitness up, we went out to do some light runs before taking part in an eight-a-side game on the grassy area behind the goal at the east of the ground. Now, I do not know if it applies to all sports but certainly those employed to prepare and maintain football pitches are very protective of their surfaces and only allow the most limited of intrusions upon such an area. An incident occurred that very morning that tended to validate that hypothesis.

At one point during the eight-a-side game, the ball ricocheted off somebody's shins and ran onto the pitch proper towards the eighteen-yard line. Willie Wallace had just run on to pick it up when he heard a roar from the direction of the main stand: 'Get aff that park!' Wispy looked up to see head groundsman Hughie Docherty standing at the foot of the tunnel and gesticulating towards him. He yelled back: 'Gie us peace. It's the end of the season and we've just won the European Cup.' But Hughie was not to be denied and got the final riposte in: 'Ah don't care what time o' year it is or what you've won . . . just get aff ma bloody pitch!'

Eight days later, we were in the warmth of Madrid, doing another light warm-up, this time on the pitch at the Bernabéu. Even in those days, it was an impressive stadium, the all-embracing stands very sheer in their appearance. I felt that the guy in the top row could have dropped something on my head without leaning over too far. In the *Celtic View* published on the day of the game, Jock Stein stated that the purpose in playing the match was two-fold:

'To help to pay tribute to one of the world's greatest footballers of modern time, Di Stefano, and to gain further experience of the very highest class of football.' He added that it was only right that 'the vast body of our supporters, the great majority of whom were unable to travel to Lisbon and would not be in Madrid, should be the first to welcome the European Cup-winning team in an actual match (i.e. in August) and so, at least one change would be made from the Lisbon line-up'. Stein also revealed that Celtic had had to turn down a host of invitations to play other famous European clubs within the following few weeks, including requests to play against Barcelona in the Nou Camp on 17 June and against Ajax in Amsterdam on 20 June.

In the end, Jock Stein made two changes to the Lisbon line-up, replacing Ronnie Simpson with John Fallon in goal and bringing in Willie O'Neill for Stevie Chalmers. The rejigging meant Celtic lining up as follows: Fallon, Craig, Gemmell, Clark, McNeill, O'Neill, Johnstone, Murdoch, Wallace, Auld, Lennox. The Real Madrid side was: Junquera, Calpe, De Felipe, Sanchis, Pirri (Pachin 78), Zoco, Serena, Amancio, Di Stefano (Grosso 15), Velazquez, Gento.

The hard edge of professionalism that Jock Stein had displayed prior to taking the field in Lisbon two weeks earlier was in evidence again in Madrid. Determined to protect Celtic's prestige – which was always paramount for him – he rejected out of hand Real's proposal that, in order that the Spanish giants could wear their iconic all-white strip, Celtic should use blue shorts (part of Real's alternative strip at the time) in order to facilitate the black-and-white TV coverage. (The match was shown live in Spain.) Quite apart from the unthinkable prospect of the visitors taking to the field garbed even partly in the colours of their greatest domestic rivals, Jock Stein was set on demonstrating that Celtic would not be pushed round, even by the mightiest of European clubs.

An estimated crowd of some 120,000 turned up on that Wednesday evening of 7 June to pay tribute to Di Stefano – and presumably also to see their idols put these upstarts from Scotland to the sword. Di Stefano, who was nearly 41 at the time and had recently become the coach of Spanish side Elche, was made captain of Real for the night in an event that was not only for his financial benefit but also designed to set the final seal on his reconciliation with the club from which he had departed three years earlier in high dudgeon as a result of Santiago Bernabéu's refusal to grant him a new contract. It was a beautiful evening after an afternoon of thunderstorms that had turned the streets into rivers. On the stroke of 9 p.m. local time, the teams came out onto the field, led out by Di Stefano to a fantastic ovation from the huge crowd. As both teams lined up on the pitch, Di Stefano headed for the VIP box to meet the dozens of personalities who had turned out to honour him. When he returned to the pitch, the great Alfredo stood on the centre spot and accepted another incredible bout of applause from those present. Then the noisy acclaim was repeated when the Celtic players lined up to give their own salute to the Argentinian-born star. While these glamorous proceedings were taking place, back in Glasgow – somewhat poignantly and ironically – the junior team from which Bertie Auld had joined Celtic, Maryhill Harp, was playing out the final moments of its existence in a Central League match against Greenock, the club from the north-west area of the city having become the victim of Glasgow Corporation's compulsory purchase of their ground for the building of flats.

Eventually, the referee managed to clear the pitch of the horde of photographers, Di Stefano won the toss and Celtic got ready to face some of the all-time greats of football. Real Madrid were wearing royal-blue shorts. From the outset, the home side strived with all their craft and determination to mark the occasion for the great man, with Amancio in particular in dazzling form.

Di Stefano played for only a short time, making what was essentially a token appearance. In the 15th minute, as the ball came to him he bent down and picked it up; I was so wrapped up in the contest, I nearly claimed for a foul! He held the ball high in the air as the photographers raced onto the field to take the appropriate shots, then made his way off the pitch. All through these emotional moments, the huge crowd was waving white handkerchiefs in appreciation of what he had done for the club. After going up the tunnel, Di Stefano eventually appeared in the directors' box, from where he watched the rest of the match.

The whole of the Celtic team played well that night. I was particularly pleased with my own performance against Gento, reckoned to be among the world's best left-wingers. Di Stefano, though, would have been really impressed by two Celtic stars in particular. The agility and acrobatics of John Fallon repeatedly defied the Real attack, while Jimmy Johnstone mesmerised the Real defence, his performance constantly bringing the crowd to its feet to applaud his artistry. The 'Special Correspondent' of the *Evening Times* (Glasgow) used an appropriate metaphor when he noted how, after Di Stefano exited the stage, the spotlight switched to Johnstone, whose tremendous display of right-wing play had the crowd roaring its appreciation:

> With all the skill and confidence of a top toreador facing a brave bull, Johnstone faced the tough, and often rough, treatment meted out by the baffled Real Madrid defence. Time and again the wee Celt went down in a flurry of legs, arms and outraged indignation after receiving the full treatment from Real players. Never for a single second did Johnstone show any sign of retaliation in the face of such treatment.

In its report of the match, *Real Madrid*, the club's official magazine, despite claiming that the home side did not deserve to lose, described it a 'splendid night of football between true champion sides', while in his *Scottish Daily Mail* account of 8 June 1967 Alec Young described it as 'a dazzling exhibition by Celtic which was only marred by the sending off of Auld and Amancio after a 61st-minute clash'. The incident, however, did not diminish a spectacle during which, as Alec Young noted, 'Celtic moved the ball around with a breathtaking precision which astonished the Real fans, who have been for so long accustomed to football of the highest standard . . . Celtic's stamina was amazing after such a long, hard season.' The Real players, he added, were 'almost on their knees' before the final whistle, while 'the Parkhead men were still going hard and fast at the finish'.

Celtic's drive and determination had proved to be crucial factors in the victory, as indeed had been the case throughout the season. Bobby Lennox netted the only goal of the match, scoring in the 70th minute with a low drive after a pass from Jimmy Johnstone. That goal, said the aforementioned *Evening Times* correspondent, 'ended the scoring, but not the delightful football of Celtic, who treated Real Madrid's attempts to equalise with almost contempt, the hallmark of the true champions which Celtic showed they are'. Lennox's finishing power had chalked up Celtic's 201st goal of the 1966–67 season, which had begun with a 4–1 victory over Manchester United in a friendly at Celtic Park on 6 August 1966:

	P	W	D	L	F	A
European Cup	9	7	1	1	18	5
League	34	26	6	2	111	33
League Cup	10	10	–	–	35	7
Scottish Cup	6	5	1	–	20	3
Glasgow Cup	3	3	–	–	12	0
Friendlies/ Challenge Matches	3	2	–	1	5	2

The Spanish sports newspaper *Marca* seemed to be in no doubt as to the quality of Celtic's performance in the Bernabéu: 'Celtic have reinvented football. It was a beautiful night of football. We thank Celtic and are grateful to Real Madrid for being worthy of the occasion. The Scots played stronger and better and deserved their victory. May the football which Celtic play stay among us. Amen.'

I think I can speak for all the Celtic players when I say that we all felt ten feet tall that night. It was our first outing as Champions of Europe, we were facing one of the world's most famous sides – one that had asked us to play them! – in a marvellous stadium. Who could fail to rise to the challenge? And we needed to! Real were excellent on the night but I felt we always had the edge, matching them not only in ability but surpassing them in pace and power.

My own opponent had been the great Gento, by that time well into his thirties but still capable of a dazzling turn of speed. I met him again at the City Chambers in Glasgow just before the 2002 Champions League final at Hampden and, speaking through an interpreter, he remembered the match well, in particular the performance of 'John . . . stone!' Like Gento, when I recall the events of that trip, I also remember the name of Johnstone, but for a different reason.

Jimmy's wife Agnes had come over for the match, as they were going on holiday the next day. On the morning after the game, as I was making my way along a corridor of the hotel to the lifts, a door opened and Jimmy came out, staggering under the weight of a couple of cases. I picked up one of them and accompanied Jimmy and Agnes down in the lift, then over to the front door, where Jimmy asked the concierge to get him a taxi. When the cab came, he put the cases in the boot, made sure Agnes was comfortable in the back then turned to me.

'Thanks a million, Cairney. See you at pre-season training!' He then got into the back beside Agnes and said to the driver, 'Benidorm.' The resultant look on the driver's face is one I will never forget. Madrid to Benidorm is around 230 miles . . . but, for Jimmy, anything was better than flying!

* * *

The symbolism of that particular match is often overlooked. Real Madrid, under Santiago Bernabéu, had been the dominant force in the European Cup during its first decade, making the trophy virtually their private property (apart from winning six finals, including the first five, they had twice been finalists). Other clubs from southern Europe – Benfica, Inter Milan and AC Milan – had intruded on Real's supremacy. However, in May 1967, Celtic, from northern Europe, became the first club from that part of the world to win the prestigious trophy. Then, in that match in Madrid, against the first holders of the Cup, they showed why they had become champions, their play – just like their display in Lisbon – inspiring every other aspirant club in northern Europe to follow suit. In any event, apart from the triumph of AC Milan in 1969, teams from that part of the Continent won every European Cup competition for the following 17 years!

In its coverage of the European Cup final, the Lisbon-based sports daily *Mundo Desportivo* revealed that both Alfredo Di Stefano and Ferenc Puskás had been present in the stadium that afternoon and both had agreed that Celtic were worthy winners. Furthermore, Di Stefano was of the opinion that Inter had been awarded a 'non-existent' penalty! Now, what have I been telling you for all these years?

CHAPTER 17

'These Yins Ur No Mugs!'*

New phrases that came to our attention in 1970: 'black hole', defined as 'in space, an exhausted and collapsed star that sucks in life and matter'; 'jet lag', defined as 'tiredness and general malaise resulting from switching time zones during long-haul flights'.

Readers can make up their own mind as to whether one team in that year's European Cup final suffered a 'black hole' moment or was affected by a 'general malaise', but a shattering blow for Scottish football was balanced by the Stewarts restoring a measure of Scottish sporting prestige two months later with gold medals in the 5,000 metres (Ian) and 10,000 metres (Lachie) at the Commonwealth Games at Edinburgh's Meadowbank Stadium.

* * *

It was one of the most disappointing days in both my career (Jim Craig) and the history of Celtic Football Club. The date was 6 May 1970, the venue the Stadio San Siro in the western part of Milan; the occasion was the European Cup final; the result Celtic 1 Feyenoord 2 after extra time.

The outcome was something of a surprise, or perhaps shock, to most Celtic fans, who had expected that their side, victors by a 3–1 aggregate over the competition favourites Leeds United in the

---

* This chapter title is taken from the overheard reaction of a Glaswegian in the San Siro when Celtic's European Cup final opponents showed early signs of causing an upset.

semi-finals, would win their second European Cup in the space of four years. On mainland Europe, though, the final score raised fewer eyebrows, as there was a recognition that Dutch football was on the way up and that their teams were to be respected.

Indeed, Celtic's opponents on the night were not inexperienced at this level. In season 1962–63, Feyenoord had reached the penultimate stage of the same competition before going down to Benfica 1–3; AC Milan defeated Dundee 5–2 in the other two-legged semi-final. And certainly, over the 120 minutes of that evening in Milan in 1970, they rose to the challenge very effectively.

The events of the match itself can be summed up fairly briefly. In front of a crowd of 53,187, Celtic were upstaged by the Dutch side, which seemed to be much more at ease on such a big occasion, their midfield in particular making life in that area very difficult for their immediate opponents.

Tommy Gemmell gave Celtic the lead in thirty minutes from a free kick; midfielder Israel made it 1–1 two minutes later; and that was still the score at the end of normal time. Feyenoord again looked the more promising side during extra time and eventually striker Ove Kindvall got the winner four minutes from the end.

As you can imagine, the atmosphere in the Celtic camp afterwards was dreadful. There was little talking among the players; the management – obviously disappointed by the performance – kept themselves at a distance from the 'culprits'; while the directors, normally happy to be associated with success, were nowhere to be seen at a time of failure.

As the bus left the stadium for the return trip to our base in Varese, those fans still milling around outside, normally so boisterous, had been stunned into silence, with only a few voicing their disapproval. Back in the hotel, the post-match meal was devoured in almost funereal silence, the players wolfing the food down before retiring to the relative anonymity of their rooms.

To say that the players were disappointed was an understatement. In all the years since that eventful evening in Milan, during the 'what if?' or the 'do you recall?' conversations that take place between teammates of successful sides, the events surrounding that particular match are seldom mentioned. After all, who would want to talk about a defeat when there were so many successful occasions to remember?

So, as I (Jim Craig) attempt to answer some of the questions that were raised after the loss to Feyenoord, let me stress that these are entirely my own views on the situation.

Was the preparation right?

Celtic had lost to Aberdeen in the Scottish Cup final on 11 April 1970. Four days later came the return leg of the European Cup semi-final against Leeds at Hampden, a 2–1 win putting the Hoops into the final on a 3–1 aggregate. And on 18 April, the club played the final match of the domestic season, a league encounter against St Mirren at Love Street, which the Buddies lost 3–2.

As the final in Milan was not until 6 May, that meant that eighteen days – or just short of three weeks – would pass before the players would once again be in action in a competitive game. Granted, a couple of 'friendlies' were arranged but unfortunately after one of these, in Fraserburgh, some incidents occurred that caused friction between the manager and the players.

Only a few players were involved in the indiscretions, but for some reason the manager sent trainer Neilly Mochan round the rooms to wake everyone else up and bring them all to a meeting – held at around 1.30 a.m. – where we were told that some players had been discovered in the company of some young ladies. The Boss, Jock Stein, imparted this information to us and then went on a rant about the importance of the game coming up, etc.

Unfortunately, he did not get the reaction he anticipated. Instead of sitting quietly – like the guilty ones! – other players, myself for one, expressed annoyance that we had been woken up and brought along to this gathering to be told something that had nothing to do with us. The manager was not happy with our attitude; the innocents were raging that we had been woken up; the guilty ones were delighted that their supposed misdeeds were not receiving as much attention as they had expected. All in all, it was not a night that did much for team spirit or morale.

CELTIC: PRIDE AND PASSION

Was the choice of training camp the right one?

We were stationed at Varese, some 30 miles or so away from Milan, in a hotel situated at the top of a hill, reached by a series of hairpin bends. The club had stayed there in February 1969, when we had been drawn against AC Milan in a European Cup quarter-final but the venue had proved unpopular with the players, being very isolated. 'Even monks would find this hard going' was a comment I remember from one of the younger guys in the squad and there was more than an element of truth in the words.

Certainly, it was private and there was some space for light training but it was completely detached from the atmosphere building up in Milan and the players missed this. Even more annoyingly, the Boss decided not to travel up to the stadium for a training session before the 1970 final. This was a trip much looked forward to by most players, who appreciated a session on the pitch and also liked to take in the atmosphere being created by the fans gathering for the game.

So, it might have been a very relaxed atmosphere around the hotel – too much so, some reporters suggested – but it was also fairly boring, not what players were used to.

Was the team over-confident?

I think there was a definite feeling in the camp that the defeat of Leeds United in the semi-final had removed the chief obstacle to Celtic becoming European Champions again. This had been reinforced by the sporting press. Before the semi-final – naturally built up as a 'Battle of Britain' encounter – the Scottish reporters had been united in their belief that Celtic would go through. There had also been enormous interest from the English press in the two matches, with nearly all of them anticipating a Leeds win. After the clash, though, they switched their thoughts to a Scottish victory. Few gave the Dutch champions much of a chance. Players and managers always say they don't read the papers. Yes, they do; and their views are often influenced by what they read. This might have been one occasion when that occurred.

Was there an under-estimation of Feyenoord's quality?

Yes. At that time of football's evolution, players simply did not have the opportunity to see matches on TV involving possible opponents like they can today. We had to rely on the words of those who had been sent to see our rivals. Jock Stein had travelled to Holland to witness Feyenoord draw 3–3 with Ajax and was keen to stress to us that they had played well. At the same time, I can clearly recall an impression being given that Feyenoord, while a competent side, were not as good as some of the others we had already faced. Jock Stein's description of Wim van Hanegem, the much-capped and respected playmaker, as a 'slow version of Jim Baxter' suggests a certain degree of complacency at the time!

Was the team too concerned with making money?

Certainly, there was a feeling among the troops that we should try to take advantage of any of the proposed marketing deals that were slowly creeping into the game then. Most of the squad remembered the paltry 30-odd pounds that we received for wearing Adidas boots in Lisbon, a deal struck only on the day of the match – and our only such arrangement. So, if there was any extra money to be made in such fashion before Milan, then I, for one, was all for it. However, having said all that, I do not think for one minute that thoughts of such deals had any effect on our pre-match preparations. By 1970, most of the squad had more big-game European experience than any other group of Celtic players before or since and were very good at compartmentalising. The deals had their place in our everyday lives, but the main aim of that group of Celtic players was to win the European Cup for the second time in four years!

Why did Celtic play so poorly on the night?

The difference in approach before the match was perhaps illuminating. While the Celtic players were in and out of the dressing-room, having a look at the pitch and the stands or chatting to some pals gathered near the front door, Feyenoord manager Ernst Happel kept his players in the changing-room, presumably trying to keep them focused on the match and their performance.

There can be little doubt that Celtic were disappointing on the night. It was also true that Feyenoord were really up for the game and hustled Celtic all over the pitch. When a side does that, it can knock any quality side off its game. However, for whatever reason, it would also be true to say that individually – and collectively – the performance of most of the Hoops stars was below their normal standard.

The collective display was not helped by an injury (a chipped ankle bone) to Jim Brogan, one that obviously affected his game, a circumstance seemingly unnoticed by the manager. In his column in the *Evening Times* of 12 May 1970, the reporter Malcolm Munro declared:

> Before the European Cup final with Feyenoord, Jock Stein told me that the key man in his entire set-up was Jim Brogan. Brogan was to be the 'extra man'. When he was needed in defence, he was to fall back. But here's the surprise! When Celtic were on the attack, Brogan was to be their ace-in-the-hole. The surprise packet. The man least expected to burst through. The trouble was that Brogan was so keen to do the job that, when he burst through in virtually the first attack of the game, he was injured. And it says a lot for Brogan's gameness that although he was obviously in pain, though he was capable only of limping thereafter, he finished the game as full of fight as anyone else.

Now, while every member of the squad had respect for Jim Brogan's determination and drive in the cause of Celtic, we could also see – particularly those of us sitting on the bench – that he was struggling to run with any fluency. As the match progressed, the substitutes – Callaghan, Hood, Fallon, Connelly and myself – were talking about it quite openly on one of the benches, with the management on the adjoining bench seemingly oblivious to the problem.

Jock Stein could have got round the problem in a number of ways. He could have decided on a straight swap, George Connelly for Jim Brogan. Or he could have brought me on at right-back and moved Davie Hay into Brogie's role. In either case, it would have provided a fit player in a position where the incumbent was obviously struggling. Eventually, he did decide on a change, bringing on George Connelly for Bertie Auld in the 75th minute, leaving Brogie *in situ*, to try to last another 15 minutes of normal time – plus another possible 30 minutes of extra time – with an obvious injury.

The players on the field that evening were quite despondent afterwards but also very aware of the side's poor performance. In an interview with journalist Hugh McIlvanney printed in *The Observer* of 10 May 1970, three were particularly brutal in their assessment.

Bobby Murdoch: 'Where could you fault them? They were strong everywhere. They seemed to outnumber us whether they were attacking or defending and they were marvellous in the middle of the park.'

Billy McNeill: 'The score was a travesty. Two–one in extra-time makes it seem close but we know the real difference was about four goals. We weren't at the races. It was a whitewash!'

Bertie Auld: 'The only time I saw the ball was when I took a throw-in.'

Whatever the reasons, the loss to Feyenoord marked a watershed in the history of Celtic Football Club. From the 1966–67 season right up to the Leeds match, the club had been known and recognised not only for its successes but also the style, flair, pace and excitement with which those wins had been achieved. One European Cup triumph was all very well but, on that evening in Milan, there had been the opportunity for the name of Celtic to be bracketed alongside those of the truly great European teams – and multiple winners – like Real Madrid, AC Milan and Ajax. Unfortunately, the chance was lost.

* * *

Thursday, 7 May. On the much-delayed journey home to Glasgow, the undercurrent of disappointment among the support was again evident, both at Malpensa Airport in Milan and in Glasgow; while, on the plane itself, various journalists were vying for the players' attention, keen to hear their ideas on why it had all gone so wrong. It was quite stressful for all of us and, to be honest, it was a much-relieved squad of players who eventually reached the comfort and security of their own homes.

In Glasgow, the local paper, the *Evening Times*, had a major story to impart: 'The Celtic goalkeeper Ronnie Simpson has announced his retirement from the game due to a shoulder problem. Simpson, 39, was one of the co-commentators with the BBC for the European Cup final in Milan. On the Tuesday before the final, he was retained as the Conservative councillor for the Corstorphine Ward in the Municipal Elections in Edinburgh.'

Friday, 8 May. The players reported to Celtic Park for training, as the squad was due to head off to North America and Bermuda on tour two days later. There was little enthusiasm for the trip and I do not ever recall a quieter dressing-room. There was still an air of deep disappointment and more than a touch of envy directed towards Jimmy Johnstone and Jim Brogan when it was announced that both would miss out on the tour due to injury. And, as usual, in the press the inquests continued.

Sunday, 10 May. The touring party gathered at Celtic Park and tried on the new blazers specially made for the trip. Frankly, they did not fit too well. I ended up swapping with Tommy Callaghan and that helped a bit. Then, just to compound our lack of enthusiasm, the plane was delayed and we were four hours behind schedule when we arrived in Toronto, to be greeted by a crowd of around 200 fans.

Monday, 11 May. The first match of the tour, in the Varsity Stadium, where Manchester United proved stronger and fresher and won 2–0. An own goal by Billy McNeill in the 11th minute and one by John Aston ten minutes from time gave the Reds the Toronto Cup.

The crowd of 20,000 witnessed a good game, though, and I held my own against George Best for about 70 minutes, during which he was constantly asking me how I was feeling! I realised near the end what he meant, as my legs suddenly felt as if they did not belong to me and I was glad to hear the final whistle.

Tuesday, 12 May. A short, early morning flight took us to New York, where it was 85 degrees. Our hotel was the 43-storey New Yorker and we had a day round the city sight-seeing.

Wednesday, 13 May. At Randall's Island, we faced Bari, who played with seven men in defence at the best of times, ten back when we attacked! They opened the scoring through a doubtful penalty – no, not me! – but Harry Hood knocked in a fine goal to give us a draw. A bit of jersey-tugging, the occasional spit, a vociferous Italian section of the crowd, man, it's grand to be on tour!

Friday, 15 May. After some days in sweltering New York, it was back to Toronto, 50 degrees and raining! We did some training in preparation for our second match against Bari on Saturday, which was at the Canadian National Exhibition Stadium, a good wide pitch with fine grass.

Saturday, 16 May. Due to a thunderstorm, the match was postponed for 24 hours.

Sunday, 17 May. Two players sent off, some ridiculous decisions by Vancouver referee Reg Clark and the game eventually abandoned. Oh! And it was 2–2 at the time. There were fights all over the pitch, a penalty given in my favour was the trigger for the Italians to walk off the park . . . and Jock Stein left 15 minutes before the end to head home.

Monday, 18 May. We flew back to New York. The players were given little information as to why Jock Stein had returned home but the rumours certainly flew around. That he had gone back to deal with transfer requests by Jimmy Johnstone and Tommy Gemmell was one theory. That he was looking for another job south of the border was another. Or did his injured ankle really need some sudden – and urgent – treatment? Whatever the reason, his ears should have been burning back in his home, as the players were not impressed either by his walk-out or its timing!

Wednesday, 20 May. We were in action again. A quick flight up to Boston and a match against New England All-Stars. They were by no means a good side and the 7–1 win, with hat-tricks for Harry Hood and Vic Davidson, helped lift the mood of the camp. On the following morning, Hood's first goal was memorably described in the *Boston Globe*: 'Hal boomed a left-footed kick into the upper left corner of the cage.'

Back in Uddingston, when asked about reports of his being linked to Newcastle United, wee Jimmy declared, 'I'm not interested. I'm quite happy where I am' (*Evening Times*).

Thursday, 21 May. The management made the decision to give us a light workout and we reported in the foyer kitted out in shorts and T-shirts. We were divided into groups of four – each foursome with a ball – and packed into taxis with the instruction to meet in New York's Central Park. Once set down by the driver, my group of four passed the ball around for what seemed like ages while we waited for the others. Eventually, we called another taxi and headed back to the hotel, where other groups of four explained that they were also waiting for us! Seems like no one worked out just how big Central Park was! Still, I enjoyed the fresh air.

Back in Glasgow, it appeared wee Jimmy had changed his mind: 'If I don't get a new contract from the club, I won't play for them again.' But Jock Stein was not for budging: 'Johnstone has completed only two years of a twelve-year contract he signed with Celtic in 1968. The next move is up to the player.' (Both quotes from the local *Evening Times*.)

In the States, the players attended a supporters' function in the evening at Kearney, New Jersey, where the behavioural patterns of a few players gave cause for concern for one reason or another. The following day, Tommy Gemmell and Bertie Auld were sent home by Sean Fallon for 'misdemeanours'. Both players have since given their version of the events and I have no reason to doubt their sincerity. However, my own recollection was that the old Scottish maxim – 'when guid drink goes in, guid sense goes oot' – proved once again to be right on the button.

Friday, 22 May. According to the *Evening Times*, Brian Clough, the manager of Derby County, had been in touch with Jock Stein about Johnstone and Gemmell.

Meanwhile, the remaining members of the travelling party – boosted by the arrival of Davie Cattanach – played the final match of the North American segment of the tour. This was against Eintracht Frankfurt, again in New York, and ended with another defeat, this time by 3–1.

It was difficult to decide whether they were very good or we were really off-song. Perhaps a bit of both would be an easy way to explain our indifferent result. Frankly, most of the players were by this time thoroughly unsettled by the whole tour. The travelling between Toronto and New York, then up to Boston; the poor condition of the pitches; the lack of control by the referees; the sterility of Bari's play, in both games, added to their undoubted talent for fouling; the constant haggles over expenses, which most of us thought were insufficient for our daily needs; the shock of the Boss disappearing without warning and the concerns over his future with the club; the unsettling newspaper stories from back home, initially some extremely critical ones about the performance in the European Cup final and then some fanciful tales about the futures of Johnstone and Gemmell; all of these in some way contributed to our feeling of disillusionment.

Apart from the young ones like Kenny Dalglish, George Connelly, Vic Davidson and Lou Macari, everyone else felt like a condemned man as we took our seats in the plane at the airport in New York, heading for Bermuda and two further matches. Even the prospect of spending time on that tropical paradise did not seem enough to shake the gloom away from the players . . . but that beautiful island soon worked its magic!

Sunday, 24 May. In the brand-new National Stadium in Hamilton, the capital of Bermuda, on a pitch surface that could have been used for bowling, we gave an outstanding performance to thrash a Bermuda National side 7–1, the goals coming from Vic Davidson (3), Willie Wallace (2, including 1 pen.), Lou Macari and Harry Hood.

The local press were most impressed by our form and over the following few days there were editorials exhorting our next opponents, national champions Somerset, to rise to the challenge and beat this team from Scotland! We read the comments, of course, and did some light training to keep in shape. To be honest, though, the whole party was more caught up with sunbathing, sailing, golfing, sight-seeing or sampling the various delights of the wonderful Princess Hotel.

Sunday, 31 May. On that same superb pitch, Somerset had a real go but we rose to the challenge again, winning 4–1, Tommy Callaghan, Lou Macari, Bobby Lennox and a penalty from Kenny Dalglish doing the damage. It was an outstanding display and the local crowd, while desperate to see their own side do well, was completely won over by our play and cheered us off the pitch. A memorable end to what was mostly a disappointing tour.

Monday, 1 June, early morning. In the foyer of the Princess Hotel, at 6 a.m., the various members of the travelling party were sitting or standing round, waiting for the bus that would take us to the airport. We were all looking forward to seeing our loved ones again but the over-riding impression at that time of the morning was tiredness and there was little chat.

Suddenly, the relative quiet was shattered. 'You're kidding me,' a voice roared. 'Most of that has nothing to do with me!' When we looked across, we saw physio Bob Rooney, obviously angry, at the reception desk, shaking this piece of paper at the young lady behind the counter. And we all suddenly realised that we knew the reason for his anger. I had been rooming with Tommy Callaghan and Harry Hood and whenever we had ordered cheeseburgers and cokes, which we did not infrequently, we had been in the habit of signing the chit in the name of Bob Rooney, adding his room number as well. Unfortunately, we had not been alone; apparently, most of the squad had been doing the same, under the impression that the club officials with us would pick up the tab. This they refused to do, so, to prevent poor Bob being out of pocket, we had a whip-round in the foyer that morning to settle the bill, although not everyone paid up with good grace.

Monday, 1 June, evening. We had been away for nearly three weeks and everyone had bought a number of presents, etc. for the folks back home. Now the problem was to get them past customs without paying any duty and we came to a collective decision in the final few days of the tour. We would each carry just two bags, cramming our training gear and ordinary clothes in one and the presents in the other. Then, on our arrival in Britain at Heathrow Airport, we would keep together and all walk straight through the Green Channel. On that Monday evening, the procedure was put into operation and seemed to be going well. Suddenly, though, one of our number received a tap on the shoulder from one of the customs officers, followed by a request that he put his bags up on the counter. As he did so, the rest of us breathed a sigh of relief and headed through to where the bus was waiting to take us to the Glasgow flight.

Eventually, we were joined by our unfortunate teammate, who told us that he had had to pay a considerable fine before being allowed to join the rest of us. It was sheer bad luck but the player refused to accept it as such, moaning and complaining all the way to the plane. Eventually, we told him in no uncertain terms to give us peace and, to be fair to Billy McNeill, he soon resorted to his normal equanimity.

* * *

The European Cup final was a disaster for Celtic. Nothing could be more futile than to try to deny this. It was a disaster for the players, for the management and perhaps for the supporters, many of whom had made tremendous sacrifices to see the game . . . Surely never in recent years have so many Celtic players been off-form in such an important game . . .

This is not the end for Celtic. The heroes of Lisbon and of the tie against Leeds have not suddenly lost their skills. Nor has Mr Stein lost his great knowledge and shrewdness. . . San Siro, 1970, may yet be seen not as an irreversible tragedy but as the start of a road to new greatness.

Celtic View *editorial, May 1970*

CHAPTER 18

A Final Flourish

The Scottish supporters celebrated the final whistle by promenading *en masse* across the Wembley turf and perching on top of the crossbars, which quickly fractured under the pressure. Ally MacLeod had a swift opportunity to contemplate the force he had unleashed when he attempted to retreat to the sanctuary of the players' tunnel at full-time, only to be restrained by a security man who was disinclined to believe that MacLeod was the Scotland team manager. Only when the England team manager Don Revie intervened was MacLeod permitted to reach the visitors' dressing-room where he was astounded to discover four Scottish supporters sharing the bath with the goalkeeper, Alan Rough.

Roddy Forsyth on the aftermath of Scotland's 2–1 victory in June 1977, in his The Only Game, *1990. Forsyth described the recent appointment of the exuberant MacLeod in succession to Willie Ormond as reflecting 'the mood of a newly assertive and bombastic Scotland on the upward curve of one of its periodic revivals of nationalism'.*

The year 1977 was a remarkable one in British sport. In Wimbledon's centenary year, Virginia Wade won the ladies' singles title that July. No one from Britain has reached that final since then. In August, English cricketer Geoff Boycott notched up his 100th century, achieving it in a Test match against Australia at the Headingley ground, Leeds, in his native Yorkshire. The most heart-warming triumph, however, for the British public had come in April that year when the hugely popular racehorse Red Rum won the Grand

National for the third time, prompting the bizarre sight of the director of one betting firm bursting into the press room to announce that 'We've lost a quarter of a million and I don't care!'

* * *

As a statement of intent it could hardly have been blunter:

> Celtic jerseys are not for second-bests. It's the jersey that was worn by men like McNeill, Gemmell, Clark, Auld, Wallace, McBride and Chalmers. And it's not going to shrink to fit the inferior player. If it isn't filled to our satisfaction it will go to someone else. We're reaching out for Lisbon standards and we're not going to settle for something less . . . All down the years Celtic's success has been based not only on skill but also on attitude. Players didn't just play for Celtic – they wanted more than anything else to play for Celtic. It's absolutely vital that the same spirit still permeates our dressing room. It may be that we have to recruit from outside the club. But nothing will be done in a hurry. It's important that we get the right man and that takes time . . . One thing the fans can be sure of – there will be no passengers. Nobody will be taken along for the ride.
>
> Celtic View, *summer 1976 edition*

Jock Stein was back in business after his year-long absence spent in recovering from a horrendous car crash the previous summer, and his exasperation at Celtic's recent slide into mediocrity was a measure of his determination to wrest back Scottish football supremacy from a Rangers side that had won the 'treble' in season 1975–76 when, as he acknowledged (in rather odd wording), his deputy Sean Fallon had experienced, during what was essentially a holding operation, 'a lot of the wrong kind of luck'. That sympathy did not prevent the latter's badly handled replacement as Stein's assistant by the former Partick Thistle manager Davie McParland, whose main responsibility was viewed as the supervision of training sessions formerly conducted by a manager still feeling his way physically as part of the process of re-evaluating his life after the trauma of a brush with mortality had brought about a change that was obvious to the likes of the Lisbon Lion Jim Craig. A more subdued and cerebral Stein was firmly in charge of team affairs, though, and, now that he was back in harness, he soon showed that he was true to his word in the matter of recruitment and that his unrivalled appetite for football had not been diminished. He set about a rebuilding job necessitated by the loss in recent seasons of so many experienced – and, in some cases, exceptional – players, a seepage that had started in January 1973 when the lively forward Lou Macari, once a member of a group of promising young Celtic reserve-team players known as the 'Quality Street Gang' who had been given a terrific grounding in professional football under the tutelage of Stein, his backroom staff and the 'Lions', left for Manchester United. In July 1974, another member of the 'Gang', the tigerish midfielder David Hay, was transferred to Chelsea, the second exit in an exodus of what Billy McNeill described in an interview with Kevin McCarra in *Champions* magazine (August/September 2005) as the raw material that might have produced another European Cup-winning side at Parkhead:

> They were terrific and they were coming into an ideal situation. When they were introduced to the first team there were good players around them. They were protected and they didn't feel as if they had something to prove to themselves. If players like Lou Macari and David Hay had been paid as they should have been, then there would have been the basis for mastery in Europe for many years. The truth is that Celtic were often a selling club.

That parsimony was perhaps symptomatic of a directorate that was ill-equipped to build on the club's new-found status post-1967, in the years that followed a European Cup triumph that one suspects caught the board completely by surprise, as the forthright football journalist Gerry McNee has suggested: 'When Celtic were on the cusp of greatness, in spite of dinosaurs like their then chairman Bob Kelly and thanks only to the genius of Jock Stein, they lacked the calibre of directors with vision and imagination who could have consolidated the club's position in Europe' (*The Herald*, 16 September

2003). In May 1975, McNeill himself, the most successful captain in the club's history, retired, and within weeks both the inimitable Jimmy Johnstone and the sturdy defender Jim Brogan had departed for pastures new. In the autumn of 1976, another 'Gang' member, the supremely gifted George Connelly, dubbed the 'Scottish Beckenbauer', would walk out on the club for the third and last time, his contract torn up at the age of 27 after he finally gave up his struggle to come to terms with the pressures of professional football at a time when he should have been enjoying his peak years in the sport. And now only the evergreen Bobby Lennox remained of the Lisbon Lions side that had given the name of Celtic a worldwide dimension. It seemed a daunting task for a manager who in that same article in the club newspaper had expressed his concern that 'the lions' roar has become muted'. But the shrewd Stein had identified the immediate pressing need as being that of 'getting the backbone right', with a focus on adding ballast to a leaky central defence and on acquiring a spearhead up front who would not only score goals but also give more thrust through the middle and take the weight off a player on whom he thought the team had become over-dependent, namely the multitalented Kenny Dalglish, equally adept in midfield or up front and a captain around whom the manager was intent on building the new Celtic. Destined to become the most notable graduate of the 'Quality Street Gang', the fresh-faced youngster, whom Jim Craig remembers as one of a trio of famous future players to whom he gave lifts to training in his car (Danny McGrain and Graeme Souness were the others) in the late 1960s, had 'developed' an unmissable early self-confidence to the extent of becoming by the mid-1970s one of the most effective operators on a football field, a player with, in Craig's opinion, an uncanny knack of shielding the ball from opposing players and an unrivalled ability to bring teammates into the game with his laying off of the ball. He also, Craig recalls, had an eye for an opening, a verdict shared by Billy McNeill shortly before his retiral: 'Kenny is absolutely brilliant. I have played so long with him that even his most glorious goals from crazy angles no longer mystify me.'

If Dalglish was the vital cog in Stein's plans to resurrect Celtic, the man he chose to add stability and experience to the heart of the Celtic defence was the versatile Pat Stanton (equally at home in defence and in midfield), who was approaching his 32nd birthday when he came from Hibernian in early September 1976 in a player swap with Jackie McNamara, a defender-cum-midfielder whose skills Stein acknowledged while categorising him as 'a slow developer'. Out of favour at Easter Road, where he had been playing reserve-team football, Stanton was relieved to escape his fractious relationship with an abrasive manager in Eddie Turnbull, whose tactical acumen the player admired but about whose man-management he harboured distinct reservations. Stein had remembered his days as manager of the Edinburgh club in the mid-1960s when he noted Stanton's capacity to 'tidy up' behind the big, rugged ex-Celtic defender John McNamee, and he clearly envisaged Stanton's skill and strength as being ideally suited to performing a similar anchoring role in tandem with Roddy MacDonald, Billy McNeill's successor. Two weeks after completing this deal, Stein paid £60,000 for the transfer of Joe Craig from Partick Thistle, in the expectation that the 23 year old would prove to be as prolific a goal-scorer as John 'Dixie' Deans had been prior to leaving Parkhead three months earlier, in addition to hoping that Craig's movement off the ball would create space for his former Firhill teammate Ronnie Glavin to 'drive through' from midfield to provide an extra attacking threat.

A first-round UEFA Cup exit at the hands of Wisła Kraków would prove to be a blessing in disguise by clearing the decks for an assault on the domestic prizes, although the prospect of the club's first 'treble' since season 1968–69 evaporated in early November 1976 with a League Cup final extra-time defeat (1–2) by Aberdeen. A significant factor in that reverse was the absence of both Stanton and Craig, who had been cup-tied with their previous clubs and who had already been proving their worth in a title challenge that had got off to an uncertain start before gaining momentum in the autumn, but which now seemed to be given an extra spur by the disappointment of that setback at the hands of the men from the north-east. Celtic quickly shook off any lingering hangover by embarking on a thirteen-match unbeaten league run (twelve wins, one draw) that laid the foundations of their success that season. Their championship mettle was evident two weeks later when they came from two goals behind on the half-hour to overcome Heart of Midlothian 4–3 in thrilling fashion at Tynecastle Park, thanks to a dazzling equaliser engineered by Scotland colleagues Danny McGrain (already regarded by many judges as Europe's most complete full-back) and scorer Kenny Dalglish and a late 'blistering' winner by Ronnie Glavin. Celtic followed that up with an equally dramatic, and morale-boosting, victory at Ibrox Park four days later, when Joe Craig swivelled to curl a 20-yarder past Kennedy to give Celtic their first victory over the Light Blues since January 1974. Another 1–0 victory over their greatest rivals in mid-January 1977, on a Celtic Park pitch only made playable by using bales of straw as protection against the frost, propelled Celtic to the top of the table, a position from which they would not be dislodged for the remainder of the title race. Dundee United's pursuit of the men in green and white foundered at Celtic Park on 26 March 1977, due in no small measure to the erratic behaviour of their goalkeeper Hamish McAlpine, whose 25th-minute penalty-kick attempt was smothered by his Celtic counterpart Roy Baines when the match was goalless. Celtic edged in front just before the interval through Joe Craig, then five minutes after the resumption Ronnie Glavin sealed the points (2–0) when he blasted a penalty low and hard past McAlpine after the latter had upended Johnny Doyle. Doug Baillie, writing in the *Sunday Post*, stated that 'The Scottish League offices can order the engraving for the championship medals as soon as they like.' With Celtic now five points ahead of Dundee United, eight of Rangers and nine of Aberdeen – all of them having played at least one game more than the leaders – it was hard to argue with that declaration, particularly since Jock Stein had reinforced his squad at the beginning of that month by means of his shock 'cloak-and-dagger' acquisition of ex-Ranger Alfie Conn from Tottenham Hotspur for a modest £65,000. It was a coup that had a touch of mischief and one-upmanship about it, enabling Celtic to snatch the moral high ground at a time when Rangers were attracting criticism for their notorious signing policy

– 'Ability is the main ingredient we look for in players,' commented Stein on the controversial signing – but there was also no doubting the sincerity of the manager's claim that, in Conn, a forward-cum-midfielder, Celtic were introducing a player of the type the Parkhead crowd had not seen since the heyday of Jimmy Johnstone, one of those performers 'with a bit of flash about them, who would encourage people to come and watch them even if the team was having an ordinary time'. How appropriate, then, that it should be the combination work of two of Stein's astute signings that would deliver the title-clinching goal in mid-April 1977, only three days after a stumble at Motherwell had caused a few tremors in a Celtic support alarmed by a wastefulness in front of goal reflected in the passing up of half a dozen clear-cut scoring opportunities, a deficiency that enabled the Fir Parkers to run up a 3–0 victory made all the more notable for two bizarre, late own goals by full-back Andy Lynch. Jock Stein would admit at the end of the season that he had been concerned that tension was getting the better of his players during the title run-in, but relief was at hand for both him and the unfortunate Lynch when Celtic travelled to meet Hibernian at Easter Road on 16 April 1977.

Hibernian: McDonald; Brownlie, Brazil, Stewart, Schaedler; Bremner, Edwards, Smith; McLeod, Duncan and Scott.

Celtic: Latchford; McGrain, Stanton, MacDonald, Lynch; Glavin (Burns), Dalglish, Aitken; Conn, Craig and Doyle.

Referee: W. Anderson (East Kilbride).

Attendance: 22,306.

Hibernian, playing down their notorious 'slope', were deemed to have had slightly the better of a first half characterised by the visitors' tension-ridden display on a bone-hard pitch, the conditions being aggravated by a swirling wind. Celtic had set off at a brisk pace, but once Hibernian began to settle they showed their menace when it took a fine Latchford save to keep out Smith's close-in header. The match took on the aspect of a cup tie as half-time loomed, its end-to-end nature evidenced by McDonald's brilliant save from Conn's powerful left-foot volley in the 32nd minute being matched a few minutes later by Lynch having to clear a Duncan shot off the line with Latchford beaten. The pattern continued after the interval, with the Glasgow side's frustration becoming all too clear when their strong penalty claim after Brownlie brought down the young midfielder Roy Aitken was rejected by the referee on the grounds of 'diving' and Hibernian scampered up the pitch immediately afterwards to force two corners that kept the pressure on a conspicuously nervy Celtic. Hibernian, said Alan Davidson in his telephone-dictated report from the press box to Glasgow's *Evening Times*, were 'certainly not here to join in on any champagne party'. The breakthrough arrived halfway through the second half (the 63rd minute, to be precise), just when it looked as if Celtic would not secure the result that would put the destination of the flag beyond any doubt. It came about when a Ronnie Glavin run ended with a shot that struck the near post before rebounding fortuitously in the direction of Alfie Conn, who took the ball in his stride near the far bye-line before whipping it across goal to Joe Craig for the striker to ram the ball into the net from close range and ring up his 22nd goal in 36 appearances to date in a Celtic jersey. It was a piece of finishing that prompted what Allan Herron of the *Sunday Mail* described as 'an incredible explosion of green and white scarves, flags and caps all around the stadium'. (One observer estimated that a 20,000-strong Celtic support was present.) A more relaxed Celtic were now intent on playing out time in pragmatic fashion, taking no chances by 'killing the game stone dead' at 1–0 with 'more passes back than forward'. The final whistle set off an eruption of pent-up joy that was not dampened by Hibernian chairman Tom Hart's petty ban on the presence of both the television cameras and the Celtic Cine Club to cover the match and the celebrations afterwards for highlights purposes. Allan Herron was impressed particularly by Celtic captain Kenny

Dalglish's insistence on grouping his colleagues together and leading them towards the massed Celtic support, who gave their heroes a tremendous ovation 'under their patchwork umbrella of green and white scarves'. In a spontaneous testament to the team spirit that had brought about the triumph, the players refused to pose for photographs until the watching popular Bobby Lennox, who had featured comparatively briefly that season, joined in the festivities.

One down – and one to go. Having clinched the title with four matches to spare, Celtic could now look forward to the prospect of rounding off what many had envisaged as a transitional season by annexing the League and Scottish Cup 'double'. Celtic's road to the final had been unspectacular and at times unimpressive, taking in, surprisingly, replays against both lower-division Airdrieonians and Ayr United, who barely escaped relegation from the top division, but they were installed as favourites to win the final on 7 May 1977 against a Rangers side that had ended up nine points behind Celtic in a championship during which they had failed to beat the Parkhead club in their four fixtures (Celtic won 1–0 home and away, the other two ending in 2–2 draws). It was the first Scottish Cup final to be televised live in twenty years, as part of a four-season sponsorship deal negotiated by the SFA with Scottish and Newcastle Breweries.

Celtic: Latchford; McGrain, Lynch; Stanton, MacDonald, Aitken; Dalglish, Edvaldsson, Craig, Wilson, Conn.

Rangers: Kennedy; Jardine, Greig; Forsyth, Jackson, Watson (Robertson); McLean, Hamilton, Parlane, MacDonald, Johnstone.

Referee: R. Valentine, Dundee.

Attendance: 54,252.

The SFA had printed 85,000 tickets for sale, but the attendance was 30,000 down on the previous year's contest between Rangers and Heart of Midlothian, and 15,000 down on that for the Celtic v. Aberdeen League Cup final held at the same venue seven months earlier. The live TV transmission on BBC Scotland, STV, Grampian, Border, Ulster and Tyne Tees (north-east England), all areas from which the Old Firm drew support, obviously had an adverse effect, but on the day the weather also acted as a deterrent. A rain-swept Hampden Park presented a dismal vista to both the spectators present and to the TV viewers, an appropriate backdrop to the rather dreary spectacle that would unfold, despite the initial promise reflected in Jim Blair's report for that evening's 'Pink' edition of the local *Evening Times:* 'The football was entertaining, the pace furious, and incidents non-stop.' Celtic had an early penalty claim rejected after Dalglish's close-in volley appeared to be handled on the goal line by Watson, Edvaldsson displayed his alertness in hustling Johnstone into shooting wide when the Ranger moved in to take advantage of the opportunity presented by a Hamilton cross slithering from Latchford's grasp. A goal was in the offing, and it was Celtic who struck the vital blow in the 20th minute after a Conn free kick was punched out by Kennedy, but only in the direction of Andy Lynch, whose adroit header looked netbound until Kennedy managed to scramble it to safety, but not without injuring himself in colliding with a post as he conceded a corner kick. That kick, taken by Alfie Conn after a two-minute delay to allow the keeper treatment, was met by Roddy MacDonald, whose header back across goal was only parried by Kennedy under pressure from the inrushing Jóhannes Edvaldsson, whose attempt to force the ball over the line was blocked by Derek Johnstone. Whether it was by a hand, or whether he drew back his hands and the ball hit his knee, was not cleared up to everybody's satisfaction by TV replays, but the referee was sufficiently convinced that an infringement had taken place as to award a penalty kick to Celtic. Bob Valentine, who was refereeing not only his first Scottish Cup final but also his first 'Old Firm' encounter, and an official who had hardly endeared himself to Rangers and their fans by sending off captain John Greig at Aberdeen the previous Saturday for an 'off the ball' offence, brushed aside the Ibrox club's heated protests before blowing his whistle for Andy Lynch to take the penalty kick. The full-back, who had missed his only two previous penalty kicks (when with Hearts) and yet had volunteered to take this one, stepped up to blast the ball past Kennedy, in the process earning some lucky punter(s) a small fortune. He had been listed at odds of 40–1 at Ladbrokes to score the first goal of the final. Thereafter, Celtic bedded down their strategy for the final, a plan dictated by the absence of their powerhouse in midfield, Ronnie Glavin, who had not recovered in time from a thigh injury sustained in Scotland's friendly against Sweden ten days earlier. Jock Stein tried to play down the loss of a player who had contributed 26 goals in his 52 appearances that season ('It upset us a bit,' he said drily) as he reshaped his formation in a manner that meant, essentially, forsaking the midfield in favour of defence in depth and hitting Rangers on the break. Edvaldsson and MacDonald formed a 'double centre-half' bottleneck, with Pat Stanton detailed to cover or 'sweep' the whole defensive line, and the mercurial Paul Wilson had been restored to the team with a view to his running power stretching the defence of a side against which he had an impressive goal-scoring record, most notably two goals in their first clash of the season and two in the 1975 Glasgow Cup final. Rangers, it should be noted, also opted for caution by assigning Alex MacDonald to block Danny McGrain's surges down the right, at the expense – it must be said – of the former's goal-scoring threat. The effectiveness of Stein's tactics can be judged by the failure of Rangers' main threat up front, Johnstone and Parlane (the two Dereks), to shake off their limpet-like respective markers, Edvaldsson and MacDonald, the latter being described by Jim Blair as 'the tall Highlander' who was 'literally head and shoulders above everyone else throughout'. It helped that Rangers' approach was rather one-dimensional as they huffed and puffed in their vain attempt to secure an equaliser, their limitations ascribed dismissively and rather uncharitably by one observer to an obsession with 'long balls up the middle and into the box'. Their frustration was evident midway through the first half when Tommy McLean was yellow-carded for a 'back tackle' on Stanton, the first of four bookings (two Rangers and two Celtic) in a match that took on an increasingly attritional aspect, in other words, the niggly, uncompromising affair that has been the 'Old Firm' contest down the years – the 'beautiful game' it rarely is (if, indeed, it ever has been). Celtic, who looked the sharper side throughout, contrived to fashion more of the few clear-cut chances that became available and should have killed the match as a contest halfway through the second half when Joe Craig was clean through on goal but shot wide. He could, though, consider himself unlucky a minute later after McGrain latched on to a superb pass by Conn and drove a low cross into the goalmouth that was missed by the inrushing Wilson but collected at the far post by Craig, whose shot was partially saved by Kennedy before Jackson booted the ball clear. Celtic's failure to capitalise on the edge they had over Rangers almost proved costly after the Light Blues made a 70th-minute substitution, with striker Chris Robertson replacing midfielder Kenny Watson. The former's 86th-minute header ('of stunning power') cannoned back off the crossbar with Latchford beaten.

The final whistle, signalling a 1–0 victory, came as a considerable relief to Celtic, allowing two players in particular to savour personal triumphs. Alfie Conn had not only joined his father (Alfie senior) in becoming the holder of a Scottish Cup winners' medal, but he had also become the first player to acquire winners' medals in the competition with both Celtic and Rangers (the latter in 1973, against Celtic!). Pat Stanton had acquired both League Championship and Scottish Cup winners' medals for the first (and only) time, enabling him to put behind the memory of his agony five years earlier when, as a Hibernian player, he had been desperate for time-up as the Edinburgh side crumbled in the second half to a humiliating 1–6 defeat by Celtic. 'When I got home,' he had recalled before the 1977 final, 'I didn't dare leave the house for several days, I was too embarrassed.' As for Jock Stein, this 'Drawing board victory', as the *Glasgow Herald* match report billed it, was further vindication of his remodelling of Celtic in the face of sceptics who thought that the car crash had irreparably, or at least significantly, damaged his managerial powers. He had achieved his sixth League and Scottish Cup 'double' in an 11-year stint in charge of the club (the 1975–76 'recovery' season excluded), but as usual he refused to indulge in extravagant manifestations of emotionalism after such triumphs, contenting himself with the inner joy. He was both philosophical and laconic about it all as he emerged from his Celtic Park office the following day to conduct his regular Sunday press conference, rationalising the victory by pointing towards the trophy room and saying: 'We are all convinced it was a penalty. Andy Lynch scored and the prize is in there.' It was the brisk reaction to questions of a man who was all too aware that the life of a football manager revolves around coping with an unending series of challenges, and there was one hovering in the background that he must have known, deep down, was turning into a losing battle. Six weeks earlier, Kenny Dalglish had been the guest of honour at the Celtic FC Supporters Association annual rally, the programme for which was replete with football writers' superlatives in praise of the fans' hero: 'World class player . . . a talent that ranks with the best . . . tremendous vision . . . a pearl of a player . . . probably the most complete footballer in Britain today'. Celtic supporters would have readily agreed with the conviction of one of the contributors to the brochure, Jim Reynolds of the *Glasgow Herald*, when he stated that the best was yet to come of the player 'as he prepares to lead Celtic into the new era', thus making 'you Celtic fans, indeed, a privileged band of followers'. However, that was a prospect that would be denied to them, for Dalglish, as he states in his 1996 autobiography, had already come to the conclusion that 'By 1977 I had outgrown Celtic', adding that 'I had captained Celtic, won everything in Scotland, but nothing in Europe' and that 'it was time to move on to a club capable of giving me the European success I craved'. During the previous two years, he had made those in charge of Celtic aware of his desire to leave the club and its Canute-like stance in dealing with the situation was no match for the single-mindedness and determination of an individual who, as an apprentice joiner close to the end of a first year at the club during which he had been farmed out as a provisional signing and part-timer to Cumbernauld United for 'toughening up', insisted (successfully) on becoming a full-time professional despite Jock Stein's belief that Dalglish would benefit from another season with the junior side. Few senior players, never mind a seventeen-year-old rookie, would have relished standing their ground so firmly against the formidable personality that was Stein, and now nine years later the manager was set to lose out again to the player's resolution. Matters came to a head in the summer of 1977 when Dalglish refused to go on Celtic's tour of the Far East and Australia. His by now inevitable departure, to Liverpool that August for a £440,000 fee that turned into a thief's bargain for the Merseyside club, still came as a thunderbolt to Celtic supporters, for all that they had been prepared for the worst by ominous press speculation. Only three months earlier, in *The Observer* of 1 May 1977, Patrick Glenn had noted the sense of optimism and excitement being generated by Celtic's success that season: 'Stein's rebuilt Celtic will contest another European Champions' Cup next season and this is rumoured to be his last assault on the Continent before handing over to Davie McParland, his heir-apparent. But Europe is a drug to the big man and if Celtic have any kind of run next time he is likely to get the urge again.' But even Jock Stein, once described by one of his peers, Bill Shankly, as 'the greatest manager of them all', could not fashion miracles after the loss of Dalglish, coupled with early season injuries to Pat Stanton (career-ending) and Danny McGrain (year-long), contributed heavily to a train wreck of a season that shattered Stein's hopes of turning Celtic Park once again into a theatre of dreams on European nights and brought down the curtain in May 1978 on his distinguished reign at the club. Hugh McIlvanney, his long-time friend and admirer, had written what now reads eerily like an epilogue or epitaph for that period when he wrote the following in *The Observer* of 24 April 1977: 'For more than a decade he has led Celtic with a skill and theatrical flourish that no other manager in world football can equal. Remarkable success at home and in Europe is only part of the basis of the loyalty given to him by the Celtic support. His personal style is equally significant. Jock Stein is utterly unique, irreplaceable.' Indeed he was, but without the irreplaceable player the gap between ambition and achievement proved simply impossible to bridge. Season 1976–77 had been the twilight's last gleaming for the great man of Celtic Park.

CHAPTER 19

A Breaking of Hearts

1986 was the year that Professor Robert Grieve, himself brought up in a Glasgow tenement in the 1960s, condemned housing conditions in the city, describing them as 'a disgrace to humanity'. No less than 40,000 homes needed urgent repairs, with leaking roofs and dampness 'making life a misery for tens of thousands of families'.

Elsewhere in the world:

January 1986: The US space shuttle 'Challenger' exploded in mid-air above Cape Canaveral only 90 seconds after take-off, killing the crew of seven, including Christa McAuliffe, a mother of two chosen for the mission from over 10,000 applicants.

June 1986: Diego Maradona's 'Hand of God' brought Argentina their opening goal in their 2–1 World Cup quarter-final victory over England in Mexico City. Initially, it seemed as if he had netted with a header, but TV replays soon showed that the Tunisian referee, Ali Ben Nasser, had been deceived and that the goal had been scored illegally.

September 1986: Prince Charles, heir to the British throne, admits on television that he 'talks to plants'.

* * *

The impact that Jock Stein had on Celtic could not be over-emphasised. After all, before his arrival in the spring of 1965, Celtic had not won a single major trophy since the 7–1 League Cup final win over Rangers in October 1957. To put it another way, of the 21 domestic trophies up for grabs in the interim, Celtic had won none of them!

During the 13 years of Stein's tenure at Celtic Park, success was a largely constant feature for the fans to enjoy, although there were some disappointments. However, his overall record is an excellent one and he truly does deserve to be included in the top rank of football managers:

	League	Scottish Cup	League Cup	European Cup	Cup-Winners' Cup	Inter-Cities Fairs Cup/UEFA Cup
*1964–65	8th	Celtic	F	–	–	2nd Round
1965–66	Celtic	F	Celtic	–	SF	–
1966–67	Celtic	Celtic	Celtic	Celtic	–	–
1967–68	Celtic	1st Round	Celtic	1st Round	–	–
1968–69	Celtic	Celtic	Celtic	QF	–	–
1969–70	Celtic	F	Celtic	F	–	–
1970–71	Celtic	Celtic	F	QF	–	–
1971–72	Celtic	Celtic	F	SF	–	–
1972–73	Celtic	F	F	2nd Round	–	–
1973–74	Celtic	Celtic	F	SF	–	–
1974–75	3rd	Celtic	Celtic	1st Round	–	–
**1975–76	2nd	3rd Round	F	–	QF	–
1976–77	Celtic	Celtic	F		–	1st Round
1977–78	5th	4th Round	F	2nd Round		

* Stein took up the managerial reins at Celtic Park in early March 1965, when the Scottish Cup was the only trophy that could be won. ** Jock Stein was out of action during season 1975–76 after his car crash. His assistant, Sean Fallon, took charge in his absence.

With a record like that, the task of the successor to Jock Stein was never going to be an easy one. The spotlight fell on Billy McNeill, who was rightly apprehensive at taking on such a prestigious post with limited experience in management but 'Cesar' (nick-named for sartorial reasons after the actor Cesar Romero rather than the Emperor Julius Caesar) proved to have been an inspired choice by the board of directors and his record over the next few years was impressive:

	League	Scottish Cup	League Cup	European Cup	Cup-Winners' Cup	Inter-Cities Fairs Cup/UEFA Cup
1978–79	Celtic	QF	SF	FTQ for European competition	FTQ for European competition	FTQ for European competition
1979–80	2nd	Celtic	QF	QF	–	–
1980–81	Celtic	SF	SF	–	2nd Round	–
1981–82	Celtic	4th Round	FTQ from section	1st Round	–	–
1982–83	2nd	SF	Celtic	2nd Round		

Billy McNeill left for Manchester City in the summer of 1983 and, in a selfish way, I (Jim Craig) was pleased about that. I had not found his tenure an easy one to cope with. After all, this was a guy with whom I had played during some wonderful Celtic years. I was good friends with him, his wife Liz and their five children and have always had enormous respect not only for Billy's abilities but also for his almost unbelievable approachability and friendliness to the club's fans. However, during those five years when he was manager of Celtic for the first time, I was broadcasting for Radio Clyde and sometimes had to ask pertinent post-match questions. Even the best sides have poor days and fans want to know why such-and-such happened, so the probing questions must occasionally be asked. I did not enjoy doing so to an ex-teammate and friend, particularly as I could tell from his face that the blood pressure was still up in the rafters, even though the match had long finished.

Billy's departure rather shocked the Celtic support but those of us at closer quarters could see that he was unhappy. As he has mentioned in several interviews since, his relationship with chairman Desmond White was 'iffy' to say the least, the obvious generation gap compounded by conflicting views on that perennial Celtic problem of the period – money! In any case, while extremely disappointed that he was leaving a club for whom he had been an excellent player and manager, Billy was looking forward to a new challenge and possibly a better relationship with his new chairman.

The Celtic board's next choice was something of a surprise . . . and another ex-teammate. Davie Hay took over the reins at the start of season 1983–84 but, unlike his predecessor, he did not win a single trophy during his first season:

	League	Scottish Cup	League Cup	UEFA Cup
1983–84	2nd	F	F	3rd Round

The following season's campaign was more promising, with a trophy in the cabinet, although Davie's rather laid-back attitude did receive some criticism. Those of us who played with him were not surprised by his reserved approach to the job. Even as a player, Davie was calmness personified, although that did not prevent his becoming a very tough, aggressive and talented performer. And to be honest, while fans seem to be impressed by managers who leap and dance on the touchlines, the vast majority of players just ignore such antics, knowing they do little to help the team.

The Scottish Cup final against Dundee United, on 18 May 1985, was a memorable day for the Celtic fans in the crowd of 60,346. They suffered the agony of seeing their team go one down in 54 minutes, felt a sense of relief in 76 minutes when a wonderful curving free kick by Davie Provan gave them the equaliser and then experienced ecstasy six minutes from time when Frank McGarvey headed home the winner. It was the 100th Scottish Cup final and Celtic's 27th victory in the competition.

	League	Scottish Cup	League Cup	Cup-Winners' Cup
1984–85	2nd	Celtic	QF	2nd Round

Davie's third season in charge got off to a poor start, when Celtic went out on penalties to Hibs in the quarter-finals of the League Cup. That disappointment was compounded by the loss in the first round of the European Cup-Winners' Cup to Atletico Madrid. Then, in early March 1986, came another defeat at the hands of Hibs, this time in the Scottish Cup at Easter Road. At that time, too, the league position was also looking less than promising, with the latter's great rivals Hearts on top and going well, although Celtic did have some games in hand:

	P	W	D	L	F	A	Pts	Pos.
Hearts	28	14	9	5	44	28	37	1st
Celtic	26	12	8	6	41	31	32	4th

However, the Celtic players really rose to the challenge over the next nine matches, winning seven and drawing two, so that, as the sides went into the final day of the season, Celtic had pulled to within two points of Hearts (two points for a victory):

	P	W	D	L	F	A	Pts	Pos.
Hearts	35	20	10	5	59	31	50	1st
Celtic	35	19	10	6	62	38	48	2nd

For the final matches of the campaign, on 3 May 1986, Hearts travelled to Dens Park and Celtic to Love Street. Much to my disgust, I was sent by Radio Clyde to Dundee to report on the league leaders' match and I journeyed through by car in a foul mood. Like many others, I could see no logical reason for Hearts to drop any points against the men from Dens Park. At that point, Dundee were in mid-table, 17 points behind the leaders, having let in a massive 51 goals in 35 games. So, it looked as though I would have to watch my dad's *bete noire* from Gorgie Road – as a man from Leith, he had always been a Hibs fan – pick up the title for the first time since 1959–60. Celtic could only snatch the title on goal difference if, in football parlance, they 'did the business' by obtaining a three-goal margin of victory while Hearts went down to defeat. In a sense – with the pressure being on Hearts – the Parkhead men had nothing to lose, a potentially crucial factor in deciding the outcome.

Dens Park was packed for the occasion, the official figure given as 19,567, with maroon scarves very much in evidence everywhere. During the hour before the kick-off, I was on air several times to describe the scene and I also listened with some envy as the commentary team at Love Street – not surprisingly, Radio Clyde, a West of Scotland station, had chosen St Mirren v. Celtic as their main game that day – told us of the great atmosphere down in Paisley, swathes of green covering the ground.

Once the match started at Dens Park, though, my mind was on the action there and I very quickly realised that Hearts were struggling. A rumour had gone round the press box before the match that some form of sickness bug had rampaged through Tynecastle during the week – a virus confirmed as fact after the match by manager Alex MacDonald and which had ruled out central defender Craig Levein (a hero of Hearts' run of 27 matches undefeated) – but, whatever the reason, the fluid movements that had characterised Hearts' play during the season were just not there. The players looked slightly cumbersome, passes were going astray and they were making little headway against a determined Dundee side delighted to be at the centre of attention after such a disappointing season.

I was quick to report back to the studio that Hearts were not performing well and went on air several times in the first half. Meanwhile, news was coming through almost constantly that Celtic were putting St Mirren to the sword. Brian McClair got the first in six minutes, heading home from an Owen Archdeacon corner; Mo Johnston made it two in the thirty-second minute after good work by Paul McStay and Brian McClair; Johnston rounded off a superb 'box-to-box' bout of interpassing to make it three a minute later, then McStay drove home the fourth seven minutes before half-time. Inevitably, the crowds at both venues had access to transistor radios and there was a real buzz about Dens Park, the Hearts fans desperate to get the one goal that would make all the difference. But by half-time it had not arrived . . . and Celtic were four up!

The Hearts players had obviously received a rocket from Alex MacDonald at the interval, as they started the second half at full throttle. Dundee responded well, though, and a real battle ensued. Then, a further blow to Hearts morale; the news that Celtic were five up, Brian McClair getting his second of the game in the fifty-third minute. The maroon section of the crowd, still shouting their favourites on, was now in a bit of a quandary, with a dilemma no doubt also affecting the management team in the dugout. Should they will their boys to go all out for a win or should they merely settle for the scoreless draw that would give Hearts the title?

On 83 minutes, though, Albert Kidd solved the problem for them. A Connor corner, a downwards header by Brown and Kidd lashed it home, although goalkeeper Smith got a touch. The Hearts fans were stunned, to say the least, and a silence descended on most parts of the ground, only those occupied by Dundee fans showing any emotion. Over at Love Street, the transistor radios were on and, when news of Kidd's goal came through, the information went round the Celtic support, who responded with glee, waving, shouting, gesticulating and cheering.

Back at Dens Park, Alex MacDonald raced out to the touchline to pass instructions on to his side but, frankly, the players were stunned and tired, in no state to make a comeback. Two minutes later, Albert Kidd struck again, this time playing a one-two with Harvey before shooting home. And that was it; the Dundee players just kept possession up till the final whistle.

When the referee blew for time-up at Love Street, the Celtic players and management hugged each other and waved to their supporters, who were in a mood for celebration, with large numbers of them invading the pitch to 'mob' their heroes. By contrast, as the whistle went in Dundee, the Hearts players sank to the ground in despair as the Dundee side tried to give them some comfort.

For the final ten minutes or so, our producer had been switching back and forward between the two matches and for all concerned it was an exciting few moments. What I saw afterwards at Dens Park, though, was quite unbelievable. Somebody was crying in the directors' box; all over the stands and the terracing, Hearts fans – male and female – were sobbing into hankies and holding on to each other for support. From my position in the front row of the press box, I could hear them crying uncontrollably as they made their way out of the ground. It was truly astonishing.

From the Celtic point of view, it had been an amazing comeback after months of the bookies offering pretty long odds on their chances of winning the title. The players, though, had stuck to their task, seen it through to the end and fully deserved the praise that was being heaped on them. It was Celtic's 34th league title and a first for manager Davie Hay – and won by the proverbial skin of their teeth, a superior (+3) goal difference.

Football is a wonderful game, played and enjoyed throughout the world. Those who play in teams enjoy the camaraderie; the supporters of professional clubs can live out their own dreams by following their heroes. Occasionally, though, the tension and pressure surrounding a big match can lead to a few fans dropping their normal standards of courtesy. Unfortunately, I was a victim of that type of poor behaviour that afternoon at Dens Park. As I made my way back to my car, parked in the Radio Tay car park, just a few minutes away from Dundee's ground, I came across quite a number of Hearts fans outside the stadium, still stunned by their side's defeat and its failure to pick up the title. As I appeared occasionally on

TV at that time, my face was a well-kent one, my background as a Celt even better known. Much to my disappointment – and disgust – I received a considerable amount of verbal abuse as I walked along, even being blamed for the defeat by one rather angry woman. 'It's all your fault' was her cry, a comment I found quite laughable as I had retired from football in 1974!

* * *

POSTSCRIPT

In his autobiography, *From the Heart*, brought out in the summer of 2012, former Hearts striker Sandy Clark claimed that referee Bill Crombie refused to award him a 'stonewall' penalty at Dens Park and that the St Mirren players had an 'unprofessional' attitude in the match at Love Street. As you might imagine, this caused quite a stushie and several ex-players involved were quick to reply. Former Dundee and Rangers defender John Brown was at centre-back for Dundee that afternoon and his reaction was scathing: 'If Sandy wants to point the finger at anyone then maybe he should have a look at himself, as he dived . . . it was a blatant attempt to win a penalty.'

Ex-Buddies star Tony Fitzpatrick was equally dismissive: 'There's no way any player I played beside at St Mirren gave anything other than 100 per cent for the jersey . . . What Sandy is saying is a disgrace and he should look at his own team's performance that day . . . they only had to avoid defeat and it was all over, but they didn't . . . they bottled it!'

And ex-Celt Frank McGarvey, who played in the colours of the Paisley side that memorable afternoon, was as blunt as ever:

Maybe Sandy should look at his own performance that day . . . Celtic were a much better team than St Mirren and there was no surprise that they beat us . . . when the Old Firm have had to score goals to win league titles, they have scored goals . . . it was all in Hearts' hands that day . . . the question that should be asked is, did their players bottle it? I think football fans know the answer.

CHAPTER 20

The Playboy of the Eastern World*

In August 1989, Manchester United fans waiting for the start of their opening league match against Arsenal were astonished by the sudden appearance on the Old Trafford pitch of 'a rather overweight, mustachioed 37 year old with a bouffant hairdo' who was wearing United training kit. He saluted the crowd, then proceeded to do a bit of ball juggling before dribbling the ball towards the Stretford End (the section of the stadium associated with the club's most passionate fans) and shooting the ball into the empty net. It was a stunning piece of self-publicity on the part of Michael Knighton, a hitherto obscure businessman based in the Isle of Man whose £20 million takeover bid for the club came to naught at a time when English football was unfashionable, its clubs still serving a ban from European competition as its game struggled to recover from the tragedies of Heysel and Hillsborough and the ravages of hooliganism. Within three years, with the advent of a Premier League underwritten by Sky TV, there began an astonishing transformation in its fortunes, leading to Manchester United being valued by the mid-1990s at £460 million and in 2011 at between £1.5 billion and £2 billion.

* * *

---

* The chapter title is taken from a tag given to Jacki Dziekanowski of Celtic by an unidentified Scottish journalist, being a parody of the title of a play by the Dublin-born J.M. Synge, namely *The Playboy of the Western World*. Jacki, it was rumoured, was a regular frequenter of Glasgow nightspots.

The 1980s – a memorable decade for slang. Among the terms introduced to the English language were the following: 'airhead' (a dim-witted person), 'couch potato' (a TV addict), 'yuppie' (a 'young upwardly mobile professional') and – also appropriate for what became known as 'the decade of aspiration' – 'wannabe' (someone desperate for fame, wanting to imitate someone in the public gaze, e.g. a pop star such as Madonna).

* * *

'It was the morning after the night before.' The opening sentence of a novel or a fairytale? No, it was a journalist articulating the prevailing mood at a football club as a prelude to describing the rather pitiful sight of 'a sad, solitary figure' making his way across the litter-filled car park at Celtic Park with a look on his face of someone who was suffering from a hangover and had suffered a restless night in the wake of ejection from European competition. For that wretched-looking individual and his teammates, 1989 was turning into the antithesis of the old Sinatra song 'It Was a Very Good Year'. The memories of a Scottish Cup final victory over Rangers a few months earlier at a sunlit Hampden Park were fading rapidly. It was a development that would have come as no surprise to one of that player's colleagues, namely Tommy Burns, who only two months earlier had granted an interview to Kevin McCarra of *Scotland on Sunday* that was prophetic in terms of his fears about the impact on his beloved club of a Rangers revival spurred by major financial investment and driven by the fierce ambition of manager Graeme Souness, who had embarked on the recruitment of buying established players of international standard:

> The potential at Ibrox is frightening. There is a chance that they could just run away with the championship for years ahead. Football is unpredictable and we will certainly compete, but you have to recognise the standard of player they are buying . . . It's bound to bring down your failure rate. They are signing people for one and a half million while Celtic have to operate in the £600,000 range. That's just a fact of life. Celtic will always be a different sort of club,

but I wouldn't want to see them hiding behind the family image. They have to find a way of competing for the best.

Scotland on Sunday, 30 July 1989

Burns, a footballer raised within the proverbial stone's throw of Celtic Park – 'You don't play for Celtic, you live for Celtic,' he once said – was obviously still reeling from the damage inflicted to the club's credibility only three weeks earlier by a stunning Rangers' coup, that of snatching the former Celtic striker Maurice 'Mo' Johnston from the Parkhead club to which he had been set (seemingly) to return from Nantes after being paraded in the green-and-white hoops at a press conference at the stadium two months earlier. Bill McMurdo, Johnston's agent and a figure whose role in the affair is still a matter of suspicion and controversy, would later accuse the Celtic board of the time of incompetence and of having 'tried to save face by blaming me for it all . . . none of them understood the workings of Freedom of Contract, they had previously [in 1987] let Maurice, Brian McClair, Alan McInally and Murdo MacLeod go out of contract at the same time, which tells you something'. A 'prodigal son' transfer was essentially hijacked by Rangers manager Graeme Souness, who, on the 20th anniversary of the most sensational transaction in British football history, admitted to *The Herald* that he had been as much intent on delivering a 'devastating psychological blow' on Celtic as on ending the Ibrox club's long-standing sectarian recruitment policy: 'There was an element of mischief. I believed we were hurting Celtic by signing him. It wasn't just signing a Catholic, it was signing a Catholic who had played for Celtic. It was a double whammy.'

Celtic's attempt to counter the resurgence of their greatest rivals resulted that summer in the signing of four players. In mid-June, a fee of £500,000 was agreed with Heart of Midlothian for the services of the tall and aggressive Shropshire-born midfielder Mike Galloway, who would be joined at Parkhead a few weeks later for £600,000 from Pisa by a London-born central defender, Paul Elliott, and, surprisingly, in mid-August from Aberdeen for £250,000 by John Hewitt, whose greatest claim to fame had been as the striker who came off the bench to score the winning goal in extra time for 'The Dons' in their 1983 European Cup-Winners' Cup final against Real Madrid, but whose best days were now considered to be behind him (as proved to be the case, with no goals in 21 appearances for Celtic). The most immediate impact, however, was to be made by a tall, 26-year-old powerfully built Polish international striker with 'Hollywood film-star looks' and a 'playboy' reputation that was to dog his Parkhead career, namely Dariusz Dziekanowski, whose signing from Legia Warsaw for £600,000 only four days after the resolution of the Johnston saga hinted at Celtic's desperation to shore up the ebbing faith of their fans. 'Jacki', as he was understandably dubbed by Celtic supporters baffled by the pronunciation of his name, became an instant hit with those same fans, who left Celtic Park drooling after their first sight of the new acquisition, particularly his spectacular 81st-minute conversion of Alex Mathie's cross with 'an exquisite bicycle kick', which not only made the final score 2–2 in a pre-season friendly with Dynamo Moscow, but also prompted the unfurling of a Polish flag on the terracing. Amid all the excitement few supporters were inclined to listen to the note of caution (and, perhaps, scepticism) introduced after the final whistle by Celtic's assistant manager Tommy Craig: 'Dziekanowski showed what he has in flashes, but he'll have to come to terms with the fact that the game is more frantic in Scotland. If he can adjust, the quality will come out.' Just as pertinent, perhaps, for the more perceptive fans had been the alarming sight of Celtic, a team just six weeks away from their European Cup-Winners' Cup tie against Partizan Belgrade, struggling to cope with the fluency of another Eastern European side, with the movement of the Russians on and off the ball leaving the home side looking leaden-footed far too often for comfort. Nevertheless, at the start of the season, the Celtic manager, Billy McNeill, pronounced himself satisfied with the playing resources at his disposal: 'I feel we now have a first-class squad of players who will make their presence felt in the coming months.' And he had ample reason to look forward with confidence to the challenge from the Balkans, for Celtic had yet to lose a European tie against a Yugoslav club, having disposed of Dinamo Zagreb in the same competition in season 1963–64 and both Vojvodina (1966–67) and Red Star Belgrade (1968–69) in the European Cup. Partizan Belgrade also appeared to be a club in turmoil, languishing as it did in second-bottom place in their domestic championship, largely as a result of the haemorrhaging of players that summer, with seven members of the team having departed (or being in the process of departure). The coach, Momcilo Vukotic, may genuinely have been venting his exasperation, and not merely indulging entirely in the tiresomely predictable mind games that normally precede European ties, when he threatened to resign during that summer, claiming that 'This club has no ambition', for he would only have been reflecting the reality of the dire economic situation that had prevailed in the native game for several decades and which had been responsible for an endless procession of their talented players to the more lucrative pastures of Western Europe. After all, had not the club lost virtually a whole team, eight players to be exact, after losing the 1966 European Cup final to Real Madrid, in the process becoming the most notable part of an exodus of no fewer than one hundred players from Yugoslavia in the following twelve months? Players from that country had long been highly prized by richer foreign clubs for a technical skill and strength to which ex-Celt Bobby Murdoch, a veteran of Celtic's three previous jousts with Balkan opponents, attested in a preview of the first leg of the tie in September 1989: 'Hard, hard teams. I was sick of the sight of them. There's no end to the supply of players in that country.' Indeed, there used to be a saying in Yugoslavia that when the stork delivered a male baby to a household it also brought a football.

Nor could Celtic draw comfort from the fact that the first leg of the tie would not take place on Partizan's own ground, the Serbian club having been ordered to play it 300 kilometres from Belgrade as a result of fireworks sparking a fire in a stand of their Stadion JNA, and a visiting player being struck with a missile while taking a corner kick, during their previous season's UEFA Cup tie with AS Roma. When the draw had taken place in mid-July, the clubs seemed to have come to an initial agreement (though more reluctantly on Partizan's part, apparently) for the first leg to be played in Skopje, in the south-east of Yugoslavia, but in early August it was announced by UEFA that it would be held in the south-west, in the city of Mostar, famous for the sixteenth-century bridge (Stari Most) that straddled the River Neretva. Celtic manager Billy McNeill suspected that Partizan had secured the venue that really favoured them, one located in a part of the country noted for exceptional heat at that time of the year. As it happened, the humid weather in Mostar on 12 September 1989 broke shortly before kick off in the Stadion Gradski, resulting in torrential rain almost flooding the uncovered terracings and the pitch to such an extent that McNeill said afterwards that at one stage he thought the match might be called off.

First leg:

Partizan Belgrade: Omerovic (Pandurovic), Zupic, Milanic, Spasic, Petric, Vujacic, Dordevic, Milojevic, Durdevic, Durovski, Bogdanovic (Pantic).

Celtic: Bonner, Morris, Rogan, Aitken, Whyte, Grant, Galloway, P. McStay, Dziekanowski (Walker), Burns and Coyne.

Referee: H. Kohl (Austria).

Attendance: 15,000.

The thousand or so Celtic fans present, many of them wearing T-shirts emblazoned with a caricature of their new hero 'Jacki' Dziekanowski, looked on anxiously as the Serbian side set about their favourites from the off, literally so at times with some scything tackles (Zupic 'nearly cut playmaker Tommy Burns in half') that were overlooked by an indulgent referee whose failure to crack down early upon the approach of Partizan – albeit four of their players were eventually booked – 'opened running sores around the pitch', according to Graham Clark of Glasgow's *Evening Times*. Anton Rogan's aerial clash with goalkeeper Omerovic, which led to

Omerovic's replacement through injury early in the match, was hardly conducive to pacifying matters either. Billy McNeill's pre-match statement of intent to the effect that Celtic were set on displaying 'a more thoughtful, Continental approach' was unravelling rapidly against 'up-and-at-them' opponents. Just as concerning to the Celtic support was a perceptible edginess, and sometimes slackness, in their favourites' play that had been in evidence from the very first minute when Roy Aitken conceded a free kick that resulted in Milanic's effort deflecting off the defensive wall and looping over the bar, much to Pat Bonner's relief. Celtic's fallibility was duly exposed in the 20th minute when the ball was virtually given away, Dziekanowski's wayward crossfield pass behind Burns enabling Milojevic to stride forward virtually unchallenged into the counter-attack and evade two tackles before firing the ball under Bonner from some twenty yards out. Celtic were rocking, and they could have lost more goals through defensive shortcomings had not Dordevic and Durovski squandered fine opportunities before the visitors equalised three minutes from the interval through Mike Galloway, shortly after he had been yellow-carded for a rash challenge on Spasic. Galloway had acquired the reputation of being a 'Euro-specialist' after his five goals for Heart of Midlothian the previous season in the UEFA Cup, including one at the same Mostar ground – and at the same end – where he now scored on his European debut for Celtic by curling a 'thigh-high' left-foot shot high into the corner of the net after a Chris Morris free kick aimed at the far-post area was headed back cleverly into Galloway's path by Tommy Coyne. Sadly, Celtic could not capitalise on the psychological value of this well-timed goal, surrendering the initiative only eight minutes after the restart when Durdevic, with his back to goal, found space to manoeuvre in the penalty area and turn on a pass from his captain Durovski to whip a shot well out of Bonner's reach for the winning goal (2–1). Thereafter, Celtic never really threatened to get on level terms, a symbol of their frustration coming on the hour mark with the taking off of Dziekanowski, whose failure to impress had been highlighted by his getting involved throughout in a 'needling match' with Vujacic.

The Celtic party journeyed home confident that, having notched up a precious away goal, Partizan's narrow advantage would be overturned in Glasgow, but the former's recent European record left little room for complacency. The days leading up to the return leg were replete with warnings as to the pitfalls awaiting Celtic, including an acute observation by Ian Paul of the *Glasgow Herald* on the match day itself, 27 September 1989: 'The nature of the club and its supporters has ever been more suited to the thrills of aggression rather than the science of sophistication.' A few days earlier, Tommy Burns had poured cold water on the rising optimism of all connected with the club when he commented in the *Sunday Post* on the absolute necessity of Celtic striking a balance between attacking and keeping things tight at the back: 'In the past 12 years we've cut our own throats so often, I take nothing for granted.' He would also have had in mind a sobering demonstration of the resilience of Yugoslav footballers only days before the first leg when the Scottish national team had taken a first-half lead in a World Cup qualifier in Zagreb, only to collapse spectacularly to a 1–3 defeat in the space of nine minutes early in the second half. In addition, there were two other factors compromising Celtic's hopes of bringing the crucial element of composure to their performance in an encounter surrounded with so much expectation. The team was going into the match short of genuine self-belief, judging by a run of seven successive matches without a victory (they had advanced to the League Cup quarter-finals by means of a penalty shoot-out), and their striving to get their season back on track after four opening victories was being bedevilled by disciplinary problems, with three players having been red-carded in three successive domestic matches that September, two of them involving highly experienced campaigners. Shortly before the first leg, the eloquent Tommy Burns had displayed a lack of self-control during the league defeat (0–1) inflicted by St Mirren at Paisley, in circumstances that drew the wrath of his manager. Burns vented his anger after the yellow card brandished by the referee (J.F. McGillivray) to teammate Derek Whyte following an 'off-the-ball' incident. He remonstrated with the linesman who had drawn the matter to the attention of the referee and he could consider himself fortunate to be only given a yellow card when he continued to argue his case with the latter. An exasperated Billy McNeill took off Burns 'for his own protection', but the player, still in a state of agitation, compounded his folly by 'mouthing off' – at the Celtic bench, according to at least one account – within earshot of the referee, who promptly issued Burns with a red card that did not disadvantage Celtic numerically, the substitution having already taken place. Seven days before the return leg, Celtic were defeated (0–1) by Aberdeen in a League Cup semi-final at Hampden Park that was marked by two manifestations of indiscipline, the first concerning Joe Miller, a forward so mortified on finding himself a 'substituted substitute' that he came close to committing the unpardonable sin in supporters' eyes of removing his jersey as he gestured his displeasure to the Celtic dugout, and the second involving Roy Aitken, the captain no less, who was red-carded in the closing stages of the match by referee Brian McGinlay for a foul on Jim Bett. Some sort of malaise was infecting Celtic Park, which was in stark contrast with the breezy confidence exuded by Partizan on their arrival in Glasgow, as personified by their new coach. Ivan Golac, who five years later would become a hero to Celtic fans when he guided Dundee United to a Scottish Cup final victory over a treble-seeking Rangers, was the replacement for Momcilo Vukotic, who had resigned on the weekend before the return leg. The bullish Golac, who had recent experience of British football, making his name as a full-back with Southampton in particular, was an advert for self-belief, telling the Scottish press that Partizan would go through to the next round on the basis that, in his opinion, Celtic should have lost by three or four goals in Mostar and that his players had the ability to increase their slender aggregate lead at a stadium that held no fears for a side that had recently played in front of a 90,000 crowd in a local derby with bitter rivals Red Star.

Second leg:
Celtic: Bonner, Aitken, Rogan, Whyte, Elliott, Grant, Galloway, P. McStay, Dziekanowski, Walker and Miller.

Partizan Belgrade: Pandurovic, Stanojkovic, Spasic, Milanic, Petric,

Vujacic, Durdevic (Bajovic), Milojevic, Scepovic, Durovski, Bogdanovic (Dordevic).

Referee: K. Peschel (East Germany).

Attendance: 49,500.

Far from heeding Billy McNeill's pre-match warning about the Slavs being 'masters of waiting and breaking', Celtic committed defensive suicide in spectacular fashion on the evening of 27 September 1989, unable as they were to pin down the Partizan danger man Milko Durovski, who, in the words of the *Daily Record*'s Rodger Baillie, 'pranced in and out of Celtic's rearguard, causing chaos with every touch of the ball'. This rollercoaster of a match unfolded as follows (Celtic score first, aggregate score in brackets):

7th minute, 0–1 (1–3): Durowski's torment of a Celtic side featuring central defender Paul Elliott, who as a result of injury was making only his second appearance in a Celtic jersey since his July signing, began with his taking a corner from which Vujacic, 'given the freedom of Parkhead' according to one report, headed the opening goal.

25th minute, 1–1 (2–3): The home side's frantic efforts to regain a foothold in the tie bore fruit when Paul McStay's free kick was headed on by Paul Elliott for 'Jacki' Dziekanowski to power a header past Pandurovic into the roof of the net. Ten minutes later, Durovski turned sinner when he failed to round off a Partizan breakaway by 'skying' the ball over the bar from twelve yards out, with Bonner helpless.

46th minute, 2–1 (3–3): Celtic sprang like greyhounds out of the trap after the interval and Dziekanowski set in train a sensational twenty-minute spell in which four goals were scored by pouncing on a loose ball after Pandurovic could only parry a Peter Grant shot.

51st minute, 2–2 (3–4): Advantage restored to Partizan when Derek Whyte lost possession in his own half, enabling Durovski to speed down the right to lay the ball into the path of Durdevic, who netted easily.

56th minute, 3–2 (4–4): Dziekanowski secured his hat-trick when he drove home Roy Aitken's cross from the right, but Partizan were still ahead on the 'away goals' rule.

61st minute, 3–3 (4–5): The Yugoslavs seem firmly in control, with Celtic needing two goals without reply to win the tie, after a somewhat dubious goal scored on the break by Durovski, who looked offside as he rounded Bonner to score, with Anton Rogan striving desperately to clear the ball off the goal line.

65th minute, 4–3 (5–5): Celtic clawed their way back into the tie when Andy Walker, destined to become the forgotten goal-scorer in this epic match, given Dziekanowski's personal triumph, latched on the latter's pass from the right to lash the ball into the net from close range.

81st minute, 5–3 (6–5): Pandemonium at Celtic Park! Dziekanowski, irresistible on the night, appeared to have swung the pendulum decisively in Celtic's favour after he flicked a Mike Galloway cross past a bewildered Pandurovic for his own fourth goal. Surely those spectators engrossed in this breathtaking spectacle had just witnessed its climactic act? Graham Clark summed up the prevailing mood in his *Evening Times* report: 'So Celtic had won an amazing tie and all the awful defensive errors they had committed had merely added to a spectacular night's entertainment. Or had they? It seemed impossible there could be anything else left in this match . . . '

88th minute, 5–4 (6–6): Celtic's name, said Rodger Baillie, 'was in the silver champagne bucket for tomorrow's draw then suddenly it was snatched out again'. It is impossible to miss the lingering tone of incredulity when Doug Baillie, ex-footballer turned journalist, looked back a few days later in the *Sunday Post* on the bizarre finale that resulted in Celtic's exit from the Cup-Winners' Cup on the 'away goals' rule:

> The shock scoreline, however, cannot be put down to inexperience. Most of the side had been over the course before, and often. What a pity the enthusiasm of the huge Parkhead following got under the players' skins and continued to drive them forward *after* the tie had been clinched. At 5–3, with round two beckoning, big Roy [Aitken] continued his cavalry charges down the right. On the left, Anton Rogan got carried away in the excitement of it all as well. With time running out it was the Irishman who dashed to the ball boy to grab the ball off him so that a quick throw-in could be taken.

Celtic's recklessness, their incredible naivety and lack of concentration, was duly punished in the visitors' final attack when Durovski – who else? – exploited the resultant 'unforgiveable gaps' (Graham Clark) to set up a Scepovic header past Bonner that plunged the ground into a stunned silence. At the final whistle, the Partizan players danced around the pitch in triumph, the shell-shocked Celtic players headed for the tunnel in a state of absolute dejection, and the crowd trooped out in a mood of utter disbelief. A distraught Billy McNeill delivered a pithy verdict on the unbelievable outcome of a match in which his players had consistently come from behind only to shoot themselves in the foot: 'We climbed three mountains and then threw ourselves off.' One supporter quoted in *Scotland on Sunday* provided a terse summing-up of Celtic's fatally cavalier approach: 'The attack swashed and the defence buckled.'

* * *

The Partizan Belgrade party returned to a Yugoslavia in the throes of disintegration as a result of rising ethnic tensions – a riot eight months later at a Dinamo Zagreb v. Red Star Belgrade match is widely seen as a catalyst for the Balkan Wars of Independence during which a prominent figure in the prolonged siege of the city of Sarajevo was, bizarrely, one Radovan Karadzic, the former psychologist of the local football club (FK Sarajevo) turned leader of the Bosnian Serbs. Celtic themselves were left to pick up the pieces of a setback to the board's attempts to appease fans still hurting after the Johnston debacle and stubbornly unconvinced that those at the helm were capable of coping with the pace of change being forced by Rangers' flexing of their financial muscle, a turning of the screw that threatened to eclipse the Parkhead club for many years to come. The unmistakable smell of fear in the air culminated in an angry demonstration of a type that had not been seen at Celtic Park in a quarter of a century, since 17 August 1963 in fact, when the dam had burst over frustrations about the 'Kelly Kids' era and where it was leading the club. The tipping point for disgruntled fans on 27 January 1990 was the home defeat (the third successive one at Parkhead without Celtic scoring a goal) by a Motherwell side playing a far more attractive brand of football. That left Celtic, whose indifferent form had continued in the wake of the exit from Europe, hopelessly out of contention for the championship, trailing ten points behind Rangers in the title race, thus prompting, according to *The Scotsman*, 'demonstrations, cat-calls and general abuse hurled in the direction of the Celtic directors, not only by those in the park's famous "Jungle", but by some among those in the normally more sedate ranks of the season ticket holders'. In retrospect, it is the reaction of the latter that can be seen as the first signs of the crumbling of dynastic rule at Celtic, leading to the demise of the Kellys and the Whites who had controlled the club for many decades; in the words of W.B. Yeats, 'Things fall apart, the centre cannot hold.' The initial response from the boardroom was far from reassuring, since it only succeeded in reinforcing the growing impression of them as a complacent body of men wholly out of touch with the supporters, a group of custodians who were seemingly bewildered, outraged even, at their stewardship of the club being called into question and, more alarming still, uncertain in their approach to the challenge that was facing the club. The 'special statement' issued in the name of chairman Jack McGinn adopted a tone of *noblesse oblige*: 'Fans have a democratic right to voice their opinions, but staging demonstrations, as was seen at

CELTIC: PRIDE AND PASSION

Celtic Park on Saturday, is not the answer . . . [we need] unity in an effort to put things right, not ripping ourselves apart and doing things we may later regret.' His assertion that 'Celtic have never settled for second best and never will' made uncomfortable reading for many who interpreted it as an admission that the club was indeed settling for mediocrity. His claim that 'the players are undergoing a crisis of confidence' was but a confirmation of the patently obvious, but did not explain why the traditional will to win in adversity had been so markedly absent in recent months. Certainly, he could point to the loss of two stalwarts as a factor in Celtic's increasingly feeble challenge to the Ibrox men, as reflected in the team finishing no higher than third in the years spanning 1989 to 1995. Tommy Burns, who had more often not found himself on the sidelines in the months following his dismissal at Paisley, had left for Kilmarnock in December 1989, to be followed a month later by the departure to Newcastle United of captain Roy Aitken, the culmination of an increasing disenchantment with life at Parkhead, which perhaps made it no surprise that he should have been the 'sad, solitary figure' seen approaching Celtic Park by the *Sunday Post*'s Doug Baillie on the morning after Partizan had administered a body blow to the confidence articulated by the captain himself in the match programme: 'I believe we have the strength in depth and the style to crack the European code.' But, however unpalatable it might have been to those charged with the leadership of the club, the truth was that the Yugoslavs had laid bare the falsity of such optimism and exposed a shallowness in Celtic's resources that would not be rectified over the next five years due to financial debility and, now that the supporters' mood was one of growing restlessness, insurrection in the shape of 'people power' was soon to administer the death blow to a regime that was rapidly running out of answers. The genie was out of the bottle.

CHAPTER 21

No Place Like Home

For whom the bell tolls – the early 1990s were notable for the disappearance from the landscape of British football of terracing areas made famous for being the parts of the ground where the most passionate and vocal fans congregated. Their replacement by more comfortable seating accommodation has not significantly diminished the feelings of nostalgia on the part of fans who tend to think that the atmosphere at the grounds has suffered since. The most famous of these terraces were as follows (date of 'last stand' indicated): The North Bank, Arsenal, May 1992; The Stretford End, Manchester United, May 1992; The Kippax, Manchester City's Maine Road ground, April 1994; The Kop, Liverpool, May 1994; The Shed End, Chelsea, May 1994; The Holte End, Aston Villa, May 1994; The Jungle, Celtic, June 1993.

The 'Jungle' was described by the *Weekly News* (Glasgow edition) in April 1966 as 'that corrugated-iron roofed shelter which houses 10,000 fanatical green-and-white scarved Celtic fans whose support for their team can get through the toughest hide of the most hardened of opposition'.

The history makers: 1995 was the year that two famous footballers paid severe penalties for breaches of discipline. In January that year, Manchester United's French international forward Eric Cantona aimed a 'kung-fu-style' kick at a Crystal Palace fan as he left the field after being sent off during a match at Selhurst Park. In addition to hefty fines imposed by both his club and the FA, Cantona was suspended for eight months. It was thought to be the first time in the history of English professional football that a player had assaulted a spectator, albeit it was said in Cantona's defence that the target of his wrath had been shouting abuse at the player from the front row of the grandstand. In October, the Everton striker and Scottish international Duncan Ferguson was sentenced to three months, of which only forty-four days were served, in Glasgow's notorious Barlinnie Prison for head-butting an opponent, John McStay of Raith Rovers, while playing for Rangers at Ibrox Park in April 1994. Both the referee and his linesmen had missed the incident. It was reported that Ferguson was the first British footballer to be jailed for an on-field offence, one committed while he was on probation for previous misdemeanours.

* * *

It could all have been so very different – or was it all really just pie in the sky? For almost two years, a beleaguered Celtic board clung, albeit with varying degrees of enthusiasm on the part of its members, to a hope of salvation – both for the club and themselves – that they had invested in a planned move from the club's hallowed Parkhead ground (nicknamed 'Paradise') to a new, all-seated home to be built a few miles away at Cambuslang. One director, Michael Kelly, described the attractions of the project for a club that was becoming manacled by debt at a time when the implications of the Taylor Report's recommendations on stadium seating were becoming a matter of real concern:

Here, there was space for everything to make it possible for Celtic, the football club, to survive with its traditions, while its financial needs were met by commercial activities that could co-exist around a magnificent multipurpose stadium complex. The old thinking that every club needed to own its own ground, which lay unused for 13 days out of 14, could be supplanted by a new vision, a leisure and recreation centre in a much-neglected part of Glasgow where not only football but other sports and also musical and any large-audience events could be staged . . . a major and permanent new asset for the city . . . it would rival the best of European and world-class facilities and it would put Ibrox [the home of Rangers] in the shade.

The main features of the proposed £100 million development certainly sounded impressive when unveiled in April 1992: a circular stadium seating 52,000 in 2 tiers; integrated leisure and sports facilities within the stadium; a 200-room hotel; a 'retail village'; an 8-screen cinema complex and a 30-lane tenpin bowling alley; parking for more than 4,500 vehicles and 2 'park-and-ride' railway stations. But it was a dream fated never to come true as the club's fortunes on the pitch deteriorated and doubts about the viability of the Cambuslang proposal surfaced, with concerns being expressed about its financing and the possibility of the site being contaminated, being described as 'a toxic timebomb' in environmental terms. Joe Sullivan, looking back at the situation that prevailed in the early months of 1994, highlighted the prevalent disaffection that proved fatal to the project, which turned into a pipe-dream: 'A stinging 4–2 home defeat at the hands of Rangers [on Ne'erday] only fuelled the fire of discontent, which ranged from the embers of disinterested fans who just couldn't be bothered to the full-blown flames of organised boycotts' (*Celtic View*, 21 December 1994). A perfect metaphor for the gloom surrounding a skint club going nowhere, and playing in a huge barn of a stadium that was becoming more and more anachronistic, was the 15 January 1994 league match with Aberdeen at a fog-shrouded Celtic Park where only the tumbleweed was missing as an under-20,000 crowd watched a rather anaemic contest between a title-challenging outfit and a home side mired in fifth position and which was fielding a player who was the most potent symbol of Celtic's penury, namely the veteran Yorkshire striker Wayne Biggins, a November 1993 signing by new manager Lou Macari that involved a part-exchange deal with Barnsley for an unsettled Lancashire striker (Andy Payton). The hapless Biggins failed to score in any of his 11 outings for Celtic (including this truncated affair) before being moved on to Stoke City for an estimated £125,000 in March 1994. In the view of many, the match itself should not really have started, the visibility being such that spectators at both ends could not see the full length of the pitch. Hugh Keevins of *The Scotsman* described the conditions as 'akin to spectating through frosted glass'. Despite repeated choruses of 'Where's the ball, where's the ball, where's the ball?' from the thinly populated terracings, which only added to the unreal, ghostly atmosphere, it took referee Hugh Williamson until the 61st minute to call a halt to the farcical proceedings with neither team having found the net and with little prospect of doing so. The headline in the *Sunday Post* spoke of more than an abandoned football match: 'Celtic fans lost in Paradise'.

Caught by now in a pincer movement involving disillusioned fans chanting 'Sack the board' at matches, demonstrations by the 'Celts for Change' supporters' pressure group, expressions of discontent expressed in fanzines such as *Not the View*, and a takeover bid by an investor group led by expatriate North American-based businessman Fergus McCann, the board's demise was inevitable following the failure in late February 1994 to secure 'cornerstone' funding for the Cambuslang venture, on the site of which not one brick had yet been laid. In contrast to the perceived shortcomings of the previous administration, McCann's air of brisk, no-nonsense efficiency and strong leadership after taking charge in early March 1994 quickly commended itself to Celtic supporters. They readily endorsed his plans for the revitalisation of the club, to the extent of backing a December 1994 share issue with a £14 million investment that contributed massively to the capital base needed for the realisation within a few years (1998 as it turned out) of an all-seated, 60,000 capacity Celtic Park after McCann, now installed as the virtual owner of the club and the Chief Executive of Celtic plc, scrapped the Cambuslang plan. He soon proved that he was not a man to be trifled with when he reacted vigorously to sniping in *The Herald* (23–24 December 1994) at his plans for reviving the club. He replied instantaneously by letter to insinuations that the finance was not in place to 'support both the rebuilding of the team and the redevelopment of the park', rebutting in detail the 'inaccuracy and innuendo' he saw being peddled by a newspaper whose most ludicrous claim, bordering on snobbery, was that the benefits being offered to attract Celtic fans to take up the share issue could be compared to the Indian caste system: 'In effect, five exclusive social classes are being offered to supporters – with rankings on a sliding scale, and dependent on ability to pay. Some classes, literally, will be armchair supporters, with food and drink to hand in seated sections of the new North Stand.' It was as if the wealthier fans had not patronised the seated areas of stadia from the earliest days of football as a spectator sport and private boxes had not been introduced into the British game in the mid-1960s (at Manchester United's Old Trafford), the latter increasingly becoming the norm as the big clubs in particular sought to broaden their revenue streams. After all, were Celtic not engaged in an attempt to close the yawning gap that existed, both commercially and on the field of play, between them and Rangers, who had been raking in the money from full houses at their modernised, all-seated stadium and from their annual participation (with its enhanced potential from sponsorship, etc.) in the lucrative Champions League, a prospect hitherto denied to Celtic as a result of their mediocre performances in the domestic championship? The truth, however unacceptable as it may have been to the sentimentalists, was that the days of turning up at the turnstile, 'paying a few bob and wandering off on to the terraces', as one football writer put it, were well and truly over, 'consigned to history, just like gaslights'.

Work on the early stages of the rebuilding of Celtic Park was already under way before the team had started to fulfil its fixtures for season 1994–95 at Hampden Park, a largely miserable sojourn that cost the club £600,000 according to McCann, a man who was fulfilling his promises to such effect that, within 18 months of his arrival on the scene, the number of season ticket holders had trebled and by the time of his departure in 1999 had risen to the 50,000 mark. In the space of little more than a year, the demolition of three sides of the stadium – the two terracing ends and the 'Jungle' enclosure (seated as recently as the summer of 1993), with only the main, south, stand being retained – was followed by the erection of that aforementioned £17 million, near-27,000 capacity North Stand, described at the time as the biggest of its kind in Britain and which would become the most visible symbol, initially at least, of the Celtic renaissance. It was a massive two-tier structure that, according to one writer and consultant on football stadia, the highly respected Simon Inglis, 'required 900 concrete piles and 1,000 boreholes, so riddled was the site with mineshafts'. (Celtic Park really had rested on shaky foundations!) When completed, it would house a restaurant, hospitality boxes and lounges, and in the rear of the lower tier (in its middle section) rows of seating characterised as 'heated armchairs'. It was all a far cry from the basic facilities endured for generations by the denizens of the 'Jungle' enclosure that the new stand replaced. Fast-forward, then, a mere 18 months or so from that Parkhead arena shrouded in the mists of despair in January 1994 to a Celtic Park shimmering in the sunshine as Newcastle United hanselled the team's return from its mercifully brief exile at Hampden Park. For the sell-out crowd that filed into the ground on 5 August 1995 for the gala opening of the 'new' stadium, albeit only half completed at that stage, their first look at the majestic North Stand was truly breathtaking. They looked on with obvious pleasure and delight as the 'Celtic-daft' rock singer Rod Stewart cut the ribbons on the new stand as part of an opening ceremony that included 4,000 green and white balloons being released into the skies above to announce that Celtic Park was back in business. First impressions count, so they say, and ex-Ranger Doug Baillie's match report in the *Sunday Post* conveyed the dramatic impact on those present of what was reported to be British football's largest free-standing structure:

> Awesome! That's the only way to describe this homecoming for Celtic after a season in the wilderness at Hampden. Emotions were sky-high. The relief and joy of it was a wonder to behold. And with every shade of green on parade, the new multimillion pound stand was a mind-boggling sight. Impressed? You bet, and I don't mind admitting that the obvious pride of the faithful returning to their spiritual home was enough to make the hair stick out on the back of my neck. It was a wonderful experience.

Celtic: Marshall, Boyd, McKinlay, McNally, Mowbray, Grant, Vata (Donnelly), O'Donnell, van Hooijdonk, Thom (Walker) and Collins.

Newcastle United: Srnicek, Hottiger, Beresford, Peacock, Fox, Howey, Lee, Beardsley, Ferdinand, Ginola, Sellars.

Referee: H. Dallas (Bonkle).

Attendance: 31,000. A near-capacity crowd, comprising the total of spectators in the main (South) Stand and the new North Stand. The opening of the stadium's east-end Lisbon Lions Stand in 1996 and the west end's Jock Stein Stand in 1998 brought the capacity to over 60,000.

Within 30 seconds the elegant winger David Ginola, the target of booing throughout by Celtic fans angered by his alleged 'using' of a reported £14,000 per week offer by the Glasgow club to improve his terms on Tyneside, hit a long-range shot that Gordon Marshall tipped over the bar. Undeterred, Celtic, showing verve and inventiveness throughout a first half they dominated, moved quickly into the attack and retaliated with a thunderous shot by the Dutch striker Pierre van Hooijdonk that thudded off Srnicek's bar. With John Collins, the most influential player on the park, spraying the ball about in midfield, they just would not be denied, and in the 29th minute the pace, directness and sublime ball control of a new signing, German midfielder cum forward Andreas Thom (£2.3 million from Bayer Leverkusen), enabled him to latch on to 'Tosh' McKinlay's clever through ball and surge past Peacock, who promptly and rashly brought him down with a crude tackle inside the box. Collins sent Srnicek the wrong way from the penalty spot, drawing a wry observation from Doug Baillie about the growing cosmopolitanism of British football: 'A German fouled by an Englishman, and a Scotsman beating a Czech from the spot.' Celtic's ascendancy did not last into the second half, when the visitors showed just why they would be challenging for the top honours, though a Premier League season that started with their explosive attacking power and vibrancy taking them 12 points clear of the rest in January 1996 ended with their being pipped by Manchester United for the championship. (This was the season when the noted 'mind games' of the latter's manager Alex Ferguson 'spooked' his Newcastle counterpart Kevin Keegan at a crucial stage of the title run-in.) The equaliser arrived only ten minutes after the restart, thanks to the intuitive Ginola, who released Sellars on the left with a 'killer' ball inside Mark McNally. Sellars' cross was perfection itself, allowing the leaping English international striker Les Ferdinand to head the ball firmly past Marshall. Celtic, who were acquitting themselves well on this landmark day in the club's history, could have snatched the winner 13 minutes from time when Srnicek fumbled a McKinlay free kick but McNally couldn't prod the ball over the line from close range. Instead, they could have found themselves the victim of a last-minute smash-and-grab raid when the rampaging Ferdinand embarked on a solo run that ended with his shot striking a post while Celtic Park held its breath.

After the 1–1 draw, Kevin Keegan expressed his delight in being part of a great event: 'It was fantastic to see a great club being re-born.' Equally pleasing for all those connected with Celtic was the visible and audible proof that afternoon of the genesis of an atmosphere that would come to intimidate visiting sides, earning the stadium the title 'Fortress Parkhead'. It was ample vindication of the transformation wrought in the club's fortunes, a perception underlined in Patrick Barclay's profile of Fergus McCann ('the wee man who thinks big') in the *Sunday Telegraph* of 7 April 1996:

> You can see it in a stadium that has suddenly, even in the process of construction, become Britain's most impressive. And the only reason you did not hear it if you were listening to Radio 5 Live on Monday evening is that the roar acclaiming a goal by Portuguese international debutant Jorge Cadete managed to smash the BBC's sound equipment.

Silenced too were any lingering notions that Celtic would have been better off moving from Paradise. Celtic would not be Celtic anywhere else.

CHAPTER 22

Lightning Strikes

Disaster: (1) A sudden event such as a flood, storm or accident that causes great damage or suffering. (2) Something that is very bad or a failure, especially when this is very annoying or disappointing.

Longman's Dictionary, *fifth edition*

The word 'disaster' is often used in football commentary to describe various circumstances. Probably, it is often an over-used word. Frankly, if we take cognisance of the first of the definitions stated above, then very few of these circumstances could be included. Possibly only serious injury could come under that heading.

Definition two, though, is a different matter. Words like 'very bad' or 'failure' can accurately be used to describe defeat; while the reaction of fans to those setbacks could most decidedly come under that description. During the first decade of the new millennium – roughly speaking – Celtic Football Club employed five managers: John Barnes, Martin O'Neill, Gordon Strachan, Tony Mowbray and Neil Lennon – plus one caretaker manager, Kenny Dalglish. By the advent of the new century, John Barnes was coming to the end of his tenure (June 1999–February 2000), while Kenny Dalglish only held the position, as a caretaker manager, from February 2000 to June 2000. The others had longer spells in the role and, of these, two had considerable success, one had a poor time and the last one only arrived just before the end of the era. However, no matter how long or short their period of tenure, all four had at least one match that could come under the heading – in football terms – of a 'disaster'.

After the disappointing decade of the 1990s, when Celtic Football Club won only four out of a possible thirty domestic trophies and was never involved in European competition after the turn of the year in each season, the arrival of Martin O'Neill gave the club and the support a great boost. The board decided to relax the purse-strings a little, allowing O'Neill to spend some big money on new players and, equally importantly, provided the cash to pay wages to match.

The result was a domestic 'treble' in his first season, 2000–01, the first since the Jock Stein era, and further successes in succeeding years, although main rivals Rangers were never far behind in terms of trophies won. Of the twelve major domestic trophies up for grabs in the first four full seasons of the decade, only Livingston's League Cup success in 2003–04 prevented a clean sweep by the Old Firm.

	League	Scottish Cup	League Cup
2000–01	Celtic	Celtic	Celtic
2001–02	Celtic	Rangers	Rangers
2002–03	Rangers	Rangers	Rangers
2003–04	Celtic	Celtic	Livingston

There were also some great moments in the European arena, particularly the UEFA Cup run of 2002–03, when the Hoops reached the final in Seville and their estimated 80,000 fans turned the occasion into a marvellous festival despite the outcome, although there were also disappointments in failing to reach the last 16 of the Champions League in each of the above seasons. However, domestically, as has always been the case for many years, the Old Firm were the main participants in the race for the trophies.

As the two sides prepared for the season of 2004–05, the press and fans were full of anticipation. It was expected that the whole campaign would be a close-run affair and that is exactly what happened. Rangers struck first blood by knocking Celtic out of the League Cup (CIS Cup at that point) on 10 November at Ibrox, then went on to thrash Motherwell 5–1 in the final in March 2005. In the league, the sides were nip-and-tuck for most of the season; a fine 2–1 win by Celtic over their oldest rivals at Ibrox on 24 April giving them a fairly substantial lead with only four matches left:

	P	W	D	L	F	A	Pts	GD
Celtic	34	28	2	4	79	29	86	50
Rangers	34	25	6	3	68	19	81	49

A headline in the *Scottish Sun* probably summed up the mood of most Old Firm fans at that time:

O'Neill won't admit it
McLeish won't concede it
But we'll say it . . . Celtic are
Champs!

The following three weekends were full of tension and interest. On 30 April, Celtic went down 1–3 to Hibs at Celtic Park; a day later, Rangers won 3–1 at Aberdeen. On 7 May, Rangers beat Hearts 2–1 at Ibrox; on 8 May, against Aberdeen at home, Celtic won 2–0. On 14 May, it was Rangers 4 Motherwell 1; on the 15th, Hearts 1 Celtic 2. So, with one match left, that left the table looking as follows (three points for a victory):

	P	W	D	L	F	A	Pts	GD
Celtic	37	30	2	5	84	33	92	51
Rangers	37	28	6	3	77	22	90	55

For the crucial matches on the final day, Sunday, 22 May 2005, both the Hoops and the Light Blues would be away, Celtic against Motherwell at Fir Park and Rangers against Hibs at Easter Road.

The odds still looked to be tipped in Celtic's favour, although an (accurate) front-page *News of the World* story (apparently leaked by an 'insider' at Celtic Park) on the day of the match about Martin O'Neill leaving at the end of the season hardly boosted the players' morale. Still, most Celtic fans were quietly confident, as the Hoops had won all three of their league meetings that season against Motherwell. They also, though, had a two-point advantage, albeit with an inferior goal difference – victory at Motherwell would bring Celtic the title outright. However, in the back of the minds of many of the Celtic players must have been the painful memory of their greatest rivals pipping them to the title on goal difference only two years earlier, that severe blow coming just a few days after Celtic had suffered the heartbreak of an extra-time defeat at the hands of Porto in the UEFA Cup final in Seville.

The Celtic team sent out that day at Fir Park was Rab Douglas, Didier Agathe, Bobo Balde, Stan Varga, Jackie McNamara, Stiliyan Petrov, Neil Lennon, Chris Sutton, Alan Thompson, John Hartson and Craig Bellamy. Celtic took the initiative right from the whistle, made a few early chances and then went ahead on the half-hour mark thanks to a goal by Chris Sutton. After the interval, Motherwell seemed to step up a gear but Celtic matched them and play swung from end to end. The Celtic fans were tense; a one-goal lead was cutting things a bit fine; then news came through that Nacho Novo had scored for Rangers at Easter Road and the fans' nervousness increased.

Celtic were playing nice football but failed to press home their advantage. Then, disaster struck! With only two minutes left, a Richie Foran shot was not dealt with adequately by the Celtic rearguard, the loose ball falling to Scott McDonald, who struck an overhead volley behind Rab Douglas. Motherwell were level, Rangers now had the edge in the dying minutes of the title race and the Celtic fans just knew, deep down, that it was all over for their favourites.

Celtic pushed men up but failed to create any chances. Then 'The Steelmen' sprang forward again, a long ball allowing McDonald to race beyond Stan Varga, who struggled to recover. Before he could do so, McDonald looked up and fired a shot towards goal that hit the outstretched leg of Varga before looping over Douglas. It was 2–1 to Motherwell and within seconds referee Hugh Dallas had blown the whistle for time-up. Celtic had lost the title or, to perhaps phrase it more accurately, Celtic had failed to take advantage of a golden opportunity.

As the home support cheered their heroes, the Celtic players looked stunned, the manager and his staff appeared completely gob-smacked and the fans just stood silent as though they could not believe what they had just seen. High in the skies, the helicopter that had been bringing the SPL trophy to Fir Park now changed direction and headed for Easter Road, where the delirious Rangers fans would not let their stars leave the pitch after their 1–0 victory.

It had been a terrible day for Celtic. Judging by definition (2) from the start of the chapter, this certainly could be described as a 'disaster'. Indeed, eight years after the event, Martin O'Neill apparently still regards it as an episode too painful to discuss. A few days after 'Black Sunday', as Celtic fans dubbed it, Chief Executive Peter Lawwell announced that Martin would leave the club after the Scottish Cup final (due to be played on 28 May 2005 and won 1–0) and that Gordon Strachan would take over on 1 June 2005.

* * *

Gordon Strachan became Celtic's 15th manager since Willie Maley first assumed the role in 1897. His appointment did not go down too well with all of the support, as he had played for Aberdeen in Scotland and had often been a thorn in the flesh of the Celtic side of the time. He would have a tough job on his hands to win over quite a number of the fans.

Strachan quickly made his presence felt:

14 June: Jackie McNamara transferred to Wolves
17 June: Joos Valgaeren moved back to Belgium, to Club Brugge
19 June: Neil Lennon made club captain
21 June: 'Mo' Camara arrives from Burnley. Strachan's first signing
1 July: Jérémie Aliadière comes in on loan from Arsenal

7 July: On-loan signing Craig Bellamy departs for Blackburn Rovers
8 July: Maciej Zurawski arrives from Wisla Kraków
20 July: Adam Virgo, in from Brighton
22 July: Paul Telfer also arrives from Brighton
29 July: Shunsuke Nakamura joins from Reggina

As players came and went, the pre-season matches got under way:

16 July: Fulham 0 Celtic 0
19 July: Leicester City 0 Celtic 0
21 July: Celtic 2 Sporting Lisbon 2
24 July: Celtic 0 Leeds United 0

Three days later, Celtic would face Artmedia Bratislava, named after a subsidiary of their wealthy backer's publishing company, in a second qualifying round tie for entry to the Champions League, with the first leg being held at Tehelné Pole, the Slovakian national stadium, since Artmedia's stadium (Stary Most) was deemed unsuitable by UEFA for European matches. The Slovaks had beaten Kairat Almaty of Kazakhstan in the first round – fighting back from being two goals down – but they did not have a European 'pedigree' and everyone connected with Celtic was fairly confident that the Hoops could prevail quite comfortably. On 27 July 2005, the teams took to the field on a hot evening in Bratislava, the Celtic side showing four changes from the one that had won the Scottish Cup back in May, the final match of the 2004–05 season. David Marshall replaced Rab Douglas in goal; Paul Telfer and Mo Camara made up the full-back pairing, in place of Didier Agathe and Jackie McNamara; up front, Maciej Zurawski took the striker role in place of the departed Craig Bellamy.

Celtic got off to the worst possible start when Chris Sutton had to be taken off early with a suspected fractured cheekbone after an accidental collision with Neil Lennon. Aiden McGeady came on as substitute. Artmedia took early control and limited Celtic to the occasional break. The Slovaks opened the scoring just before half-time, Halenar netting from close range. Being only one down at half-time gave Celtic's travelling support some hope, but missed chances early in the second half by Maloney (on for Zurawski) and McGeady seemed to lift Artmedia, who got a second in 57 minutes, Halenar cutting the ball back for Vascak to score. Three goals in the final quarter of an hour seemed like the nails in Celtic's coffin: the third in 75 minutes, again through Halenar; a fourth by substitute Mikulic three minutes later and a fifth in the last minute by that man Juraj Halenar again to complete his hat-trick. It had been a night to forget for Celtic fans and few had any hope that the 0–5 deficit could be overturned in the second leg at Parkhead.

ESPN's Soccernet succinctly summed up the evening: 'Gordon Strachan made a *disastrous* start as Celtic manager tonight after watching his new-look side slump to a humiliating five-goal Champions League qualifying drubbing and arguably the worst European night in their history.' In strict statistical terms, it was, edging out the previous biggest margin of defeat set in October 1991 when Liam Brady's Celtic collapsed to a 1–5 UEFA first-leg away loss at the hands of Swiss side Neuchatel Xamax, whose striker Hossam Hassan also, like Halenar, netted a hat-trick (indeed, he scored four times). Remarkably, Celtic almost made what would surely have been the greatest comeback in the club's history, winning the return leg 4–0 at Parkhead. For Gordon Strachan, however, that night on the banks of the Danube was – and is still – a haunting one. Some nine months later, Glasgow's *Evening Times* reported him as telling one journalist that 'It is 10 past 11 on my watch, it stopped at the end of the Artmedia game', adding that he kept it like that as a reminder of 'how football can kick you in the guts'. Gordon has a reputation for a quirky sense of humour, but you never know . . .

* * *

The arrival of Tony Mowbray as Gordon Strachan's successor in time for the start of season 2009–10 was greeted with approval by the Celtic support. As an ex-player and originator of the famous 'Huddle', he certainly had the Parkhead background many fans – deep down – liked to see. In addition, his work in transforming

Hibs and West Bromwich Albion into free-flowing sides was regarded with appreciation. However, he had a hard act to follow. Gordon Strachan might never have completely won over the fans and the press with his comments and attitude but there was no doubting his record. Three consecutive league titles had only been managed before by Willie Maley and Jock Stein.

As Mowbray tinkered with the players he had been left – and brought a few in – the team played a few pre-season matches, against Brisbane Roar (3–0 in Australia), Cardiff City (0–0 in Wales) and both Al-Ahly (5–0) and Spurs (2–0) to win the invitational Wembley Cup.

Then came the qualifying ties for the Champions League: Celtic beat Dynamo Moscow 2–1 on aggregate in the third round but fell to Arsenal (1–5 aggregate) in the play-offs. That result consigned Celtic to the Europa League group stages, where they were drawn against Rapid Vienna, Hapoel Tel-Aviv and SV Hamburg. It did not look on paper to be a very onerous section but, sadly, Celtic frequently failed to rise to the various challenges, finishing with a record of P6 W1 D3 L2 F7 A7. Those poor figures meant that they failed to progress in the competition.

In the CIS (League) Cup, a convincing 4–0 thrashing of Falkirk at their new stadium was followed by a poor showing versus Hearts at Parkhead, the visitors getting the only goal of the game to send Celtic crashing out of the competition.

Form in the league had also been indifferent. By the end of January 2010, Celtic were trailing Rangers by nine points, the difference in consistency quite apparent from the table:

	P	W	D	L	F	A	Pts	GD
Rangers	20	14	5	1	48	13	47	35
Celtic	19	11	5	3	38	20	38	18

The three defeats, all of them by two goals to one and all away from home, had come against Rangers, Dundee Utd and Hearts. The draws were against Dundee Utd (H), Motherwell (H), Falkirk

(H) & (A), and Rangers (H). All in all, it was not a convincing campaign and the fans were beginning to become restless, to say the least.

They would be slightly mollified by the victories over Dunfermline and Kilmarnock that put the Hoops into the semi-final of the Scottish Cup but league form still tended to be uncertain. Of the following ten matches in that competition, there were seven wins, one draw and two defeats. Unfortunately, Rangers kept up the pressure and towards the end of March they were still in prime position in the table, well ahead in nearly every category (three points for a win):

SPL Table at 20 March 2010

	P	W	D	L	F	A	Pts	GD
Rangers	28	20	7	1	64	16	67	48
Celtic	29	17	6	6	56	29	57	27

Realistically, the league was lost, but, with a Scottish Cup semi-final coming up, it was important to maintain both form and morale, which made the league trip to New St Mirren Park on 24 March 2010 so important. Saints had had a poor season and were in third-bottom place in the table and still feeling a hangover from a League Cup final defeat at the hands of a nine-man Rangers; if ever there was an opportunity for Celtic to put some form together and knock in a few goals, then this was surely it. The starting line-up on the night was: Lucasz Zaluska, Mark Wilson, Josh Thompson, Darren O'Dea, Edson Braafheid, Aiden McGeady, Ki Sung-Yueng, Landry N'Guemo, Paul McGowan, Robbie Keane, Georgios Samaras.

There were only 5,018 in the stadium to see Celtic dominate the early play without taking advantage of their territorial control, albeit the home goalkeeper Paul Gallacher made two crucial saves. Then, in 38 minutes, Josh Thompson and Saints striker Billy Mehmet challenged for a ball at the edge of the box, it broke clear to Andy Dorman, and he fairly rifled it home for the first goal. Obviously, instructions were put over in no uncertain terms in the Celtic dressing-room at half-time as the Hoops started the second period brightly but Saints kept plugging away and got their second in 58 minutes through Steven Thomson. It was now starting to be a rough night for the Celtic players. All the play was directed towards their opponents' goal but not only were they finding the Buddies' rearguard difficult to break down, but also their own supporters were not enamoured by what they were seeing and were beginning to show it in no uncertain terms. As usually happens when teams become desperate, too many players pushed forward and that left the defence highly vulnerable. In the eighty-fourth minute, Andy Dorman found himself in acres of space inside the box and knocked in number three; and only three minutes later Steven Thomson, again unchallenged in the penalty area, lashed in number four. For the Celtic players, the final whistle must have come as something of a relief and they made their way off the pitch with the jeers of their support ringing in their ears. It was Celtic's 13th defeat of the season in the 46 matches played to that point in all the major competitions.

Afterwards, in his interviews, Tony Mowbray looked embarrassed but did not attempt to make any excuses. 'I take full responsibility,' he said. 'I left some very young defenders exposed.' When asked about his own position, he replied, 'I don't think I want to get into that tonight. I don't think it is a pertinent question.' The Celtic board obviously did; within 24 hours, Mowbray had been relieved of his duties as manager.

* * *

Following Tony Mowbray's inevitable departure the following day, Neil Lennon was appointed as interim manager and immediately brought in Johan Mjallby as his assistant. Only three days after that 0–4 hiding in Paisley, Celtic were in action again, this time at home to Kilmarnock. A crowd of 41,000 turned up to welcome the new man in charge, who made some changes from the 11 who had taken the field against St Mirren. Artur Boruc replaced Lucasz Zaluska; Andreas Hinkel came in for Mark Wilson; Lee Naylor took over from Edson Braafheid in the other full-back position; Scott Brown was in place of Ki Sung-Yueng; with Marc-Antoine Fortune replacing Paul McGowan. The whole team gelled well and gave an effective performance. Two goals by Robbie Keane, in 36 and 62 minutes, plus one by Scott Brown in 66 minutes gave Celtic a well-merited and much-needed 3–1 win. Eight days later, the team travelled to Easter Road, where a rather disappointing crowd of 10,523 were present to see Celtic record another win, a Robbie Keane penalty in 63 minutes bringing the only goal of the game.

The next match was against Ross County in the Scottish Cup semi-final. When meeting a team from a lower division, the likes of a Celtic are always regarded as firm favourites but in the *Celtic View* preview of the match, Neil Lennon was rightly on his guard.

I saw them at Partick Thistle and they got beaten but deserved to win. They have got good players, are well organised and all know their jobs. I know semi-finals can be very nervy occasions. They are different and have a different atmosphere in a different stadium, so we won't be taking anything for granted. There will be no complacency on our part. While we keep pushing Rangers for the title, this is our most realistic chance of silverware so we want to get to that final. It's the most important game of the season for us now.

The Celtic team that afternoon of April 10th 2010 was Lucasz Zaluska, Andreas Hinkel, Darren O'Dea, Josh Thompson, Lee Naylor, Scott Brown, Aiden McGeady, Landry N'Guemo, Georgios Samaras, Marc-Antoine Fortuné, Robbie Keane. A disappointingly small crowd of 24,535 was scattered throughout the national stadium at Hampden but they would have enjoyed a fascinating first half, with both teams looking comfortable on the ball yet strangely reluctant to commit the opposing defence in the final third. With five men in midfield, Ross County were perhaps the steadier side and Lennon moved McGeady in off the wing to counteract that, playing him just behind Keane with Samaras moving wide. Minutes before the break, the Celtic manager made a tactical switch, taking off Landry N'Guemo and replacing him with Marc Crosas. However, by the time the whistle went for half-time, neither side had made a real chance.

That all changed in the 55th minute when Steven Craig burst through from midfield and cracked a fierce shot past Zaluska. Immediately, Celtic upped the tempo but the players, both individually and collectively, seemed uncertain, allowing Ross County to control the proceedings and eventually get a second in the 89th minute through Martin Scott.

It was a performance that stunned the Celtic fans in the ground. To say they were disappointed is an understatement; that word 'disaster' tripped off the lips of many Celtic supporters over the next few hours and days. In defeat, Neil Lennon was composed, diplomatic and ruthlessly truthful: 'We were not good enough from the first minute. Ross County played a lot better than we did and deserved to go through to the final. I can't say anything except the 11 players on the park didn't play to their full potential and Ross County wanted it more than us.'

'Wanting it more' has always been a prerequisite at Celtic Park. Second best has never been an acceptable part of the club's DNA.

* * *

Unfortunately, for Celtic Football Club, such difficult afternoons and evenings were not confined to the decade of the 2000s. Each of the final five decades of the twentieth century had such moments, occasions when the support was bitterly disappointed by a result. They can be listed as follows:

1950s I (Jim Craig) can clearly recall the acute disappointment among my uncles when Celtic lost 0–1 to Clyde in the Scottish Cup final replay of 1955. The old adage about the Old Firm never losing in replays was still in vogue at that period, so the result came as a severe blow. Possibly even more agonising was the 4–0 defeat by St Mirren at Hampden in the Scottish Cup semi-final of 1959.

1960s Take your pick. The loss to Dunfermline in the Scottish Cup final replay in 1961; the 3–1 defeat by St Mirren in the Scottish Cup semi-final of the following year; the 3–0 thrashing by Rangers in the Scottish Cup final replay of 1963; or the unbelievable 4–0 humiliation at the semi-final stage of the Cup-Winners' Cup in Budapest at the hands of MTK in 1964, after Celtic had won the first leg 3–0.

1970s One bad afternoon at Hampden rises well above the rest: Celtic 1 Partick Thistle 4, League Cup final, 23 October 1971. A day when the victors really lived up to the tag 'The Maryhill Magyars' given to them in the early 1950s (after the great Hungarian side of that era) by a local football writer and Thistle fan, Malcolm Munro.

1980s Four possibles. Losing (on the 'away goals' rule) in the second round of the Cup-Winners' Cup in 1980 to a team that few had ever heard of, Politechnica Timisoara of Romania; or the three painful defeats by Aberdeen in the Scottish Cup in consecutive seasons, 1982 (4th round), 1983 (semi-final) and 1984 (final).

1990s Frankly, a decade of disappointments, but two stand out. That horrible night in Switzerland on 22 October 1991 when Neuchatel Xamax hammered Celtic 5–1; and one dreadful afternoon at Ibrox on 27 November 1994, when Celtic lost a penalty shoot-out to Raith Rovers in the League Cup final.

The hardback edition of this book had barely been published when Celtic's heaviest margin of defeat in European competition was equalled by their 1–6 Champions League reverse at the hands of FC Barcelona at the Camp Nou on 11 December 2013. An 'angry and disappointed' manager Neil Lennon pulled no punches afterwards in the *Guardian* when giving his verdict on an ignominious performance: 'I wouldn't say some players gave up, but it certainly looked that way at times . . . There was no bravery on the ball tonight, we started off nervously and it looked like our heads went down at 2–0'. Conceding possession cheaply in the early stages, Celtic were duly punished by a Pique goal after only six minutes. Two goals shortly before the interval torpedoed Celtic's hopes of making it a contest, the scorers being Pedro and the £71.5 million (including 'extras') Brazilian signing Neymar, who went on to complete his hat-trick on the hour mark. Tello made it 6–0 some twenty minutes from time, prompting nightmarish visions of the proverbial 'cricket score', but Barcelona did not thereafter cash in on their domination and pressure. Georgios Samaras's header in the dying minutes brought a consolation goal for the visitors. This result meant that Celtic finished bottom of group H ,with only three points and three goals from six fixtures which produced five defeats and only one victory for the loss of fourteen goals.

Brian Marjoribanks, reflecting in the *Scottish Daily Mail* of 23 May 2014 on the announcement the day before of the manager's departure from the club, suggested that the wounding defeat in Barcelona and the outcome of the group had left its mark; 'Perhaps Lennon asked himself then how much further he could take the club'.

CHAPTER 23

A Question of Identity

Counting the cost of rivalry:

75: percentage of 'Old Firm' fans whom a Scottish police chief thinks could be arrested [presumably for conduct during a Celtic–Rangers match].

17: percentage of Scottish population who are Catholic.

140: percentage leap in domestic violence complaints when Celtic–Rangers games kick off at Saturday lunchtime [presumably the same applies to Sunday matches].

229: arrests after 'Old Firm' match last month.

50: distance in miles 'troublemakers' had to be transported to find available accommodation after all the cells in Glasgow were filled in the wake of February's game.

The Times, *21 March 2011*

Francis McKee, in his *Bellgrove* (1991), depicts the looming – and still lingering – culture clash set in train by the Irish leaving their native land in cattle boats to escape famine, cholera, evictions and coercion Acts in a desperate bid to seek a better life as the providers of muscle in the digging of ditches and as navvies on the roads and railways in the West of Scotland. Glasgow, the city that would become known in the late nineteenth century as 'The Workshop of Empire', was a particular magnet, given the opportunities provided by such large enterprises as Parkhead Forge, the famous factory whose noisy output was such, it was said, that every house in the area shook with the impact of 'Goliath' and 'Samson', its two giant hammers:

> Their arrival was perceived in almost biblical terms by the Presbyterian city fathers. Old Testament punishments provided the metaphors as the Irish came to be seen as a swarming mass of pauperism or a devastating plague of locusts sent to impoverish the city. Catholic leaders quickly tried to foster a sense of pride among the displaced masses. Celtic Football Club was founded to provide a focus for the fledging community. Symbolically, the club's grounds became established in Parkhead – a hieroglyph for Catholic, Irish family values set squarely in the industrial heartland of the East End. Celtic's rapid success played an important role in the formation of the East End community. The team offered a sense of identity and an alternative to the punishing factory work schedule.

One of the club's founders, John O'Hara, a native of Faughanvale in County Derry, left the Ireland of the mid-century Great Famine era with his family to eventually become a shoemaker in the Calton district adjacent to Parkhead before becoming a trades union official in both the Operative Shoemakers Society and the National Union of Boot and Shoe Operatives. He acquired clerical and organisational skills, not to mention powers of persuasion and a reputation for hard work, which made him an obvious choice as the club's first secretary, in which capacity he promoted the drive for subscriptions that underpinned the early funding of the club in addition to taking a prominent role in recruiting players (most notably James Kelly, the first captain) for a venture that, without the determined efforts of O'Hara and his colleagues, could easily have gone awry, so quickly did many football clubs disappear almost without trace in those days. Those pioneers were parishioners of St Mary's in the Calton, a church in which O'Hara was secretary of the Catholic Union. The influence of Catholicism in the founding of the club, as highlighted by the crucial role of a Marist – Brother Walfrid – was thus no coincidence; indeed there was a sense of inevitability about it, given this assessment by two Church of Scotland ministers

A QUESTION OF IDENTITY

(Andrew L. Drummond and James Bulloch) in their 1975 book *The Church in Victorian Scotland 1843–1874*:

> In Victorian Scotland the Roman Church gave its people the faith which alone gave dignity and hope to lives otherwise spent in the midst of hardship, brutality and squalor . . . Not only were they [members of the clergy and the various religious orders] pastors of their people, they were also their leaders in a desperate struggle to raise them from squalor and the slums through education, into a more prosperous and comfortable existence.

The quasi-mystical link between the club and St Mary's was brought into sharp focus on the evening of 6 November 2012 when, as Celtic manager Neil Lennon told Martin Hardy in *The Independent* some seven weeks later (22 December edition), during the moving and inspirational event (promoted by the Celtic Graves Society) held in the church to celebrate Celtic's founding there 125 years earlier, he began to 'think the impossible', that his team could defeat the mighty Barcelona in a crucial Champions League group match at nearby Celtic Park the following evening. 'I just started to believe there was going to be something special,' said Lennon of the service, 'it just compounded the atmosphere going into the game . . . you just felt the whole club was really united that particular night.' Celtic, very much the underdogs before kick-off, duly won the match 2–1, a result that sent shock waves throughout European football.

That cultural bond was attested to graphically by Matt McGinn (1928–1977), 'singer, songwriter, humourist, raconteur, novelist, playwright, and above all Glaswegian', than whom no one had a greater sense of the place from whence he came. He was one of a family of nine living in a two-roomed tenement flat at the corner of Ross Street and Gallowgate in the Calton, the district in which Celtic FC was born. His growing-up in the rather defensive, inward-looking and poverty-stricken Catholic community of the time, long before the Church took on a more ecumenical outlook with the advent of Vatican II and social change in the 1960s, was not untypical of life in those working-class areas of industrial Scotland from which the club drew its overwhelmingly Catholic support, albeit the club has always counted on a fairly large degree of Protestant backing. In his autobiography, McGinn said:

> We were brought up Catholics and that in Glasgow also meant Celtic supporters, and there were plenty of objects and ornaments about the house to indicate to any stranger who came our way what we were at a glance, like holy water fonts, scapulars, pictures of the Sacred Heart and the Virgin, and a picture of the Celtic team in full colours which graced an ornamental plate beside the set-in bed.

In the small, self-contained neighbourhood in which he grew up, 'Irish accents were rare, most of the people speaking the Glasgow "glottal stop", but the names left no doubt as to the genealogical origin of the Dochertys, Donnellys, Reillys, Connellys or the Quinns.' It was an Irish Catholic world of fish on Fridays, the wearing of shamrocks on St Patrick's Day, and the feverish (and apprehensive) atmosphere that surrounded the Orange Walks as they 'stomped up the Gallowgate', not to mention the confrontations with pupils of the local Dovehill school 'who did not share the religion of my forebears'. Celtic FC was the most visible symbol of that minority community and McGinn was to become accustomed to his favourites, the representatives of the 'underdogs', being dominated by the 'Protestant' Rangers FC, whose supremacy from the 1920s onwards became so pronounced that it came to be regarded as the natural order of things. This was so much so that it was somehow indicative of that situation that as late as the 1950s Celtic Park should be a ground in which Catholic hymns such as 'Faith of our Fathers' and 'Hail glorious St. Patrick' should be sung with a particular fervour and, sometimes, from the 'Jungle' enclosure there emanated the cry of 'Come on the sons of Dan!', a plea that, bemused listeners would soon come to learn, was a reference to Daniel O'Connell, the nineteenth-century Irish patriot and champion of Catholic emancipation.

It was, then, somewhat appropriate that, after Celtic finally emerged from the shadow of their greatest rivals, Cinderella-like, in the Portuguese sunshine in May 1967, Matt McGinn should lend his talents as a balladeer to a song entitled 'The Bhoys of Lisbon'. A contemporary of McGinn and a fellow Caltonian, Glen Daly (1920–87), born Bartholomew Francis McGovern McCann Dick in Tobago Street and a product of St Mary's School, close to where Celtic FC was formed in November 1887, worked in the city's shipyards, where he displayed his love of Celtic by welding inside the framework of ships that he worked on the names of the 1938 Exhibition Trophy-winning team, before taking up a career as an entertainer. In October 1961, 'The Celtic Song', which had its origins in a humble little record shop (Clifford Music Ltd.) in the Gallowgate, was first given its airing over the loudspeakers of Celtic Park. Sung from the heart, in the authentic voice of a fan (Glen Daly) who also happened to be an entertainer by profession, it struck an immediate chord with the club's supporters through its unmistakable tone of pride and defiance in that early part of the decade when adversity was the norm. Who then could have guessed that, six years later, the walls of the Celtic dressing-room in the Estádio Nacional would reverberate, much to the astonishment of a foreign press unused to such raucous celebration, to a passionate rendition by the victorious players of that very song, the choruses of what became one of the world's most famous club anthems heralding the arrival of a new force on the European scene? On his appointment as a Rangers director in March 1963, Matt Taylor, a haulage contractor and the club's second-biggest shareholder, had made no bones about the acquisition of the Cup being the only acceptable reward for his years of following his club all over Europe. Instead, one of his colleagues, chairman John Lawrence, would be waiting at the foot of an aircraft's steps at Glasgow Airport to congratulate their hitherto less illustrious rivals on their achievement of becoming the first British club to lift the trophy. They had returned from a continent enraptured by television images of the Glasgow club's exciting brand of football, which had, by general consent, brought a breath of fresh air to a competition that had gone stale, earning Celtic the description from the venerable Parisian sports daily *L'Équipe* of *l'ouragan* (the hurricane). The Madrid daily

Ya headlined its match report '*El Celtic, brillante vencedor de la Copa de Europa*'. Heady stuff, indeed, and from then on the community from which Celtic sprang was enabled to walk a little taller. Their team, drawn from a 30–40-mile radius of Glasgow, had achieved the impossible – and, in true Celtic tradition, by coming from behind. In his 1994 book *Paradise Lost*, Michael Kelly, a former chairman of the club – a member of the family that had produced both the club's first captain (James Kelly) and its chairman in 1967 (Bob, James's son) – was in no doubt about the social impact of this triumph. When growing up, he had 'inherited' the philosophy that 'Celtic represented the Irish Catholic in Scotland. Celtic stood for the underdog. Celtic was anti-establishment. Celtic represented social justice and opposed discrimination.' But, in the wake of Lisbon, all seemed to have changed: 'The objectives of those who established Celtic in the poor East End of Glasgow had been achieved. The discriminated had equalled the best. The outcasts had been accepted. The oppressed could hold their heads high. The dissenters were part of the establishment.'

No need then, surely, for that community to look back. Just as Celtic would have to come to terms with the new, international status conferred on a hitherto homely, unpretentious and rather parochial club inhabiting a far from palatial stadium, it was time for their supporters to stride on confidently, to finally leave behind their forefathers' sense of being 'strangers in a strange land'. That is the nature of the expectation articulated by two well-known figures when, twenty-five years on, they reflected on the significance of Celtic's triumph. Tony McGuinness, a businessman who was both a noted supporter of the club and a confidant of Jock Stein, asserted that the reaching of this pinnacle had given Celtic supporters more faith in themselves – 'If Celtic could achieve this in football, maybe we could achieve more in other ways'. Jim Craig, Celtic's right-back in Lisbon, added the following perspective: 'It helped the community which supported Celtic to be proud of the tradition from which they came. And it is a Scottish tradition, rather than an Irish one. It encouraged them to believe that they could do things' (*The Herald*, 16 May 1992). Certainly, while Willie Maley, born in Newry and a member of the first-ever team, could assert in a 3 March 1931 *Daily Express* article that the Celtic of which he had been in charge for over 30 years was a 'great Glasgow-Irish club', its most famous manager, Jock Stein, Lanarkshire-born and a figure of unquestionable patriotism who was proud beyond measure that during his reign Celtic had reached the pinnacle of its achievement with 11 native-born players, would have shared Craig's underlying perception that several decades of assimilation had seen Celtic metamorphose into a quintessentially Scottish club. As it transpired, the club's directorate lacked the necessary drive, imagination and determination to build on Jock Stein's legacy and to elevate Celtic to a place in the pantheon of truly great European clubs. Its comparatively abysmal record since the mid-1970s (reaching the UEFA Cup final in 2003 and the odd Champions League highlight apart), led Hugh MacDonald of *The Herald* to reflect in the autumn of 2011 on the club's diminished reputation in that sphere by remarking of a run of only one victory in thirty-one away matches that 'Celtic's travels have taken on all the tragedy of some desperate mythic search that is fated to end in disaster, a sort of Jason and the Argonauts meets the *Titanic*'. The same could not be said of the community (or at least a significant section of it) to which McGuinness and Craig referred. The Glasgow University Celtic Supporters Club was formed in 1972 at a time when, it was said, Catholics were becoming the 'largest social grouping' at the university, and the executive boxes and lounges at a wholly transformed Celtic Park are nowadays heavily populated by what might be termed the 'post-1967 generation', namely the sons and daughters who have attained prominent positions in the legal, business and, particularly, political life of Scotland, so much so that there have been frequent accusations that local government in Glasgow was under the control of 'a Catholic Mafia'. Yet their air of self-confidence, the impression they project of being completely at ease in the land of their birth, does not appear to be shared by a sizeable portion of the aforesaid community, which still regards itself as outsiders, a dichotomy that finds an oblique reflection in the Scottish–Irish 'division' hinted at in Jim Craig's quote. Indeed, this is a state of affairs that has existed from the earliest days of the club's history, judging by *Scottish Umpire*'s 20 November 1888 characterisation of Celtic v. Queen's Park Glasgow Cup semi-final as 'an international battle', a description that underlined the writer's contention that 'blood is thicker than water', a 'truism' that, he averred, 'has over and over again been proven, not only in our social dealings, but also in our national and international relations'. For him – and, doubtless, many others – this was a contest with both a racial and (though unspoken) religious dimension: 'The clubs engaged were the premier club of Scotland, the famous, the redoubtable and popular Queen's Park, and the best combination of Irishmen that has ever been raised in Scotland, knitted together by an unquenchable desire to do honour to the Emerald Isle from which they spring.' Kevin McMunigal, 110 years on, writing in *The Scotsman*'s weekend supplement of 16 May 1998, captured the growing assertiveness of those who adhered passionately to, and clung determinedly to, the club's Irish Catholic heritage, which they believed was under threat of erosion at the hands of those who ran what was now Celtic plc and whom they suspected of trying to rebrand the club for commercial purposes. He visited Matt McGinn's old stamping-ground, once the heart of Catholic Glasgow, on a day that has passed into Celtic folklore, the day when St Johnstone were beaten 2–0 at Parkhead (through goals by two foreigners, the Swede Henrik Larsson and the Norwegian Harald Brattbakk) to prevent Rangers creating a new record of ten successive championships and to restore the league flag to Paradise:

> The Gallowgate of old, when houses and communities filled the gaps between the shops and the market place [the famous Barras], was an area known to be predominantly Catholic. Its people were all for Celtic Football Club. In less sober moments they'd be heard recalling the struggles across the sea, each song a ballad to a country not their own. Perhaps that of their great-grandfathers, perhaps not.

As the new millennium loomed, it was now a part of the city where the bulldozing of the tenements had sucked much of the vitality out of a famous district, leaving it an area from which in large parts the people had virtually disappeared, giving it a ghostly appearance at night-time. It only came to life now at weekends when people flocked to the Barras and men clad in green and white, members of 'the great clan Celtic', congregated on match days in the local pubs. McMunigal was in a near-deserted Saracen Head bar, one of Glasgow's most famous hostelries, when – as noon approached – 'upward of a hundred people' suddenly burst in to listen to an advertised recital by Charlie and the Bhoys:

> The singing begins. Rallying in numbers, in a pitch higher than the sun, they sang: 'Soldiers are we, whose lives are pledged to Ireland, some have come – where from? – from a land beyond the wave. Sworn to be free . . . ' Each song trails into another, every man a rabble-rouser at the chorus and mute at the verse. I remember those songs. From my father's record player – for it was his, and his alone. Much softer then, more a lament than a threat, a ballad rather than a chant.

This manifestation of unease about the direction of the club was given a public airing only a few months later in an episode which underlined that the debate was inextricably intertwined with an 'Old Firm' rivalry whose bitterness had refused to go away. It was made unmistakably clear to the club's managing director (and virtual owner Fergus McCann) when he was barracked by a section of the crowd at Celtic Park during the league flag-unfurling ceremony not only for a perceived lack of activity in the transfer market that summer but also for a reason contained in a banner that read: 'We're Irish and we're Celtic fans but not bigots, Mr McCann'. Its unfolding was seen as a backlash against the 'Bhoys against bigotry' campaign initiated by McCann two years earlier, a campaign that its critics saw, for all its worthy intentions, as veering towards a blanking out of the club's Irish connection, but which had its genesis in the dismay felt by McCann that the problem of 'sectarianism' should still be festering in the Scotland to which he returned over thirty years after he left to make his fortune in North America. In the 29 April 1996 edition of the Toronto-based *Maclean's* magazine, he had articulated the reasons for his determination to tackle what he described as a 'bizarre' situation. The writer noted that McCann had instructed security staff to eject 'anyone leading sectarian chants', a clear challenge to those who shared the contention of one individual who was quoted in the article as saying that the singing, presumably of Irish rebel songs, was 'not being threatening', since, 'when you're singing those songs, you're singing about your identity'. McCann was adamant about the need to confront his critics: 'You can't change the minds of people who are mindless, but nor can you turn a blind eye when people are screaming this stuff. It creates a bad atmosphere at the park. It's bad for families, bad for corporate hospitality, and that is bad for business.' He was again in an unrepentant mood after the stinging abuse directed at him during that August 1998 ceremony, while being at pains to rebut 'misguided' claims that he and his associates were attempting to ignore the club's roots. Indeed, he prefaced his remarks with the observation that he was a Celtic supporter who understood the fans, that he had been a fan who used to travel on supporters' buses and knew what it was like to stand in the rain in the 1950s and early 1960s while Celtic were losing to 'minor' teams: 'This club is non-sectarian and it is against bigotry. I don't deny our Irish heritage or put down our fans from Ireland. I was over there at a charity function recently. But there is no hatred, no nationalism, no political agenda, no bias and no prejudice here.' As if to underline his assertion, the club was embarking on a recruitment policy that would mean players from all corners of the globe (no fewer than 50 or so nationalities) had arrived at Parkhead by 2012, giving rise on the part of subtler minds to the question as to whether Celtic could now be described as a Scottish club or a club playing in Scotland. The increasing cosmopolitanism of Celtic FC was also reflected in its reaching out to the wider community as the demographics of Scotland underwent significant change, as evidenced by a current SNP Member of the Scottish Parliament (MSP) for the Glasgow region and Parliamentary Liaison Officer to the Office of the First Minister of Scotland, namely Humza Yousaf, a Muslim and a son of Pakistani and Kenyan immigrants who came to the city in the 1960s, being described recently in *Debrett's People of Today* as a 'keen Glasgow Celtic fan'. For all its ring of authority, however, McCann's impassioned statement was destined not to be the final word on the matter of Celtic's identity, an issue that continued to bubble away beneath the surface before coming into sharp, dramatic focus during season 2010–11, one characterised by events that revealed starkly the dark underbelly of life in the central belt of Scotland particularly. One writer recoiled from the embarrassment of 'the world looking on in grim fascination as editorials from Manhattan to Moscow pondered why football in this north-western outpost of Europe should inspire such savagery'. This was against a backdrop of a native game described by another writer as 'an over-priced shambles that supporters are very correctly turning their backs on': refereeing blunders, claims of referee bias, referee strikes, calls for referees to 'declare their allegiances', a Celtic chairman stating at an AGM that the club would no longer be treated as 'second-class citizens' by the football authorities, a touchline 'confrontation' involving 'Old Firm' managers, a Celtic manager (Neil Lennon) who was the victim of a trackside attack by a Heart of Midlothian fan who was let off with a breach of the peace conviction after an assault charge was bizarrely found 'not proven' in the face of all the evidence, the same Celtic manager also having to receive round-the-clock security protection in the wake of bombs and bullets and various threats intercepted in the post. Oh, and not to mention the cackhanded intervention of a Holyrood Parliament more set on political grandstanding than mature reflection, judging by its ill-considered legislative remedies for a long-standing blot of Scotland's 'bigoted' image. With Celtic fans debating the club's place in a country where many of them believed that there were people running the national game who discriminated against the club, the *Celtic View* of 16 March 2011 seemed to be pinning its colours to the mast. It urged readers born in Scotland with an Irish background to 'tick the Irish box: be proud and be counted' when completing the government's Census form, citing studies that had concluded that 'Catholics of Irish descent disproportionately abide in areas of the west-central belt where there are high levels of deprivation and, arguably, degrees of religious, social economic and cultural prejudice and discord'. Intriguingly, a former editor of the club magazine, Kevin McKenna, stated in the *Scottish Catholic Observer* two months later that 'despite the sickening campaign of hatred directed at Neil Lennon this year' he was 'still not convinced that our nation is characterised by widespread anti-Catholic prejudice'. That would have cut no ice with those Celtic fans who read the opinions of contributors to the '2012–13 Season Guide' supplement to the September 2012 issue of *When Saturday Comes* in which a Heart of Midlothian fan, in an oblique reference to Rangers' demotion to the lowest tier of Scottish senior football, denounced them (Celtic fans again) as 'the other side of the bigotry coin that is/was the Old Firm . . . singing IRA songs while claiming it is their heritage, they sum up one part of what is wrong with Scottish football and society'. Meanwhile – such is the schizophrenic nature of that same Scottish society – a Dundee United fan denounced Celtic fans as 'tediously self-congratulatory' before rejoicing as he described his 'best moment' of the season just ended, the aforementioned seismic event that may well have changed the landscape of Scottish football forever: 'Watching Rangers as their season began to resemble the death throes of an ageing bull elephant: reeling around, trumpeting in pain and confusion, defecating copiously, before expiring in a soggy, fleshy heap, at which point, the vultures began their descent.'

Those who entertain the notion that developments such as the Good Friday Agreement of the late 1990s and the Queen's visit to Dublin in May 2011, the first by a British monarch to the Irish Republic, and to Belfast in June 2012 – where she would shake hands with Martin McGuinness, alleged former IRA leader turned Northern Ireland Deputy First Minister – would have a leavening effect across the water must have been seriously disabused by the disquieting aftermath to the 2011 League Cup (officially Co-operative Insurance Cup) final revealed by John Greechan in the *Scottish Daily Mail* of 21 March: 'From somewhere in the vicinity of the Rangers dressing room, the victory anthems rang out. The chorus of "Celtic are XXXXX" ["shite" being the word blanked out, most likely] provided an insight into the depth of feeling that still, for all the outward overtures of respect, underpins this fixture.' The Celtic and Scotland winger Kris Commons may have been exercising a degree of diplomacy when asked about 'the off-colour musical verdict of the winners', some of them his international teammates, by claiming that he hadn't heard the chant ('We're miles away in our dressing-room'), but there was no equivocation in the verdict of an interviewee quoted by Tony Evans, a sports journalist from *The Times* who visited Glasgow after a 25-year gap to take the temperature of the city on the day of the final and concluded after one interview that the most enduring thing about the rivalry was an appetite for conflict: 'Twenty-five years since you were here?' Donnie said. 'Come back in twenty-five years and it'll still be going on. You'll die before it does.'

In Glasgow, it seems, there is no time limit on unfinished business.

* * *

In its 14 June 1946 front-page feature on the death of the Tralee-born Father John Foley, described as 'one of the finest [ancient] Greek scholars in Britain' and 'in his younger days, a crack athlete, a first class boxer, cricketer, footballer and walker', the *Glasgow Observer* claimed that 'Celtic fans owe much to this grand old man who was one of the founders of their now world-famous club, for in its early days he frequently paid the rent of the Club's first pitch out of his own pocket'. He served in Sacred Heart parish, Bridgeton (close to Celtic Park) – during the club's foundation and early days between 1885 and 1888, according to the profile of him in Bernard J. Canning's 1979 book *Irish-Born Secular Priests in Scotland 1829–1979*.

CHAPTER 24

'All Is Changed, Changed Utterly'*

It would appear as if the newly formed Glasgow club, the Celtic F.C., has a bright future. At any rate, if the committee can place the same eleven on the field as opposed the Rangers last Monday evening or an equally strong one, the Celtic will not lack for patronage or support.

Scottish Umpire, *5 June 1888*

Fine words from the pages of the *Scottish Umpire*; indeed, just what the members of the first Celtic committee would have wanted to read. These men all came from different backgrounds, but in those early days they made several crucial – and prescient – decisions much to the benefit of the club and its future. For instance, while the vast majority (perhaps all) of that first Celtic committee would have been of a Catholic 'persuasion', they did not follow the earlier example of Hibs, whose players were originally required to have been members of the Catholic Young Men's Society. This policy not only brought the Edinburgh club into conflict with the Scottish Football Association but also limited the number of players who could be brought in. By contrast, the new Celtic committee made

---

* The chapter title is taken from a W.B. Yeats poem, 'Easter 1916'. Its tone of ambivalence about the events of the Easter Rising in Dublin could be applied equally, in a much less serious vein of course, to the feelings of a number of Celtic fans, largely of an older generation, about the seeming demise of a long and firmly held policy of building a team from home-grown players.

it clear that their club would sign players solely on the basis of their talent. And because of their early successes, which many would attribute to this policy, Celtic would attract players not only from all over Scotland but also the rest of the United Kingdom, Ireland and, gradually, various parts of the world.

Until recent times, these non-Scots players were not highly represented in a Celtic jersey because of the abundance of native talent and are listed here in alphabetical order of their birthplace. There is one rather complicated case to consider. From 1882 to 1921, all of Ireland was represented by a single side, the 'Ireland' national football team, organised by the Irish Football Association (IFA). In 1921, the jurisdiction of the IFA was reduced to Northern Ireland following the secession of clubs in the soon-to-be 'Irish Free State'. The latter was then represented by its own side in the 1924 Olympic Games and competed under that name until 1950, when its own association – the Football Association of Ireland or FAI – in conjunction with FIFA, agreed that the side would be known as the 'Republic of Ireland'.

Brazil
Ayrton Inacio, 1965–66, only played reserve-team football (OPRTF)
Marco Di Sousa, 1965–66, OPRTF

Canada
Joe Kennaway, 1931–39, 295 apps

Denmark
Bent Martin, 1965–67, one first-team appearance (Glasgow Cup), rest in reserve football

England
Jim Welford, 1897–1900, 44 apps
Jack Reynolds, 1897–98, 4 apps
Willie Nichol, 1911–12, 16 apps
George Elliott, 1918, 1 app
Ebenezer Owers, 1914, 16 apps

Tom Barber, 1918, 5 apps
Dan Shea, 1919, 1 app
Willie Lyon, 1935–44, 187 apps
Walter Jones, 1940, 3 apps
Robert Fisher, 1942, 3 apps
Peter Latchford, 1975–87, 272 apps

Iceland
Jóhannes Edvaldsson, 1975–80, 188 apps

India
Mohammed (Abdul) Salim, 1936, OPRTF

Ireland
Paddy Farrell, 1896–97, 1 app
Tommy 'Ching' Morrison, 1895–97, 16 apps
Willie Donnelly, 1900–01, 5 apps
Patsy Gallacher, 1911–27, 464 apps
Willie Crone, 1913–16, 17 apps
Mickey Hamill, 1916, 7 apps
Frank Collins, 1921–22, 2 apps

Irish Free State
Peter Kavanagh, 1929–32, 35 apps
James Foley, 1934–36, 6 apps

Republic of Ireland
Sean Fallon, 1949–58, 254 apps
Vincent Ryan, 1953–58, 22 apps
Charlie Gallagher, 1958–70, 171 apps
Joe Haverty, 1964, 1 app
Paddy Turner, 1963–64, 14 apps

Italy
Rolando Ugolini, 1944–48, 5 apps (born in Italy but came to Scotland at the age of three)

Jamaica
Gil Heron, 1951–52, 5 apps

Northern Ireland
Willie Cook, 1930–32, 110 apps
Hugh Docherty, 1946–47, 4 apps
Bernard Cannon, 1947–48, 3 apps
Charlie Tully, 1948–59, 319 apps
Bertie Peacock, 1949–61, 453 apps
John Kennedy, 1965–67, 1 app

Poland
Konrad Kapler, 1948–49, 8 apps

Sweden
Julius Hjulian, 1926 (see below)

Wales
Leigh Roose, 1909–10, 1 app

The above list – as definitive as possible – covers 42 players and around 80 years. A few of the above arrived at Celtic Park in most unusual circumstances. Take the case of Joe Kennaway, for instance. In the US tour of 1931, Celtic lost 1–0 to a team called Fall River, a match where the latter's goalkeeper, that same Kennaway, turned in a wonderful performance to keep the Celts at bay. After the tragic death of John Thomson, only a few months later, the Celtic management tried out two other keepers, Joe Coen and John Falconer, neither of whom lived up to expectations. Then, someone remembered the superb performance by 'that laddie from Fall River', so Joe Kennaway was brought over, made his debut in October 1931 and remained Celtic's keeper for the remainder of the 1930s.

Then there was the case of Leigh Roose, who only played the one match for Celtic, the Scottish Cup semi-final against Clyde in 1910. His appearance was in the way of a 'compensation'. The previous week, in the Scotland–Wales clash at Rugby Park, Jimmy

McMenemy had been injured as the result of a particularly poor tackle, with Roose's compatriot Llewellyn Davies having been named as the culprit. So, when Celtic's regular goalkeeper Davie Adams went down with an attack of influenza, it seemed logical and appropriate, by the more sporting standards of the time, for Roose, at that time a regular for Sunderland, to take his place the following week!

And Charlie Gallagher was one of the first to take advantage of the ruling that a player's parentage could be the deciding factor in choosing which country to play for. His two caps were against Turkey in Ankara on 22 February 1967 and Czechoslovakia in Dublin on 21 May of that same year.

However, there are another two 'foreign' names – not on the above list – whose stories are very unusual. The first of these was goalkeeper Julius Hjulian (1903–74), who left his native Sweden as a teenager in the early 1920s to try his luck abroad. At that period, professional football had not yet been adopted in Sweden, so after winning a league championship medal with IFK Eskilstuna in 1921, Hjulian decided to try his luck overseas, although there was speculation that the avoidance of conscription into the Army was also a factor.

Julius Hjulian turned out to be a bit of a wanderer. After a spell in the USA with Chicago clubs Pullman (Cars) FC and Harvey FC, he set out on his travels again and arrived in Scotland towards the end of season 1923–24. Why he had picked Celtic FC as his destination is a mystery, but by the start of the following season he was training with the club and ready for the call. Frankly, his chances of playing for Celtic's first team were severely limited by the fact that goalkeeper Peter Shevlin had been an ever-present in the club's fifty-three competitive matches in 1923–24 but Hjulian did wear the keeper's jersey on at least two occasions.

Despite the fact that, for reasons of false economy, Celtic did not operate a reserve side between 1922 and 1930, the club – for some reason – entered the Scottish Second XI Cup in season 1925–26 and Hjulian was between the posts for the tie against Rangers at Ibrox Park on Saturday, 20 February 1926, being listed in the local

Evening Times sports editions line-ups as 'Hjuliana'. In the match report itself – where the 'decisive' keeper was referred to as both 'Hjulian' and 'Hjuliana' – he certainly made an impression on the writer, who commented that 'his style is something new to the Glasgow crowd'.

The reporter did not elaborate on this statement but did record that, in the first half, 'only Hjulian's anticipation saved Celtic repeatedly' and that he 'dealt with everything in a capable manner'. For all Hjulian's heroics, though, Rangers netted all their goals in the second half to run up a 5–0 victory, although the match report mentioned only the scorers, with no description of the play whatsoever, probably for reasons of space. Hjulian got another outing two months later in a Celtic side containing established stars like Jimmy McGrory, Hugh Hilley, the McStay brothers – Willie and Jimmy – and Adam McLean. This was a benefit match at Easter Road for Hibs international right-half Peter Kerr, which Celtic won 2–0.

However, with his options limited by Celtic's policy of operating on a small squad, Hjulian soon returned to the Chicago area (where he spent the rest of his life) to play for Sparta ABA and Chicago Wieboldt (Wonderbolts). He seems to have taken out USA citizenship, since he represented his adopted country in their two matches at the 1934 World Cup finals in Italy, becoming the first Celtic player (albeit ex-Celtic player) to play at that level. In the first match, at the Stadio Nazionale del Partito Nazionale Fascista in Rome, the USA beat Mexico 4–2 in a preliminary round, but three days later they ran up against the host side (and eventual winners) at the same venue. 'Il Duce' himself, Benito Mussolini, 'sporting a natty white sailing cap', was present as cheerleader-in-chief as Italy, three up inside the first half-hour, proved to be simply irresistible, repelling a spirited USA fightback after the interval before overwhelming their hapless opponents to the tune of 7–1. (See Postscript to this chapter.)

Another most unusual player joined Celtic between the wars. Mohammed 'Abdul' Salim (1904/05 to 1980; sources vary as to his date of birth) was apparently the first Indian to play in Europe. A native of Calcutta, which was a hotbed of anti-British sentiment and agitation in the early twentieth century – a major factor in the capital of the Raj being moved to New Delhi in 1911 – he arrived in Glasgow in the summer of 1936. Some accounts suggest that he came to Britain on the recommendation of a friend, Hasheem (confusingly, also described as his cousin or brother), who sailed with him on the *City of Glasgow*.

The noted journalist 'Waverley', however, stated in the *Daily Record and Mail* of 27 August 1936 that it was Salim's brother, a storekeeper in Elderslie Docks at a time when Glasgow was a major shipping hub in the days of Empire, who contacted Willie Maley to seek a try-out for his relative. In his article headed 'Can He Swallow a Sword?', 'Waverley' went on to say that the new boy had been given a run-out in a trial game during which he had played '*sans* boots, *sans* shinguards and played a delightful game . . . his crosses into the goalmouth were pictures'. Sword-swallowing was an ancient Indian performance art that was popular in British music halls in the early twentieth century and this article was designed to bring out the exotic nature or appeal of Celtic's interest in Salim.

This is also the article that probably gave rise to the belief that Salim played in bare feet, whereas, in fact, he wore elasticated bandages two-and-a-half inches thick, wrapped on by trainer Jimmy McMenemy. This 'bare-feet' style may have been some form of political statement, since at least one account of football in India, by Boria Majumdar, states that the nationalists in the early twentieth century, striving to be free of colonial rule, took to the game in order to rebut British jibes that the natives were not 'manly enough' to achieve self-rule: 'The Indians played in bare feet and despite this defeated English men in boots, which was evidence that Indians were not inferior to the British.' Certainly, it is not difficult to imagine that Salim, who rose to fame locally with the Mohammedan Sporting Club in that nationalist hotbed of Calcutta, played in bare feet (or was it elasticated bandages?) against British Army sides.

Sufficiently impressed by what he had seen and undeterred by the Indian's avoidance of boot-wear and shin-guards, Willie Maley fielded him at outside-right, partnering the powerfully built John Divers, in the Alliance (Reserve) Side that beat Galston 7–1 at Celtic Park on the evening of Friday, 28 August 1936. The sheer novelty of it all attracted a crowd of 7,000 to see the man who would go down in the club's folklore as 'the Indian who played in bare feet'.

The ex-Celtic and Rangers winger Alec Bennett, reporting the match for the *Daily Record and Mail*, underlined the sense of occasion: 'Was it not unique to see a man of colour wear a Celtic jersey and, what is more, one who did his stuff in bare feet?' Bennett noted how soon a crowd 'amazed at his cleverness, were rooting for Salim; he hugged the touchline, it is true, and did not risk tackles, but in passing he seemed able to put the ball just where he wanted, while his crossing of it was, to say the least of it, just wonderful'. Three of the goals, indeed, came from 'marvellous centres from the man from India'.

The rival *Scottish Daily Express* report described the hypnotic effect of the 'ten twinkling toes of Salim' on the spectators – 'he balances the ball on his big toe, lets it run down the scale to his little toe, twirls it, hops on one foot around the defender'. Two weeks later, another splendid crowd of 5,000 turned up at Celtic Park to see the man headlined by the *Scottish Daily Express* as the 'Indian juggler', whose right-wing partner on this occasion was another player destined never to wear a first-team jersey, James Cahill. Celtic had a 6–2 win over opposing Alliance side Hamilton Academical that day and this time Salim turned goal-scorer, converting a penalty award: 'The barefooted Indian biffed the ball hard to the left of the goalkeeper.'

'Malvern', reporting for the *Daily Record and Mail*, recorded the differing reactions to the goal and, significantly perhaps, was equivocal about the winger's true worth: 'resounding cheers greeted the goal but Salim showed no outward sign of his feelings. He was clearly the main attraction again. "Give the ball to Salim!" was the slogan of the crowd but the Celtic players wisely did not overwork the Indian, who crosses a splendid ball but is far from being a complete player.'

These were Salim's only two appearances in a Celtic jersey. For someone with such obvious talent, there should probably have been more, and several theories have been put forward to explain why his career in the green-and-whites was so brief. Was he homesick? Did the club perceive a lack of robustness or stamina, very necessary attributes for those in the Scottish game at that time? Or did his lack of English prove a handicap? Certainly, he needed the constant attendance of his friend/cousin/brother Hasheem to help his understanding of the language, but the honest answer is that we just do not know. Shortly after his second match, Mohammed 'Abdul' Salim returned to India, where he continued his career with the Mohammedan Sporting Club. For the Celtic fans of that period, though, he was forever remembered as a shooting star of a player who briefly lit up an often humdrum football scene.

So, around 42 'foreign' players in the first 90-odd years of Celtic's history. Roughly from the beginning of the 1980s, though (and particularly from the early 1990s), the number of players from outside Scotland increased dramatically as the Celtic management teams and their scouts scoured the transfer markets abroad (initially the continent of Europe, but in more recent years the wider world) for the right player at the right price, once they concluded that the previously rich seam of reserve team talent had all but run dry and the club had to face the challenge laid down by free-spending Rangers as, initially under the management of Graeme Souness, the Ibrox club began to assert an alarming domination in the domestic game. Given the stunning demise of the latter club, Matt Dickinson of *The Times*, looking from south of the border in its 18 September 2012 edition at the strange new world of Scottish football, urged those in charge of Celtic to avail themselves of a rare window of opportunity to develop as a club, 'to challenge themselves to come up with so much more' (more particularly by being enabled to stretch themselves in European competition) during a unique situation where obsession with weekly results was diminished by the absence of their biggest rival and by the gulf in resources that now separated the Scottish champions from the rest of the SPL:

Time to be creative. Is the hierarchy asking hard questions about whether to stop making short-term foreign signings, such as Miku on a year's loan from Getafe, and redouble their focus on promoting youth? How about taking a few risks by pouring extra resources into teenage talents and seeking to shape them around a new philosophy? Celtic aspire to bring through their own players yet, in the first team, James Forrest is the only home grown.

CELTIC: PRIDE AND PASSION

Celtic manager Neil Lennon, however, spoke frankly about the club's current strategy when, commenting on the departure of South Korean midfielder Ki Sung-Yueng to Swansea City in August 2012, he told BBC Scotland that the reported £6 million fee was 'good business', adding that 'We cultivate players then move them on.' Hugh MacDonald of *The Herald* was blunter still, his 22 October 2012 statement that 'The reality is that Celtic are resigned to fattening up talent for the bigger leagues' prompting the more traditionally minded to wonder whether a club that once held dear, almost as a badge of honour (on behalf of its own glory, as it were), the notion of building teams around home-grown players was losing its soul, becoming in effect little more than a football factory or a finishing school for transient foreign players bound for richer pastures. In alphabetical order (with birthplace in brackets), this list covers the period roughly from the start of the 1980s to the end of the transfer window in January 2014. The list, which makes no claims to be exhaustive, excludes players born abroad but raised in Scotland (e.g. Sean Maloney, born in Malaysia) and also those born in Scotland who have decided to represent another country (e.g. Tommy Coyne or Aiden McGeady). The names in italics have only played youth or reserve-team football for Celtic:

Didier Agathe (Reunion, an overseas 'departement' of France); Jérémie Aliadière (France); Efe Ambrose (Nigeria); Ian Andrews (England); Enrico Annoni (Italy); Bahrudin Atajic (Sweden).

Roy Baines (England); Amido Baldé (Guinea-Bissau); Bobo Baldé (France, of Guinean extraction); Mohamed Bangura (Sierra Leone); Craig Bellamy (Wales); Eyal Bergovic (Israel); Wayne Biggins (England); Nir Biton (Israel); *Teddy Bjarnason* (Iceland); Andre Blackman (England); Regi Blinker (Suriname, played for Holland); Derk Boerrigter (Holland); Pat Bonner (Republic of Ireland); Stéphane Bonnes (France); Artur Boruc (Poland); Edson Braafheid (Suriname, played for Holland); Harald Brattbakk (Norway); Pawel Brozek (Poland); Paul Byrne (Republic of Ireland).

Jorge Cadete (Mozambique, played for Portugal); Henri Camara (Senegal); Mo Camara (Guinea); Tony Cascarino (born in England, played for Republic of Ireland); Cha Du Ri (West Germany, plays for South Korea); Dominic Cervi (USA); Kris Commons (England, plays for Scotland); Marc Crosas (Spain).

Fernando de Ornales (Venezuela); Paolo di Canio (Italy); Massimo Donati (Italy); Dion Dublin (England); Du Wei (China); Dariusz Dziekanowski (Poland).

Badr El Kaddouri (Morocco); Paul Elliott (England).

David Fernandez (Spain); *Islam Feruz* (Somalia, played for Scotland at youth level); *Kiartan Finnbogason* (Iceland); Darnell Fisher (England); William 'Willo' Flood (Republic of Ireland); Nicolás Ladislao Fedor Flores – better known as 'Miku' (Venezuela); Fraser Forster (England); Marc-Antoine Fortuné (French Guiana); Danny Fox (England); Holmbert Fridjonsson (Iceland).

Paul George (Northern Ireland); Rami Gershon (Israel); *Daniele Giordano* (Italy); Shay Given (Republic of Ireland); Jim Goodwin (Republic of Ireland); Jonathan Gould (England, played for Scotland); Thomas Gravesen (Denmark); Michael Gray (England); Stuart Gray (born in England, played for Scotland Under-21); Steve Guppy (England).

John Hartson (Wales); Martin Hayes (England); Colin Healey (Republic of Ireland); Magnus Hedman (Sweden); Stéphane Henchoz (Switzerland); Andreas Hinkel (Germany); Joos Hooiveld (Holland); Gary Hooper (England); *Kirk Hudson* (England); Ben Hutchison (England).

Rabiu Ibrahim (Nigeria); Jackson Irvine (Australia); Emilio Izaguirre (Honduras).

Jiri Jarosik (Czech Republic); Stefan Johansen (Norway); Tommy Johnson (England); Efrain Juarez (Mexico); Juninho (Brazil).

Lubos Kamenar (Slovakia); Olivier Kapo (Ivory Coast, played for France); Beram Kayal (Israel); Robbie Keane (Republic of Ireland); Roy Keane (Republic of Ireland); Dmitri Kharine (Russia); Chris Killen (New Zealand).

Daniel Lafferty (Northern Ireland); Henrik Larsson (Sweden); Ulrik Laursen (Denmark); Joe Ledley (Wales); Neil Lennon (Northern Ireland); Freddie Ljungberg (Sweden); Glenn Loovens (Holland); Mikael Lustig (Sweden); Mick McCarthy (England, played for Republic of Ireland); Paddy McCourt (Northern Ireland); Scott McDonald (Australia); Niall McGinn (Northern Ireland); Michael McGlinchey (New Zealand); Allen McKnight (Northern Ireland); Stéphane Mahé (France); Daniel Majstorovic (Sweden); Lee Martin (England); Adam Matthews (Wales); Mikul (see Flores); Liam Miller (Republic of Ireland); Milan Misun (Czech Republic); Koki Mizuno (Japan); Johann Mjallby (Sweden); Lubo Moravcik (Slovakia); Chris Morris (England, played for Republic of Ireland); Steven Mouyokolo (France); Tony Mowbray (England); Carl Muggleton (England); Daryl Murphy (Republic of Ireland).

Shunsuke Nakamura (Japan); Lee Naylor (England); Landry N'Guemo (Cameroon); Lassad Nouioui (France, of Tunisian extraction).

Diarmuid O'Carroll (Republic of Ireland); Darren O'Dea (Republic of Ireland); Pierce O'Leary (Republic of Ireland).

Andy Payton (England); Jean-Joël Perrier-Doumbé (born in France, played for Cameroon); Stiliyan Petrov (Bulgaria); Bobby Petta (Holland); Teemu Pukki (Finland).

Morten Rasmussen (Denmark); Marc Rieper (Denmark); Vidar Riseth (Norway); Anton Rogan (Northern Ireland); Tom Rogic (Australia); Thomas Rogne (Norway).

Georgios Samaras (Greece); Francisco Javier Sanchez Broto (Spain); *Luca Santonicito* (Italy); Rafael Scheidt (Brazil); Cillian Sheridan

(Republic of Ireland); Stuart Slater (England); Evander Sno (Holland); Anthony Stokes (Republic of Ireland); Alan Stubbs (England); Ki Sung-Yueng (South Korea); Chris Sutton (England); Mohammed 'Momo' Sylla (Ivory Coast, of Guinean extraction).

Olivier Tebily (Ivory Coast); Andy Thom (Germany); Alan Thompson (England); Josh Thompson (England); Richie Towell (Republic of Ireland); Filip Twardzik (Czech Republic); Patrik Twardzik (Czech Republic).

Joos Valgaeren (Belgium); Virgil van Dijk (Holland); Pierre van Hooijdonk (Holland); *David van Zanten* (Republic of Ireland); Stan Varga (Slovakia); Rudi Vata (Albania); Ramon Vega (Switzerland); Jan Vennegoor of Hesselink (Holland); Mark Viduka (Australia); Adam Virgo (England).

Victor Wanyama (Kenya); Tony Warner (England); Dariusz Wdowczyk (Poland); Morten Wieghorst (Denmark); Kelvin Wilson (England); Ian Wright (England).

Lucasz Zaluska (Poland); Zheng Zhi (China); Maciej Zurawski (Poland).

The above list comprises nearly 160 names in just over 30 years! With that number of players plus the extensive range of backgrounds, it is no surprise that we have to go back nearly 18 years to find the last time a team of Scots-born players ran out to represent Celtic. That occurred on 19 November 1994 at Rugby Park, where Kilmarnock were their opponents in a league match. Under Tommy Burns, the Hoops had just reached the League Cup final but, in the league, had won only four and drawn eight of their first fifteen matches.

The teams that afternoon were:

Kilmarnock (4-4-2): Meldrum; McPherson, Whitworth, Anderson, Black; Skilling, Henry, Reilly, Mitchell; Brown, McKee (Maskrey).

CELTIC: PRIDE AND PASSION

Celtic (4-4-2): Marshall; Boyd, McNally, O'Neil, McKinlay; P. McStay, Grant, O'Donnell, Collins; Walker (Donnelly), Falconer.

Referee: M. Clark (Edinburgh).

Attendance: 12,602.

The Celtic managerial duo of Tommy Burns and his assistant Billy Stark were given a predictably hostile reception by the home fans while making their first return to Rugby Park since their departure for Parkhead in the summer. The crowd witnessed a poor match in which Kilmarnock were the more threatening side, with Andy Mitchell and Tom Black squandering the best of the few scoring opportunities. The latter's came in the 47th minute after he was brought down by Brian O'Neil in the penalty box. Gordon Marshall's save prevented Celtic's fourth defeat in six league matches. Andrew Smith, in his *Celtic View* match report, noted that Marshall 'guessed Black's intention perfectly and dived to his left to block the shot', but Celtic were fortunate when the rebound from Marshall's block was driven by the inrushing Mark Skilling against the base of Marshall's right-hand post, the ball running along the goal line before being scrambled to safety.

The 0–0 result left Celtic – who had created very little despite the tireless promptings of Paul McStay, a captain who eight days later would suffer the agony of his decisive failure in the 'sudden death' penalty shoot-out in the League Cup final against Raith Rovers – in fifth place in a ten-club Premier Division, having averaged only a goal per game (only bottom clubs Kilmarnock and Partick Thistle had scored fewer), a lack of firepower that had left them eight points adrift of leaders Rangers as the competition neared its halfway stage.

Matters barely improved by the turn of the year, the need for a potent striker forcing Tommy Burns to recruit Pierre van Hooijdonk from NEC Breda in early January 1995. Thereafter, as a result of the Dutch player's popularity with the fans and his proven success as a goal-scorer, what had begun as a trickle of foreign players in the late 1980s would turn into a veritable flood. The face of Celtic had changed, perhaps forever.

'ALL IS CHANGED, CHANGED UTTERLY'

* * *

POSTSCRIPT

When Julius Hjulian's USA team was thrashed 7–1 by Italy in 1934, the coach of the winning side was Vittorio Pozzo. Thirty-three years later (at the age of eighty-one), Pozzo reported on the European Cup final in Lisbon between Celtic and Inter Milan for the Turin-based newspaper *La Stampa*.

One can only imagine his feelings when, in his match report, he duly noted the opening goal from the penalty spot netted by Inter's Sandro Mazzola, son of Valentino, captain of both FC Torino and Italy. When 18 members of that famous Turin side (known as *Il Grande Torino*) died in the Superga air disaster in 1949, Pozzo, only recently retired as national coach, had been brought in to identify the bodies, including that of Valentino Mazzola. Ironically, Valentino Mazzola's last match, a testimonial game for a Benfica player, had been played the previous day at the Estádio Nacional in Lisbon, scene of the 1967 European Cup final.

Incidentally, regarding that 1967 final, Pozzo believed at the moment of Mazzola Jr's 'ruthless' penalty conversion that Inter were destined to win but his final verdict was wholly objective, an acknowledgement that the extent of Celtic's 'deserved triumph' was not reflected in the narrow margin of victory.

* * *

Now, I (Jim Craig) know what you are all thinking, so I am going to provide the answers to the two questions that are buzzing about in your head. First, for the last Old Firm clash when all-Scottish sides featured, we have to go back to 4 January 1975, at Ibrox, a 3–0 win for the Light Blues, when the teams were:

Celtic: Hunter; McGrain, McNeill, McCluskey, Brogan; Glavin, Hood, Murray; Callaghan, Dalglish, Wilson.

Rangers: Kennedy; Jardine, Forsyth, Jackson, Greig; McDougall, Johnstone, MacDonald; McLean, Parlane, Scott.

The three substitutes – Johnstone for Hood (Celtic); Miller and Young for Jackson and Scott (Rangers) – were also Scots.

And the first time when a Celtic side without a single Scot involved in the starting 11 ran onto the field was against Dunfermline in a league match on 8 September 2001 at Celtic Park. Celtic won 3–1 and the team was: Kharine (Russia), Valgaeren (Belgium), Agathe (France), Balde (Guinea), Tebily (Ivory Coast), Thompson (England), Lennon (Northern Ireland), Petrov (Bulgaria), Moravcik (Slovakia), Sutton (England), Larsson (Sweden).

One Scot did eventually feature in this Celtic side, Stephen Crainey coming on as a substitute for Alan Thompson. The other Celtic subs were John Hartson, a Welshman, for Joos Valgaeren; and Colin Healey, born in the Republic of Ireland, for Stiliyan Petrov.